Saved, Sanctified and Serving

Perspectives on Salvation Army Theology and Practice

T0385268

PATERNOSTER THEOLOGICAL MONOGRAPHS

Saved Sanctified and Serving

Perspectives on Salvation Army Theology and Practice

Editor: Denis Metrustery

Foreword by Commissioner James M. Knaggs

Paternoster is an imprint of Authentic Media Limited
PO Box 6326, Bletchley, Milton Keynes, MK1 9GG

authenticmedia.co.uk

British Library Cataloguing in Publication Data
A catalogue record for this book is available from the British Library

ISBN 978-1-84227-845-1
978-1-78078-074-0 (e-book)

Typeset by Denis Metrustery Printed
and bound in Great Britain by
Print on Demand Worldwide

Series Preface

In the west the churches may be declining, but theology—serious, academic (mostly doctoral level) and mainstream orthodox in evaluative commitment—shows no sign of withering on the vine. This series of *Paternoster Theological Monographs* extends the expertise of the Press especially to first-time authors whose work stands broadly with the parameters created by fidelity to Scripture and has satisfied the critical scrutiny of respected assessors in the academy. Such theology may come in several distinct intellectual disciplines—Historical, dogmatic, pastoral, apologetic, missional, aesthetic and no doubt others also. The series will be particularly hospitable to promising constructive theology within an evangelical frame, for it is of this that the church's need seems to be greatest. Quality writing will be published across the confessions—Anabaptist, Episcopalian, Reformed, Arminian, and Orthodox—across the ages—patristic, medieval, reformation, modern, and counter-modern—and across the continents. The aim of the series is theology written in the twofold conviction that the church needs theology and theology needs the church—which in reality means theology done for the glory of God.

Series Editors

Trevor A. Hart, Head of School and Principal of St Mary's College School of Divinity, University of St Andrews, Scotland, UK

Anthony N.S. Lane, Professor of Historical Theology and Director of Research, London School of Theology, UK

Anthony C. Thiselton, Emeritus Professor of Christian Theology, University of Nottingham, Research Professor in Christian Theology, University College Chester; and Canon Theologian of Leicester Cathedral and Southwell Minister, UK

Kevin J. Vanhoozer, Research Professor of Systematic Theology, Trinity Evangelical Divinity School, Deerfield, Illinois, USA

"God invented The Salvation Army to save souls, grow saints, and serve suffering humanity."[1]

General John Gowans

Come join our Army, to battle we go,
Jesus will help us to conquer the foe;
Fighting for right and opposing the wrong,
The Salvation Army is marching along.

Come join our Army, the foe we'll defy,
True to our colours, we'll fight till we die;
Saved from all sin is our war cry and song;
The Salvation Army is marching along.

---

[1] *The Salvationist, (*24 July 1999), 3

Come join our Army, and do not delay,
The time for enlisting is passing away;
Fierce is the battle, but victory will come;
The Salvation Army is marching along.

William James Pearson (1832-92)
The Songbook of The Salvation Army, No 681 (verses 1, 3, 4) [2]

In the Army of Jesus we've taken our stand
To fight 'gainst the forces of sin,
To the rescue we go, Satan's power to o'erthrow,
And his captives to Jesus we'll win.

Frederick William Fry (1859-1939)
The Songbook of The Salvation Army, No 687 (verse 1)

God's soldier marches as to war,
A soldier on an alien shore,
A soldier true, a soldier who
Will keep the highest aims in view.
God's soldier goes where sin is found;
Where evil reigns, his battleground;
A cunning foe to overthrow
And strike for truth a telling blow.

We're going to fill, fill, fill the world with glory;
We're going to smile, smile, smile and not frown;
We're going to sing, sing, sing the gospel story;
We're going to turn the world upside down.

Harry Read (b. 1924)
The Songbook of The Salvation Army, No 801 (verse 1 and chorus)

---

[2] (London: International Headquarters of The Salvation Army, 1986, reprinted 1987)

For Caroline

Table of Contents

Contents

Part 3 - 'SERVING SUFFERING HUMANITY'

Acknowledgements

I would like to thank Dr. Mike Parsons, Commissioning Editor at Paternoster, for his enthusiastic acceptance of my proposal for this project in 2012, and his team for helping to translate this into the published form. Mike has done an excellent job of steering the formatting of this book; he left Paternoster in August 2015 to take up a new position, and Reuben Sneller has overseen the final stages of production.

I would also wish to express my appreciation to certain Salvation Army officers with whom I have developed a consultative relationship and who have provided welcome comment and insight into areas and issues of value to this project. Since this project has not been officially supported by The Salvation Army's leadership, it is best that these kind folk remain anonymous – you will know who you are! The encouraging words of Commissioner Jim Knaggs's Foreword are also most appreciated.

The original structure of the project was to follow the International Vision Statement and Mission Priorities disseminated by General Linda Bond in October 2011: 'One Army, One Mission, One Message'. However, in light of the unexpected and immediate retirement of General Bond in June 2013, it was felt that the outline of the project would benefit from restructuring to follow the tripartite formula of the Army's mission as offered by an earlier General, John Gowans – that The Salvation Army was called to 'save souls, grow saints, and serve suffering humanity'. This phrase and vision has become woven into the fabric of Salvation Army theology, thinking, and practice and provides a suitable framework to reconsider some important issues in the 21st Century.

The project was conceived in 2012, and I solicited the assistance and involvement of a team of international writers. Subsequent to initial acceptance of the project by Mike Parsons at Paternoster, I was advised by a senior Salvation Army source to also approach the Army's International Headquarters to discuss the proposals. The outcome was that approval was not given for active Salvation Army officers to take part in this project. This led to an urgent review of the project, and necessitated that the original writing team be reconfigured to include a group selected from senior retired officers and Salvation Army academics (some of whom were part of the original team in light of specific experience and expertise).

It should also be noted that following his election as General in August 2013, André Cox confirmed that

> I am grateful to my predecessor General Linda Bond for her
> visionary leadership, for her submission to the will of God and

for the fact that she inspired our International Vision of *One Army, One Mission, One Message* and that must continue. A change of General does not change that focus.[3]

I am indebted to the writing team who, in the midst of busy schedules, have taken the time to engage with this project and to write papers which provide a flavour of historical Salvation Army thinking as well as individual positions and concerns, and which should also help readers in ongoing discussion on issues that impact the future of The Salvation Army in its self-understanding , internal and external relations with other Christian churches, faith-based organisations, and secular bodies to which it offers – and from which it seeks – cooperation.

General Dr Shaw Clifton has noted that 'unless we know where we have come from, we cannot know who we are today… a thinking Salvationist has a knowledge of our past, a sense of our history, so that she or he can think intelligently and in context about the present and the future.' [4]

This book does not bear the official *imprimatur* of The Salvation Army, but I trust that its contents will be of some assistance and challenge to this Movement; with the rest of the Body of Christ, it needs to reflect the maxim of *ecclesia semper reformans, semper reformanda* – 'the church is always reformed and always reforming'.

May this volume help The Salvation Army celebrate the past, assess the present, and strategise for the future.

Denis Metrustery
Bangor, Northern Ireland
August 2015

[3]   Interview   with   General   André   Cox'
http://www.salvationarmy.org/ihq/news/interview060813 (accessed 6 August 2013)
[4] Clifton, S *Selected Writings* 2000-2010, (London: Salvation Books, 2010) 2.19, 21

Contributors

Dr. Andrew M. Eason

is Assistant Professor of Religion at Booth University College, Winnipeg, where he is also the Director of the Centre for Salvation Army Studies. He holds a BA (Booth College), MTS (Tyndale Seminar), BA (University of Waterloo), MA (University of Windsor), and a PhD from the University of Calgary. Andrew's publications include *Women in God's Army: Gender and Equality in the Early Salvation Army*

Dr. Roger J. Green, O.F.

is Professor of Biblical Studies at Gordon University received his B.A. from Temple University in Philadelphia with a major in English in 1965, followed by an M.Div. from Asbury Theological Seminary, an M.Th. from Princeton Theological Seminary, a Ph.D. in theology from Boston College, and a D.D. (honorary) from William and Catherine Booth College. Much of his scholarship has been devoted to the history and theology of The Salvation Army. He is co-editor of The Salvation Army's theological journal *Word & Deed: A Journal of Salvation Army Theology and Ministry*. Dr Green was a member of the Army's International Spiritual Life Commission, and was the first layperson appointed to the International Doctrine Council, and was admitted to the Order of the Founder in 2012. He is the author of *The Life and Ministry of William Booth: Founder of the Salvation Army.*

Major Dr. Alan Harley

trained for Salvation Army officership in Toronto, Canada and was commissioned as an officer 1963. Since transferring to the Australia East Territory he has held several appointments at Booth College in Sydney, serving as Senior Lecturer, Director of the School for Bible and General Studies, and Vice Principal. He also served as Territorial Holiness Teacher. Alan pursued further studies with American and British institutions, earning the Doctor of Theology degree in 1972. He has travelled extensively throughout North America and both Australian territories ministering to Salvationist congregations and centres and addressing conferences and Bible conventions.

Major Dr. Harold I. W. Hill

has worked in Corps ministry and education in Zimbabwe and New Zealand, and lives in retirement in New Zealand. He has written and lectured on Salvation Army history and theology and is currently researching the relationship between the Salvation Army and the Charismatic and Pentecostal movements. Harold holds a PhD from the University of Victoria, Wellington, New Zealand.

Dr. Ronald Holz, O.F.

completed his graduate training in historical musicology at the Cincinnati College-Conservatory of Music (M.Mus.) and the University of Connecticut (Ph.D.). At Asbury University he served as Chairman of the Division of Fine Arts from 1985-1991, having joined the faculty in 1981; he has recently retired as Professor of Music History and Literature, Orchestra Director, and Professor of Trumpet. Ron has held positions on the boards of such musical organizations as the North American Brass Band Association, the Great American Brass Band Festival, and serves as a member of the Editorial Review Committee of the International Trumpet Guild. His publications of several critically acclaimed books include *Brass Bands of The Salvation Army: Their Mission and Music, Volumes 1 and 2*. In April 2014 he and his wife, Dr. Beatrice Holz, received the highest honour granted by the international Salvation Army, The Order of the Founder, in recognition, in part, for their many years as volunteer music leaders in the denomination. He has been a commissioned bandmaster in the SA for 50 years, having been first commissioned at age 16.

Denis Metrustery

holds BTh(Hons), MTh degrees and is completing his PhD at Queen's University Belfast; he has studied at King's College, London, Union Theological College and Edgehill Theological College Belfast. He is a former Salvationist and maintains a keen interest in Salvation Army theology, and continues to undertake theological research and writing.

Commissioner Dr. Philip D. Needham

was the Territorial Commander for USA Southern Territory, and retired in 2006. He also carried responsibility for officer training and had been Principal of the International College for Officers. He is a graduate of Miami University, Princeton Theological Seminary and Emory University and holds AB, BD, ThM and DMin degrees. Phil has written widely on SA doctrine and theology, including *Community in Mission*.

Dr. James Pedlar

specialises in the study of the Church – especially questions involving reform movements, Christian unity, authority structures, and ecumenical dialogue. He is Assistant Professor of Wesley Studies and Theology at Tyndale Seminary in Toronto. James previously worked with the Commission on Faith and Witness at the Canadian Council of Churches. From 2007 to 2009 he carried out a research project on young adult attrition for The Salvation Army in Canada and Bermuda. Before that he was Community Ministries Director for The Salvation Army in the Quinte Region of Ontario, Canada. James is a part-time Assistant Pastor at Wesley Chapel Free Methodist Church, and lives in Toronto. He holds BA(Hons), MDiv and PhD degrees.

General Dr. Paul A. Rader (Ret'd)

was General from 1994-99; he spent his undergraduate years at Asbury University, then studied at the Asbury Theological Seminary and the Southern Baptist Theological Seminary, graduating with BA, BD and MTh degrees, following further study at Fuller Theological Seminary, School of World Evangelism, Rader gained the degree of Doctor of Missiology; Asbury College conferred the honorary degree of Doctor of Laws. Following retirement from international SA leadership, Dr Rader was elected President of Asbury University from 2000-06.

Dr. R. David Rightmire

is a Theology Professor at Asbury University, and holds Ph.D. Marquette University (Historical Theology), M.Div. Asbury Theological Seminary (Church History) and A.B. Bloomfield College (History) degrees. He has written widely on Salvation Army theology, including *Sacraments and the Salvation Army: Pneumatological Foundations* and *Sanctified Sanity: The Life and Teaching of Samuel Logan Brengle.*

Major Campbell Roberts, O.F.

currently works as Head of The Salvation Army's Social Policy & Parliamentary Unit in the New Zealand, Fiji and Tonga Territory. Prior to retirement in 2012, he was Territorial Secretary for Social Programme. Roberts was admitted to the Order of the Founder in 2013. Campbell is noted as a serial social entrepreneur in developing the Salvation Army's welfare and social policy initiatives in New Zealand, as well as being a leader in wider church and community initiatives on poverty and housing issues, and on prison reform. He is a frequent author of articles and publications and co-authored *Just Imagine* a book on social justice with Danielle Strickland. Campbell Roberts assisted with the establishment of the International Social Justice Commission

Major Dr. JoAnn A. Shade

was involved in pastoral and administrative roles within The Salvation Army's USA Eastern Territory until her retirement in 2012. She holds a BA in Sociology from State University of New York at Binghamton, an MA in Pastoral Counselling from Ashland Theological Seminary, and a Doctor of Ministry degree from Ashland (*'Women* in *Prophetic Leadership'*); she has been a corresponding member of the International Doctrine Council.

Aaron White

along with his wife Cherie, are Salvation Army soldiers leading 614 Vancouver, an incarnational Corps in Vancouver's Downtown Eastside. Aaron is the co-author of *Revolution*, and *The Hitchhiker's Guide to the Kingdom of God*. He teaches at The War College and speaks widely around the world. He has an Honours History degree from UVIC, and, is currently completing a Master's Degree in Theological Studies through Tyndale Seminary.

Foreword

The clearest mission descriptors of The Salvation Army flow from the pen of General John Gowans when He wrote that this movement of God is meant to be about 'saving souls, growing saints and serving suffering humanity'. Consistent with the daily offering of Salvationists for 150 years, millions of souls, saints and suffering humans have been influenced by this creative band of believers who cloak themselves in their salvation uniforms and holy love.

Their ministry, driven by their love for God and his children, has surpassed even the most ambitious prognostications of their early days on the streets of London, England. Now, fighting evil in many forms in 126 countries around the world, this determined and dedicated outfit continues to surprise even itself by the power and leading of God.

In this text, Denis Metrustery takes us on an in-depth journey of saving souls, growing saints and serving suffering humanity with the able support of celebrated contributors who have fought the good fight and for many, still are in the battle. You see, the path of The Salvation Army is aptly conveyed in its military metaphor. The course of helping, healing, and hoping for the least, the last and the lost is not a casual endeavour. As you will understand in these pages, the enemy is persistent and pervasive in his pursuit of souls. He prefers them to remain lost, confused, addicted, helpless, and mired in defeat.

The Salvationist must be a conqueror, battle-ready, courageous and convinced that by the grace of God every person can be redeemed regardless of culture, language and depravity. The saving grace of Jesus is strong enough to alleviate the heaviest burdens and tender enough not to break the bruised reed or quench the smoking flax (Matthew 12:20). His mercy, dispensed through the likes of humankind is available to all for every need, unconditional and unlimited.

Read thoroughly this expert work with a hope in your own soul that God would speak to you through these representatives who know him personally. Each voice here has enormous potential to be the one that God has chosen for you to hear. By its conclusion, you will know the encouragement to be *'Saved, Sanctified and Serving'* in the name of God.

James M Knaggs, Commissioner
Territorial Commander, USA West
April 2015

Introduction

Denis Metrustery

The Salvation Army is recognised internationally for its social services outreach, humanitarian advocacy, and emergency relief ministries. However, in essence, the Army is a Christian denomination, a church with an integrated mission to 'save souls, grow saints, and serve suffering humanity'.

Born in the midst of holiness revivalism, the Movement's founders quickly identified the need for evangelistic mission beyond the doors of contemporary churches, where middle class piety and spiritual apathy failed to reach out to the practical and spiritual needs of the vulnerable and voiceless, whose cause the emerging Army of Salvation was to champion with vigour and urgency.

Initially wanting to avoid the trappings of 'churchianity', the Army found its natural mission field among the least, the last and the lost. These Salvationist soldiers rolled up their sleeves and shared 'soup, soap, and salvation' with the masses who would never find a welcome or acceptance in the churches of Victorian England.

The Army has now grown into an international church and charity, and though comparatively small numerically, has consistently 'punched above its weight' in the various forms of ministry and service it freely offers to all without discrimination.

My hope is that this book will offer an introduction to Salvation Army theological perspectives and practice, allowing a greater insight into this important missional stream within the wider Church. It will also help Salvationists understand the development of some of the Movement's theological positions, and will engage those who wish to better understand the Army in terms of its motivation for Christian mission and practical service.

By necessity, such a volume can only begin to scratch the surface of the issues facing the Army in the 21st Century as it seeks to be both culturally relevant and remain faithful to its unique calling.

It is my hope that the topics addressed here will prompt further debate and interaction within this international Movement, and that reflection on the past will inform and help shape future planning. The Salvation Army engenders a unique level of trust from the public, governments, and other humanitarian aid organisations. It is primarily an integral part of the wider Church, with distinctive gifts to offer, but must also remember that it must flow together with other streams of Christianity to see the 'earth… filled with the knowledge of the glory of the Lord as the waters cover the sea'.[5]

---

[5] Habakkuk 2:14

Part One: Saving Souls

1. 'Raised up by God…' [1]

Contextualising The Salvation Army in the Church and in the World

Denis Metrustery

It is at work in 127 countries of the world, has 2.3million members, over 26,500 officers and almost 117,000 employees[2] – but what exactly *is* The Salvation Army?

Internationally, the Army operates local worship centres, hostel accommodation for individuals and families, addiction dependency programmes, emergency disaster response, community services (youth, unemployed, counselling, thrift shops), hospitals and clinics, schools and education programmes. This leads to The Salvation Army being one of the most visible Christian agencies, but its overall identity can be confused. Is it a church, is it a social services agency, is it a humanitarian organisation?

The aim of this chapter is to examine the Army's roots and see that it is best described as an innovative and militant Christian denomination which participates in the inbreaking of the Kingdom of God by way of its direct assault on spiritual slavery to sin and attempts to remedy the societal consequences of sin by bringing to bear God's redemptive love and justice.[3]

In recent years, there has been much internal debate seeking to clarify for contemporary members the nature and mission of the Christian organisation which became known as The Salvation Army in 1878. Founders, William and Catherine Booth, stated that their objective was not the starting of a new church, believing that many of the existing churches of their day were failing in their calling to seek and save the lost. The early Salvationists thought of their movement very much as a mission, and their unique identity was further moulded by the adoption of a military model of organisation. The Army's obvious initial mission field was the poor of London's East End, where the full range of human degradation weighed heavily on the Booths' hearts. Today's

---

[1] *The Salvation Army in the Body of Christ: An Ecclesiological Statement,* (London: Salvation Books, 2008), 5 – 'WE BELIEVE that God raised up The Salvation Army according to his purposes for his glory and for the proclamation and demonstration of the gospel.'

[2] *The Salvation Army Yearbook 2016,* (London: Salvation Books, 2015), 29 – statistics correct as at 1 January 2015. Slovakia became the 127th country where the Army's work became officially recognised in September 2015

[3] The Salvation Army's International Mission Statement can be found at Appendix A; its mission has also been summarised by pithy straplines such as 'Heart to God, Hand to Man', and 'Doing the Most Good'

Salvation Army is often referenced as 'Christianity with its sleeves rolled up', an acknowledgement from a variety of quarters, both ecclesiastical and secular, of the practical nature of the Army's approach to its calling.

Central to the Army's self-identity is the belief that it was God himself, albeit through human agency, who brought it into being to be his 'storm troops' who would have no fear of reaching out to the lowest in human society to recall them from the spectre of eternal damnation. A former international leader, General Paul Rader (Rtd), proposes that

> The Salvation Army was born of a vision. First, an idea germinating in the heart of God. Then, a living flame in the heart of a man and woman, William and Catherine Booth. Then, a compelling vision claiming the devotion of a growing Army of Salvation spreading across the world.[4]

However, as the Army has grown numerically, internationally, and in influence, some Salvationists have begun to express concern as to whether the movement has remained true to its founding vision, or has lost a certain amount of impetus by trying to emulate structures and practices of other churches – indeed, some Salvationists object to the notion that The Salvation Army is a church at all and have sought to re-emphasis the non-churchliness of the primitive movement.

Whether through inertia, routinisation of charisma, or apathy, successive generations of Salvationists have found an element of 'mission drift' within their organisation, which I reflect in my opening question: what exactly is The Salvation Army, what is it meant to be doing, and is it true to the founding vision?

Harold Hill observes that

> The life-cycles of organisations, including religious ones, follow a sigmoid curve from movement to institution as they grow. They tend to plateau and enter a period of decline, from which they may or may not recover. Commonly, with the onset of decline, some schismatic or renewal movement strikes out upon a new trajectory of growth before eventually repeating the pattern... Such reactions against the institutionalising of the original movements seek to recover their founder's vision and validate their new departure by the past.[5]

Referencing Mark Noll's critique of weak evangelical intellectualism in his *The Scandal of the Evangelical Mind*,[6] Donald Burke posits that The Salvation Army has 'been less successful at articulating the theological and intellectual

---

[4] Paul A. Rader, 'Vision', in Henry Gariepy & Stephen Court (eds) *Hallmarks of The Salvation Army*, (Blackburn, Victoria, Australia: Salvo Publishing, 2009), 65
[5] Harold Hill, 'Four Anchors to the Stern', *Journal of Aggressive Christianity*, Issue 64, December 2009, 11
[6] Mark A. Noll, *The Scandal of the Evangelical Mind,* (Grand Rapids, MI: Eerdmans, 1994)

underpinnings of [its] mission',[7] and warns of the potential consequences if the Army does not step up to the plate in terms of adequately teaching 'Christian and Salvationist heritage and identity'.

Reflecting on the vision and dynamism of the early Army and the apparent decline in holding in focus the 'big idea' of The Salvation Army's mission, General John Larsson (Rtd) suggests that

> ... perhaps the root problem lies deeper. Perhaps it won't be until the "big idea" is renewed and presented in a way that will capture the hearts and minds of this generation that the essential release of energy will occur. It is new thinking rather than new action that will stop the Army from running out of steam.[8]

More recently, Alan Burns examines Army identity[9] and proposes two broad categories of Salvationist: the 'conservative', who insists on adherence to inherited traditions and defends essential distinctives (such as the Army's traditional music and worship style, brass bands, uniform), while 'radical liberals' hold such values lightly and want to 'redesign the Army for a 21st-century audience whose world view is postmodern and future-orientated... the Army needs to reposition, reinvent, and rebrand itself'.

Burns contends that 'the answers to our current identity crisis lie in our birth story'[10] and seeks to revisit the 'founding stories and founding vision' of the Army. In this fashion, I now wish to examine the historical development of the Army and will address this in a threefold approach: the Army's ecclesial identity, its identity as a social services and humanitarian agency, and also briefly note the group's identity as a distinct legal entity from its founding legal documents and its constitution in each country or region where it operates.

The Salvation Army's Ecclesial Identity

Much has already been written on the Army's origins, and what follows here must necessarily summarise much of the existing scholarship.[11] While a proportion of what has been written reflects a certain critical distance, other works have bordered on an over-glamorised, sentimentalised account of characters and outcomes. We should therefore note the perspective of Australian officer, Grant Sandercock-Brown, when he cautions that

[7] Donald E. Burke, 'The Scandal of the Salvationist Mind', *Word & Deed*: A Journal of Salvation Army Theology & Ministry, Vol 7 No 2 (May 2005), 42
[8] John Larsson, 'Salvationist Theology and Ethics for the New Millennium', *Word & Deed*, Vol 4 No 1 (November 2001), 10
[9] Alan Burns, *Founding Vision for a Future Army: Spiritual Renewal and Mission in The Salvation Army*, (London: Salvation Army, 2013), 5-8
[10] Burns, *Founding Vision*, 10
[11] Existing works can be found in the Bibliography

> We have done ourselves a great disservice by our romanticised hagiographies of the Booths and others. The writers of such material have unwittingly held the Booths' heirs to a standard that the Booths themselves did not attain.[12]

We will preface the Army's history with that of its founders. Born in Nottingham in 1829, one of five children of Samuel and Mary Booth, William Booth's 'childhood was dark and unhappy'. A biographer, Harold Begbie, notes that, despite later more generous recollections of his mother, William in reality 'got no help at all from his father, and very little encouragement from his mother'.[13]

The family suffered severe financial hardships resulting from Samuel Booth's business life, and by the time William reached age 13, the financial circumstances were so dire that he was removed from school and placed in an apprenticeship with a local pawnbroker. From the pretentiousness of the father who often appeared to exaggerate his own position, William now found himself thrust into a lower social position than his father had hoped. William despised the trade, but his exposure to this business environment had two particular results in the analysis of Roger Green:

> First, William quickly became exposed to poverty and circumstances more dire, more difficult, and more threatening than his own. He encountered people... on the brink of ruin. He developed a special compassion for the poor... because he witnessed the tragic effects of poverty... Second... he longed for a better life... He wanted something better, looked for something more fulfilling.[14]

Nurtured by a local Methodist family within the Broad Street Wesley Chapel, William had a personal conversion experience at the age of 15 and shortly afterwards, with his friend William Sansom, became involved in preaching, open air witness, and assistance to the poor.

While John Wesley's visits had established strong renewal currents within the church in Nottingham, subsequent denominational Methodism was beginning to grow cold in Booth's day, and he began to come under the influence of itinerant Methodist preachers. Most influential on Booth was American Methodist preacher, James Caughey, who visited Nottingham in 1846. Begbie notes that Booth 'caught fire from the flame of this revivalist's oratory'[15] and Norman Murdoch goes so far as to say that

---

[12] Grant Sandercock-Brown, *21 Questions for a 21st Century Army: Being the Salvos Now*, (Freemantle, Western Australia: Vivid Publishing, 2013) (Kindle edition)

[13] Harold Begbie, *Life of William Booth, Founder of the Salvation Army*, (London: MacMillan & Co, 1920), 27

[14] Roger J. Green, *The Life and Ministry of William Booth: Founder of the Salvation Army*, (Nashville, TN: Abingdon Press, 2006), 10-11

[15] Begbie, 61

Booth was Caughey's heir. Caughey convinced Booth that converting the masses was possible through scientific, calculated means. Revivals which were planned, advertised, and prayed for would succeed... Booth was consumed with the idea of winning souls through mass meetings, house-to-house visitation, and personal witness.[16]

Booth served as a local lay preacher while remaining in employment which provided a meagre income for the family. However, his job came to an unexpected end and, failing to find alternative work locally, the 20-year-old Booth moved to London but found no immediate employment and felt like a fish out of water in the worldliness of the metropolis.

After a period of time working in another pawnbroker's in south London, a Wesleyan layman, Edward Harris Rabbits, heard the young Booth's earnest and enthusiastic preaching; convinced that Booth's approach transcended the deadly formality of contemporary Methodist services, Rabbits began to support Booth financially, allowing him to leave his employment and begin to devote himself to ministry. William's move to London was indeed providential, for it was here that he was introduced to Catherine Mumford, who with her mother, had heard him preach in their local chapel. The Mumford family had been befriended by Edward Rabbits, and so it was he who introduced William to Catherine.

As time progressed, the pair continued to frequently exchange a series of letters[17] which display their spontaneity as well as their inner feelings and concerns at the start of a relationship and their utmost desire for each other's soul and walk with God. The couple became engaged in May 1852, and married three years later in June 1855.

A significant concern for William Booth was to identify the particular church where he would undertake ministry training, "he was looking for a denomination in which he could feel at home theologically and in which his gifts as an evangelist would be used".[18]

Through Rabbits, he had become a preacher within the Reform Movement, but had reservations about the strict control exercised by church committees over preachers and ministers. He subsequently became involved with the Congregationalists, but felt unable to train for the ministry in this context in light of the denomination's promotion of Calvinist predestination. Roger Green comments that 'Booth's Wesleyan theological background... prevented him considering any doctrine of election that excluded free grace to everyone... as a roadblock to evangelism'.[19]

---

[16] Norman Murdoch, *Origins of The Salvation Army*, (Knoxville, TN: The University of Tennessee Press, 1994), 12

[17] Many are cited in Begbie; see also, the more recent: Cathy le Feuvre, *William and Catherine: The Love Story of the Founders of the Salvation Army Told Through Their Letters*, (Oxford: Monarch Books, 2013)

[18] Green, *The Life and Ministry of William Booth*, 51

[19] Green, *The Life and Ministry of William Booth*, 58

Debate concerning the relative merits of orderly church services as opposed to Booth's kind of revivalism, zealous preaching, and women preachers led to a schism among the Wesleyans in 1851.

After a brief pastorate in a Reform Movement church in Spalding, and much theological reading and reflection, Booth found appeal in New Connexion Methodism which appeared to offer William what he had been searching for in a denomination, a Wesleyan theological foundation, an emphasis on revivalism, and church governance which allowed congregational input but did not undermine ministerial authority. He entered their training college in February 1854. His mentor, Dr William Cooke, observed that the rigours of academic study were not best suited to the young Booth, and he was keen to see him engage in ministry within the London Circuit. However, Booth's own lack of confidence, especially in his administrative abilities, led to a reacquaintance with Mr Rabbits, who supported him financially to be an assistant minister, while developing his evangelistic skills, becoming the denomination's itinerant evangelist.

Some members of the New Connexion Conference appeared jealous of Booth's evangelistic success and in 1857 moved that he be removed from itinerant ministry and be assessed in circuit ministry prior to ordination. At the next year's conference, William pleaded to be released into itinerant ministry but was reassigned to another circuit; it was at this conference that he was also ordained.

However, unable to gain denominational approval for a translocal evangelistic ministry, Booth parted ways with the Methodist New Connexion in 1861. Following evangelistic campaigns in Cornwall, Wales, the Midlands and the north, during which the Booths both felt despondent about the family's lack of financial resources and the frequent separation through ministry trips, the family moved to London at Catherine's instigation in 1865.

Catherine began to gain prominence as a preacher, having fulfilled this role before especially during periods when William had been incapacitated through depression. The family also enjoyed a better standard of living, although this was in part thanks to continued frugality; consistency of income remained uncertain and both William and Catherine helped the family's earnings by way of preaching, and the sale of song books and pamphlets.

Booth was approached by representatives of the East London Special Services Committee with a view to Booth preaching in various locations in London's notorious East End, an area rife with poor housing, unemployment, illness, alcoholism, and desperation.

He rented rooms in Whitechapel for Sunday services but also continued to preach in the streets. Green notes that while Booth's primary goal was to address the spiritual poverty of the East End, he was also beginning to realise that the gospel could have significant societal impact, although 'one must be careful not to imply that the most compelling reason why Booth ministered to the poor was to create a more stable society. Booth was primarily an evangelist and revivalist, pressing the hope that spiritual regeneration would manifest itself in social stability'. [20]

Booth initially called his work the East London Christian Revival Society, but soon renamed it the East London Christian Mission. Pamela Walker comments on the Mission's distinctiveness: 'The authority it granted women, its emphasis on holiness theology and revivalist methods, its growing independence, and its strict hierarchical structure were all features that sharply distinguished it from its contemporaries'.[21] Sandall's historical review suggests that the year 1867 was the 'turning point' for it saw the formal naming of the movement as the East London Christian Mission, the acquisition of headquarters, the hiring of workers, and the establishment of a system of processing converts.[22] The intervening decade witnessed something of a transition as the movement eventually became The Salvation Army, with Booth in autocratic control.

In 1869 the Mission changed its name to simply The Christian Mission, as its remit had expanded beyond simply London's East End, and the first Conference was held in 1870. There William Booth was confirmed as General Superintendent, and while the Conference was technically in charge, 'Booth was, for all intents and purposes, in control of the Mission... an autocracy was fully established at that time'.[23]

Roger Green suggests that the survival of The Christian Mission in contrast to the durability of the many mission organisations which arose at that time can be linked to three compelling characteristics.[24] First, the Mission's constitution was rooted within Methodism, ensuring Wesleyan structure and discipline. Second, the Mission clarified its doctrine, and particularly that regarding sanctification. Third, the leadership style of the Mission helped ensure its endurance; many early leaders considered the sole leadership of Booth 'as a strength and a signal of future usefulness and growth'.[25]

A military-type of discipline was commonplace within The Christian Mission, and some of Booth's main supporters described themselves as 'lieutenant' and 'captain' and referred to Booth himself as their 'general'.[26] Booth referred to the Mission's 1877 Conference as their 'Council of War' and spoke of 'our army'. The stage was all but set for the evolution from Mission to Army: 'Before the name of the movement existed the idea of The Salvation Army leaps at one from every page... All through *Heathen England*[27] we see

[20] Green, *The Life and Ministry of William Booth*, 108
[21] Pamela J. Walker, *Pulling the Devil's Kingdom Down: The Salvation Army in Victorian Britain*, (Berkeley, CA: University of California Press, 2001), 42
[22] Sandall, *History Vol I*, 72ff
[23] Green, *The Life and Ministry of William Booth*, 114
[24] Green, *The Life and Ministry of William Booth*, 115-118
[25] Green, *The Life and Ministry of William Booth*. 118
[26] Perhaps simply an abbreviated form of 'general superintendent'
[27] George Scott Railton, *Heathen England and What to Do for it*, (London: S W Partridge, 1877)

that General Superintendent, William Booth, and General Secretary, George Scott Railton, had an army on their hands'.[28] One of Booth's biographers notes that 'a military mood was fast developing in the Christian Mission, and it reflected the wider mood of the Victorian Church and Britain generally'.[29]

Changing the description of The Christian Mission to 'a Volunteer Army' was briefly considered, but this was amended in favour of a (later The) Salvation Army.[30] William Booth became the first General, Mission Station preachers were given the rank of captain, suitable uniforms followed, and many early Army songs used a military metaphor.[31]

The Booths were convinced, especially through the evangelistic strategies of Finney and Caughey, of the need for 'adaptation of measures' or using whatever pragmatic strategies work for the saving of souls. Catherine Booth concluded that 'we have done with civilian measures... and we have come to military measures'.[32] David Taylor, in his recent book, suggests that

> Salvationists reflecting upon their ecclesiology should consider the reality that the metaphor of an army, like its forerunner, aggressive evangelistic Christian mission, emerged with an ear more tuned to the task of efficiently reaching the 'lost' and lone individual than to the life and shape of the gathered community.[33]

He further suggests that

> Booth, and his colleagues, fully exploited the potential of the military metaphor in establishing [The Salvation Army's] identity, at the expense of the predominant Biblical pictures of the church that might have added richer, and more rounded dimensions.[34]

Taylor's book addresses a 'tangled cord of three separately identifiable ecclesial strands of mission, army and church'[35] and he observes that, while

---

[28] Bernard Watson's biography of Railton, *Soldier Saint*. (London: Hodder & Stoughton, 1970), 39-40

[29] David M Bennett, *The General: William Booth*, (Longwood, FL: Xulon Press, 2003) , Vol 2, 91

[30] Robert Sandall, *The History of The Salvation Army, Volume One: 1865-1878*, (London: Thomas Nelson & Sons Ltd, 1947), 228-229

[31] Glenn K. Horridge, *The Salvation Army, Origins and Early Days: 1865-1900*, (Godalming: Ammonite Books, 1993) cites 20 different facets of how militarism attracted people to the Army, 45

[32] Catherine Booth, 'Conquest', *The War Cry*, 3 November 1881, 2

[33] David Taylor, *Like A Mighty Army? The Salvation Army, the Church, and the Churches*, (Eugene, OR: Pickwick Publ, 2014) (Kindle edition)

[34] David Taylor, *Like A Mighty Army*

[35] David Taylor, *Like A Mighty Army*

The Salvation Army has engaged in theological reflection with other Christian churches,[36]

> the metaphor of an army was the sociological and pragmatic outcome of a largely individualistic and subjective approach to salvation, [and] it does not adequately characterise the theological nature and form of the Christian community, and continues to afflict the Army's ecclesiology.[37]

Another commentator observes that 'the image of a Christian soldier is quite common in the New Testament... it presents an image of discipline, support, preparedness, dedication, and self-sacrifice'.[38]

John Briggs comments that

> In streamlining its activities in the interests of its mission, the Army had deprived itself of what other Christians regarded as essential marks of the church – particularly an ordained ministry and the sacraments of baptism and holy communion.[39]

It has been observed that The Salvation Army

> has always *acted* like a church in terms of the functions it performs for its members. It is the spiritual home for Salvationists, the place where they are converted, the place where they are nurtured, where they fellowship and serve, mark significant moments in their life, and raise their children. On the other hand, it has often maintained that it has a special vocation, to be something more than, or other than 'a church'.[40]

Henry Gariepy comments that 'through writings and international symposiums the Army has come to a new and clearer understanding of its ecclesiastical

---

[36] Such recent engagement is recorded in *Working Together in Mission: Witness, Education, and Service; Salvation Army – World Methodist Council Bilateral Dialogue report, Series II, 2011*, http://worldmethodistcouncil.org/wp-content/uploads/2012/02/Salvation-Army-Dialogue-Report.pdf (accessed 19 June 2012) and *Conversations with The Catholic Church, A record of the papers presented and recommendations made during the informal conversations between The Catholic Church and The Salvation Army 2007-2012*, (London: Salvation Books, 2014)
[37] Taylor, *Like a Mighty Army*
[38] Brian Mackey, 'The Army of God: Reclaiming a Military Model of the Church for the 21st Century', http://didache.nazarene.org/index.php/volume-5-2/722-didache-5-2-military-model/file (accessed 17 January 2013)
[39] John H. Y. Briggs in Foreword to David Taylor *Like A Mighty Army?*
[40] James Pedlar, 'When did The Salvation Army become a Church?' http://jamespedlar.wordpress.com/2012/09/21/when-did-the-salvation-army-become-a-church/ (accessed 23 November 2012)

history and identity'.[41] We will now note the development of theological reflection in some of the Army's writings on this subject.

The Army's search for self-understanding has been long and convoluted, but attention should be paid to William Booth's early statement that

> The Salvation Army is not inferior in spiritual character to any organisation in existence .... We are, I consider, equal everyway and everywhere to any other Christian organisation on the face of the earth (i) in spiritual authority, (ii) in spiritual intelligence, (iii) in spiritual functions. We hold 'the keys' as truly as any church in existence.[42]

The initial and continuing ambiguity in Salvationist ecclesiology perhaps reflects its Wesleyan heritage, where Wesley deemed his societies not to be separate churches, rather *ecclesiola in ecclesia*, Christian communities within the wider (Anglican) church. Booth confirms that 'it was not my intention to create another sect ... we are not a church. We are an Army—an Army of Salvation.'[43] However, John Coutts sagely observes that 'Booth became the founder of a new denomination, while believing—like most founders of new denominations—that he was doing nothing of the kind'.[44] Indeed, 'Booth never explicitly articulated a doctrine of the Church. It did not exist in the Methodist New Connexion's doctrines that he borrowed'.[45]

John Larsson argues that ecclesiological terminology in relation to the Army should not be a matter of words only, but that certain consequences should follow; he notes that 'in one sense it is only now—after more than 100 years of existence—that the Army in reality is evolving into a church and that we are therefore facing a time of transition'.[46] Such evolution in the Movement's thinking can be identified through statements from successive Generals in relation to the Army's understanding of its ecclesial nature.

As noted above, Booth was far from convinced of the need for another church, and sought to distance his Salvation Army from the inherent apathy of many contemporary churches toward their responsibilities in the Great Commission. He felt that many church structures and practices conspired to isolate those who most needed the Church's message, and he sought to free his salvation soldiers from such entanglements so that they could directly address the spiritual, social, and moral needs of their neighbours.

---

[41] Henry Gariepy, *Christianity in Action: An International History of The Salvation Army*, (Grand Rapids, MI: Wm B Eerdmans Publ., Co., 2009), 59
[42] Robert Sandall, *The History of The Salvation Army: Volume II: 1878–1886* (London: Thomas Nelson & Sons, 1950), 126
[43] Clarence Wiseman, "Are We a Church?", *The Officer*, Vol. XXVII, No. 10, 1976, 435
[44] John Coutts, *The Salvationists*, (London: Mowbrays, 1977), 21
[45] Taylor, *Like a Mighty Army*
[46] John Larsson, 'Salvationist Theology & Ethics for the New Millennium,' *Word & Deed*, Vol. 4, No.1, November 2001

However, both William Booth and his son and successor Bramwell stated their belief that the Army was definitely an integral part of the wider church:

> The Army is part of the living Church of God—a great instrument of war in the world, engaged in deadly conflict with sin and fiends.[47]

> Of this, the Great Church of the Living God, we claim, and have ever claimed, that we of The Salvation Army are an integral part and element.[48]

Much was made of the military metaphor, and its picture of those intensely engaged on a mission, mobile and militant; this was contrasted with a more sedentary picture of Victorian church life, where although evangelistic stirrings were breaking out, the prevailing sense of separation from the world meant that maintaining the *status quo* was to some more important than an outward, mission-orientated perspective. David Rightmire contends that during this period 'nominal Christianity hid behind the mask of excessive pietism; conformity and moral pretentiousness served to maintain order amidst tremendous social, economic, and political upheaval'.[49]

General Albert Orsborn repeatedly stated that 'we are, and wish to remain, a Movement for the revival of religion, a permanent mission to the unconverted'.[50] It should be noted, however, that his article addresses the Army's relationship to the World Council of Churches, and he is stressing the importance of the Army's distinctives and the merits of remaining separate from the churches in respect of its own governance and mission; he confirms that in terms of the Army's attendance at WCC conferences, 'we are not prepared to change or modify our own particular and characteristic principles and methods'.[51]

---

[47] William Booth cited in Wiseman, 'Are we a Church?', 436
[48] Bramwell Booth, *Echoes and Memories*, (London: Hodder and Stoughton, 1925), 79
[49] R. David Rightmire, *Sacraments and the Salvation Army: Pneumatological Foundations* (Metuchen; The Scarecrow Press, 1990), 5
[50] Albert Orsborn, 'The World Council of Churches', *The Officer*, Vol. V, No.2, March – April 1954, 74; this article was written in preparation for the attendance by an Army delegation at the WCC conference at Evanston, Chicago in August 1954
[51] Orsborn, 'The World Council of Churches', 74; The Salvation Army was among the founding members of the World Council of Churches in 1948, having previously been participants in faith & order and missionary committees that led up to the founding of the WCC. However, a dispute over the funding of guerilla groups (which in reality was an optional funding of the welfare committees of certain guerilla groups, such as the Patriotic Front in what was then Rhodesia) in Africa led to TSA stepping out of full membership and taking up an Observer role, a position that has been maintained up until this time. In particular two SA missionaries were killed in Rhodesia by guerillas and this proved to be catalytic in the Army' revised status. Following attendance at the WCC

General Wilfred Kitching subsequently noted that 'we are almost universally recognised as a religious denomination by governments and, for the purposes of a national emergency... or for convenience in designating our officers, they group us with the churches'.[52] His successor as General, Frederick Coutts, admitted that 'the subject [of the Army's relationship with the churches] has to be rethought as generation succeeds generation'[53] and he advocates that the Army must not throw away its birthright or deny the circumstances and calling which led to its founding; the insights given to Booth must be cherished, but Coutts may touch on hyperbole when he suggests that 'to abandon them now would be to commit spiritual suicide without cause'.[54]

General Clarence Wiseman explores further options for ecclesial identity and also is more explicit than his predecessors on the subject. He notes that in the beginning, they were a 'mission', and even after the change of name to The Salvation Army, there remained insistence that they were not a church, but an Army. He notes that the Army has been likened to a modern 'religious order'. He concludes that, while all of these descriptors are accurate to some degree, 'I believe also the Army can truthfully be described as a 'church' in the more circumscribed, denominational sense of the word'.[55] In 1996, General Paul Rader acknowledged that 'we have begun to come more to terms with our churchly identity'.[56]

General Shaw Clifton outlines a theological, sociological, and legal rationale for concluding that The Salvation Army qualifies to be called a church in its own right,[57] and unequivocally asserts that 'I believe that we are a church and that it is simply impossible to sustain any argument to the contrary'.[58]

I tend to agree with such a bold statement as this, for while in its early days, the Army was sectarian, and also exhibited some attributes of a religious Order, it appears now to have fully transitioned into an autonomous denominational church. While the Army does not meet one of the strict Reformation criteria 'that the sacrament should be rightly administered', it does reflect the four creedal marks of the church: 'one' – the Army accepts the

---

Conference in Korea in 2013, there are hopes that TSA may return to full membership, but this is as yet uncertain.
[52] Wilfred Kitching, 'The Army and the World Council of Churches – Part I', *The Officer*, Vol. XII, No.5, September – October 1961, 324
[53] Frederick Coutts, 'The Salvation Army and its Relation to the Churches', *The Officer*, October 1964, 649
[54] Coutts, 'TSA and its Relation to the Churches', 651
[55] Clarence Wiseman, 'Are we a Church?', *The Officer*, Vol. XXVII, No.10, October 1976, 438
[56] In Foreword to Robert Street, *Called to be God's People, The International Spiritual Life Commission: Its report, implications and challenges*, (London: Salvation Books, 1999), vii
[57] Shaw Clifton, *Who are these Salvationists? An Analysis for the 21st Century*, (Alexandria, VA: Crest Books, 1999), 10-17
[58] Shaw Clifton, *Selected Writings* Volume II (2000-2010), (London: Salvation Books, 2010), 66

spiritual unity of all true believers as part of Christ's Church; 'holy' – the church (and the churches) are called out by God to be separate from the world and dedicated to him, sanctified by the Spirit; 'catholic' – the Army is part of the universal Church, orthodox in doctrine, and international in scope; 'apostolic' – rooted in the gospel proclaimed by Christ and his apostles, and demonstrating a continuation of apostolic ministry. The Army has its own articles of faith (the eleven Doctrines), and not only seeks to evangelise and convert the lost, but also provides a structure for corporate worship and personal discipleship, spiritual growth, and pastoral care. To all intents and purposes, it has its own form of ministry (officership) which, despite holding to the priesthood of all believers, is distinct in its role and responsibilities. While all believers are called into the service of Christ, some are specifically called to teach and shepherd the flock, and within the structure of The Salvation Army, such leadership is provided by those who are identified as called and equipped for such ministry, and trained and commissioned/ordained to it. Commenting on those who have withdrawn from active officership, an old Army periodical insists that they remain divinely-appointed to proclaim the gospel, having 'entered the sacred circle,'[59] which sounds close to an understanding of an indelible ministry charism as claimed within the ordained orders of some other churches.

Jonathan Raymond comments that 'new metaphors and paradigms for leadership are emerging and changing how we think of leaders, and in particular, spiritual leaders'.[60] While still of importance, the task of Booth's early mission station preachers to focus solely on soul-saving, has developed into a multidisciplinary function for today's Salvation Army officers. It is acknowledged that each officer has received his or her own personal call to ministry, and will exercise that ministry within various facets of Army operations, and their ministry will demonstrate individual spiritual gifting and a composite of practical experience. In Corps ministry, the officer very much functions in a similar way to other ordained clergy in terms of the requirements of the position. The Army has debated the merits of ordination,[61] with some fearing a dilution of the movement's freedom and effectiveness should it try to emulate the structures and practices of other churches; we will recall the Founders' views on the importance of keeping the Army from the ineffective piety of nominal religion. Those who oppose the view that officers should be publically ordained as well as 'commissioned' stress that the main differentiation between Salvation Army soldiers and officers is not so much that of 'function' (for 'ordinary' members ought also to be able to preach and

---

[59] *Field Officer*, December 1900, 453-545
[60] Jonathan S, Raymond, 'Spiritual Leadership in The Salvation Army', *Word & Deed*, Vol. 3, No. 2, May 2001, 23
[61] Harold Hill treats the subject of the differentiation of officers in an 'ordained caste' and the consequent problems for Salvation Army ecclesiology and mission in *Leadership in the Salvation Army: A Case Study in Clericalisation*, (Milton Keynes: Paternoster, 2006)

lead meetings, etc.) that the latter have been set aside from 'secular' employment[62] to be able to offer the Army their total availability, with total disposability and appointability noted as specific marks of officership.[63] However, it is difficult to distinguish fully between soldier and officer, in the sense that both are in covenant relationship (with God and the Army), and that commitment to soldiership by its nature involves a higher degree of commitment and action than typical church membership. The differentiation must therefore include the concept of total availability of the officer for the Army's needs,[64] and we should also note that throughout church history, God has called individuals to 'leave their nets' and serve him in a special capacity which transcends the commitment of simple church membership. The Apostle Paul reminds the Ephesians that God has established certain leadership ministries within the church in order to 'prepare God's people for works of service'.[65] The goal of this is the building up of the church, unity, and maturity; while the 'works of service [ministry]' are to be done by all believers, God appoints gifted oversight and leadership to help develop this. A preoccupation with restricting officer ministry to 'soldiership writ large' can surely only have the effect of similarly restricting the potential outcome of their church-enabling ministry. Clifton observes that 'the doctrine [of the priesthood of all believers] is incompatible with any idea of there being a difference in kind, or in spiritual standing before God, between officers and others'[66] but does agree that any difference is solely one of function and the classification of role.[67]

The Army's view on 'servant leadership' notes that

> In The Salvation Army this does not mean that preaching, teaching and exercising authority cannot be part of the ministries of soldiers, but it

---

[62] See *Orders and Regulations for the Training of Salvation Army Officers* (Chapter 8, Sections 1 to 3). However, it should be noted that the officer does not then become an employee of the Army, but signs the Officer's Covenant and Undertakings, whereby the Army becomes the a means of facilitating the officer's ministry; a comparatively small allowance is paid as well as the provision of living accommodation and transport; territorial discretion allows additional benefits to be paid such as healthcare and retirement provision

[63] *The Officer*, July 1976, 290

[64] *Orders and Regulations for Officers of The Salvation Army* (Volume 1, Part 1, Chapter 1.1) - 'Officers of The Salvation Army are soldiers who have relinquished secular employment in response to a spiritual calling, so as to devote all their time and energies to the service of God and the people and who, having successfully completed the required period of training, are commissioned as officers and ordained as ministers of the gospel of Jesus Christ.'

[65] Ephesians 4:12

[66] Clifton, *Writings I*, 5

[67] In 1999, General John Gowans reviewed responses to the International Commission on Officership (previously established under General Paul Rader) and the 28 recommendations formulated for consideration; see John Larsson, *Saying YES to LIFE: An Autobiography*, (London: Salvation Books, 2007), 189-193

emphasises that an ordination to spiritual leadership is especially integral to officership. Salvation Army officers are given authority to exercise their spiritual leadership by the call of God and the confirmation of the people.[68]

Traditionally, Cadets (those training for service as officers) were 'commissioned' as officers (usually with the rank of Lieutenant) at the end of their initial college-based training. General Arnold Brown undertook a revision of the wording employed in the Army's commissioning services, allowing usage of the word 'ordain'; this attracted three main responses. Those who were against ordination argued mainly from the perspective of the functional view of officership, linking officership to availability for appointment, in contrast to the 'ordination' within other churches which remains effective unless the minister is defrocked. Brown had made the change after consultation from various territories where 'ordained ministry' was a requirement to allow the Army to hold the position it needed within church and society. Those in favour insisted that the term did not invalidate holding to the priesthood of all believers, but did recognise that certain people are to be set aside in a particular way for the service of the gospel. The term 'ordination' is also construed as 'admission to the ministry' and as such, to some extent, is probably coterminous with 'commissioning'. Others were prepared to entertain the notion of ordination but interpreted this in a functional manner, rather accepting it as a change of character or status. This view accepts the dual ordination within the church, of some to exercise specific gifts and ministries, and the greater ordination of all believers to the vocation of 'Christian'.[69]

The wording of the commissioning service was further revised and the text recited by the senior leader (usually the Territorial Commander)[70] commissioning the new officers was amended from 'In accepting these pledges which you each have made, I commission you as officers of The Salvation Army and ordain you as ministers of Christ and of his gospel' (1978 under Brown) to one of:

> Recognising that God has called you, has equipped you and gifted you for sacred service, I now ordain you as a minister of the gospel of our Lord and Saviour Jesus Christ, and commission you as an officer of The Salvation Army with the rank of lieutenant.

---

[68] *Servants Together: Salvationist Perspectives on Ministry*, (London: Salvation Books, 2002; Rev Ed 2008), 76-77

[69] Shaw Clifton summarises: 'any distinction between [clergy and laity] is one of *role* or *function*, not one of priestly or spiritual status. We do not believe that there is a special, unique or exclusive grace of God available to the ordained person, but unavailable to non-ordained believers.' *Who Are These Salvationists?*, 29

[70] Only the General, the Chief of the Staff, the Territorial Commander, or another Commissioner on active service are properly authorised to conduct commissioning ceremonies.

OR:

We rejoice that God has called you, has equipped you and gifted you for
sacred service and therefore we now ordain you as a minister of the
gospel of our Lord and Saviour Jesus Christ, and commission you as an
officer of The Salvation Army with the rank of lieutenant.

OR:

With gratitude to God for your calling into the paths of sacred service
and for his empowering and gifting in your life, you are now ordained as
a minister of the gospel of our Lord and Saviour Jesus Christ, and
commissioned as an officer of The Salvation Army with the rank of
lieutenant.[71]

Some of the optional wording represents a slight dissociation of the act of
ordination at human hands to a firm acknowledgement that the Cadet is being
commissioned because they have already been ordained and gifted for ministry
by Christ.

Ray Harris suggests that 'the Army has developed its own expression
of the church, and it is one that takes authorized ministry seriously. Officers are
commissioned in an act that is most public and most sacred. The
commissioning of officers expresses the Army's understanding of ordination,
the church and the gospel'.[72] He also posits that 'an officer has been conferred
with a new sense of identity, and this shapes [his or her] vocation'. [73]

Phil Needham's significant volume on Salvation Army ecclesiology
stresses the importance of the momentum of a pilgrim church and that the
church's *raison d'être* is the fulfilment of its mission, engaged in Kingdom
warfare as an eschatological community. He notes that his writings address a
'Salvationist ecclesiology', that is, a specifically Salvationist understanding of
what it means to be and act as church; he does not seek to promote an
'ecclesiology of The Salvation Army,' seeing such as potentially idolatrous for
'it is also a human institution and subject to many forces and influences to
which all institutions are subject'.[74] Needham also observes that a Salvationist
ecclesiology will necessarily reflect a bias toward mission, and that this 'could
never be seen as an ecclesiology for the whole Church, for no other reason than
the fact that Salvationist history and experience have created a selection of

---

[71] 2008/IA/08 Minute by the Chief of the Staff (April 2008) cited in *Servants Together*,
93-105
[72] Ray Harris, 'Identity Crisis', Salvationist (Canada and Bermuda Territory)
http://salvationist.ca/2013/12/identity-crisis/ (accessed 8 January 2014)
[73] Harris, 'Identity Crisis'
[74] Philip D. Needham, *Community in Mission: A Salvationist Ecclesiology*, (St Alban's:
Campfield Press, 1987), 3

emphases and priorities which would not be shared by all Christian fellowships'.[75]

The 1998 revision of the Army's Handbook of Doctrine, *Salvation Story*, proposes that 'Salvation Army doctrine implies a doctrine of the Church. Each doctrine begins: 'We believe . . . .' 'We' points to a body of believers, a community of faith – a church,' [76] and the *Ecclesiological Statement* of 2008 confirms that

> The Salvation Army, under the one Triune God, belongs to and is an expression of the Body of Christ on earth, the Church universal, and is a Christian denomination in permanent mission to the unconverted, called into and sustained in being by God. [77]

The ecumenical movement and the World Council of Churches' Faith and Order paper *Baptism, Eucharist and Ministry* 'proved to be a catalyst toward the... publication of a brief official clarification that seeks to outline The Salvation Army's current ecclesiological convictions'. [78]

There is a healthy tension between an organic structural entity and a dynamic missionary entity, and this has been easily observed in the Army's oscillation between self-identification as a 'mission' and its ecclesiality as a distinct denomination. Ralph Winter [79] posits that the church in its best form exists as a tension between sodality and modality, and identifies the traits of the missional thrust of early monastic orders being taken up by groups like the Cistercians, the Friars, and the Jesuits. This can be understood as the ontological and functional definitions of the church; the first evidenced within the gathered worshipping community, the second by missionary outreach. While not always ideal in doctrine or praxis, such groups 'represented the best holiness and missionary/socially engaging ideals of their time'.[80] It is interesting that Winter interprets The Salvation Army as providing a Christian community that stands between a modality and a sodality.[81]

George Scott Railton recognised the dynamics of an Order and commented that 'we have got an organisation... formed of people whose

[75] Needham, *Community in Mission*, 4
[76] *Salvation Story: Salvationist Handbook of Doctrine*, (London: UK Territory Print & Design Unit, 1998), 100
[77] *The Salvation Army in the Body of Christ: An Ecclesiological Statement*, (London: Salvation Books, 2008)
[78] Taylor, *Like a Mighty Army*; this references both the *Ecclesiological Statement* (2008) and the Army's earlier response to *BEM*, *One Faith, One Church: The Salvation Army's Response to 'Baptism, Eucharist and* Ministry' (St Alban's: Campfield Press, 1990)
[79] Ralph D. Winter, *The Two Structures of God's Redemptive Mission*, (Pasadena: William Carey Library, 1995)
[80] Robert Lang'at, 'The Salvation Army as a Christian Church with a Social Conscience', *Word & Deed* Vol. 9 No. 2, May 2009
[81] Winter, *Two Structures*, 1-16

devotion, determination and confidence at least equal that of the Jesuits,'[82] and Frances Power Cobbe observes that the organisation of the Army 'combines the inspiring military pattern with the rigid discipline and complete autocracy of the great monastic orders'.[83] Recalling the Army's early dialogue with the Anglicans, Taylor comments that 'The Salvation Army could potentially have become an order within the Anglican Church if there had been the will on both sides'.[84] However, while an Order derives its authority from the parent church, a sect has its own inherent authority structure, thus Bryan Wilson suggests that The Salvation Army represents a 'conversionist sect'[85] that would normally develop into a denomination within one generation.

In its early history, Booth and the Army's leaders were invited into dialogue with the Church of England's hierarchy, with a view to mutual recognition and respect, and to discuss the ramifications of the Army becoming a distinct sect. Also under discussion was the option of bringing the Army under the aegis of the established Church, but Booth was advised not to relinquish his control over the new movement and although they remained cordial, the proposals in respect of potential union came to nothing. Taylor notes that 'this decision clearly signalled the identity of The Salvation Army as an autonomous denomination, rather than what might have been a Religious Order in Anglicanism'.[86] He further concludes that 'in denying he was sectarian in founding a new church organisation, and whilst not formally attached to a parent church, Booth was initially and implicitly attempting to project his Army as a quasi-missionary religious order and a special service within the wider church'.[87]

Another obvious distinctive of The Salvation Army is that it does not observe the two traditional sacraments, or ordinances, within Protestantism, baptism and the Lord's Supper/Communion/Eucharist. This issue is ably addressed in a later chapter by Phil Needham, so does not need exhaustive treatment here. Suffice to note that William Booth's decision to abandon these practices was not so much theological as pragmatic, and in the early days, Salvationists did take the Lord's Supper. Booth also indicated that he had no problem with Salvationists partaking in these practices in other church settings if they so desired and found value in them.

The Army's holiness teaching and adopted 'altar theology' made it clear that holiness of life and character could not be achieved through external means or religious ritual, but simply through complete abandonment to Christ and sanctification through the baptism of the Holy Spirit. The movement's

---

[82] Sandall, *History Vol I*, 237

[83] Frances Power Cobbe, 'The Last Revival', *The Contemporary Review* (July/December 1882) 183

[84] Taylor, *Like a Mighty Army*

[85] Bryan R. Wilson, *Patterns of Sectarianism: Organisation and Ideology in Social Religious Movements*, (London: Heinemann, 1967), 27

[86] Taylor, *Like A Mighty Army*

[87] Taylor, *Like A Mighty Army*

'poet General,' Albert Orsborn, penned a hymn which has been taken as supporting the non-sacramental stance:

> My life must be Christ's broken bread,
> My love his outpoured wine,
> A cup o'erfilled, a table spread
> Beneath his name and sign.
> That other souls, refreshed and fed,
> May share his life through mine.[88]

Booth himself did not wish to make a definite, unchangeable pronouncement on the subject, citing both his desire not to foster division and his view that he was not starting a new church, suggesting that 'is it not wise for us to postpone any settlement of the question, to leave it over to some future day, when we shall have more light, and see more clearly our way before us?'[89]

Coupled with Catherine Booth's increasing concern at rituals and liturgies, the early Army's views were also influenced by the issue of who would have authority to administer sacraments (in light of the priesthood of all believers and the understanding of officership as functional not sacerdotal), the potential problems in Victorian society of women officiating at such rites, as well as the wisdom of administering communion wine to converts with a history of alcoholism. Importantly, the early leaders did not see any scriptural warrant to conclude that any special grace was received in the sacraments, nor that they were in any way necessary for salvation. It was proposed that Booth 'pointed his people to the privilege and necessity of seeking the substance rather than the shadow'.[90] This reflects a Zwinglian understanding of sacraments, where the Spirit does not need any specific channels to administer grace.

It has been argued that instead of being 'non-sacramental' Salvationists have become 'neo-sacramental'. Instead of continuing infant baptism, a ceremony of dedication of infants to God was devised; instead of adult baptism, Booth instituted a swearing-in ceremony for soldiers. Instead of the sacrament of Communion, Salvationists understood their whole lives to be 'a continual recognition of their union with Christ'.[91] The Army sought to

---

[88] *The Song Book of The Salvation Army*, (London: International Headquarters of The Salvation Army, 1986, reprinted 1987), Song 512

[89] William Booth, 'The General's New Year Address to Officers', *The War Cry*, 17 January 1883; Chick Yuill notes, however, that 'the official stance [has become] that Booth never intended his words about the possibility of further discussion on "some future day" to be taken seriously, but that he made this statement simply out of "an irenic spirit of diplomacy" to quiet the minds of those who were less sure than he was himself'. 'Sanctity and Sacrament', *The Rubicon*, Supper Club Series #4, http://therubicon.org/2007/05/supper-club-series-4-yuill/ (accessed 25 June 2012)

[90] Minnie L. Carpenter, *Salvationists and the Sacraments*, (London: Salvationist Publishing and Supplies Ltd., 1945), 5

[91] Clifton, *Who Are These Salvationists?*, 59

remember Christ's sacrifice at every mealtime (and encouraged the saying of grace and other prayers) and also held love-feasts, which was a practice among earlier Methodists. The Army's traditional terminology of 'non-observance' and 'non-sacramentalism' could therefore be deemed anachronistic and inaccurate, as the traditional sacraments of the church have, in effect, been replaced by Army ceremonies which could have the same result of transmitting God's grace to those who faithfully participate in them.

Despite a disinclination toward sacramentalism, the Army does admit that the church 'feeds upon him who is the one and only, true and original Sacrament' as it 'gathers around Jesus Christ, lives by faith in him and is blessed to be his sacramental community'.[92]

Clifton suggests that the Army's perspective is an important element of its distinctiveness when he says that 'part of [the Army's] identity is our God-given insight into sacramentalism and the relationship of outward ritual to the receiving of divine grace'.[93] He defers to Paul Rader's statement which reflects 'Salvationist sacramentalism in a nutshell.. It is closely interwoven with our understanding of mature spirituality, the sanctified life in the secular world and the blessing of a clean heart'.[94] Rader, shortly before being elected as General, concluded that 'when our hearts are made holy, all of life is a sacrament'.[95]

Again, Shaw Clifton contrasts two common perspectives when he suggests that

> ... it can indeed make sense to speak of a sacramental life even though
> the believer has never partaken of a sacramental ceremony of any kind...
> it is possible to participate in sacramental ceremonies on a regular basis
> and yet not be living a sacramental life... the Salvationist is called by
> God to demonstrate the practical feasibility of living daily and hourly a
> pure and Christlike life by grace through faith in Jesus Christ, without
> the help of sacramental ritual.[96]

Such a sacramental life is believed to be a channel of God's grace to others. However, what the Army appears to have produced is a set of sacramental ceremonies suited to its own ethos, whose purpose seems similar to existing church sacraments, and where it is anticipated that some transmission of God's grace will occur. Such practices ensure that the Army is therefore not 'non-sacramental' and believers from many other Christian traditions will testify that the administration of sacraments is continued more in obedience to Scripture and tradition, and acknowledge that these sacraments point beyond themselves,

---

[92] *Salvation Story - Salvationist Handbook of Doctrine* (London: The Salvation Army International Headquarters, 1998), 105-106

[93] Clifton, *Who Are These Salvationists?*, 60

[94] Clifton, *Who Are These Salvationists?*, 61-62

[95] Paul A. Rader, 'The Army's Position on the Sacraments', (San Pedro, CA: The Salvation Army USA Western Territory's Hispanic Ministries Seminar, 9 May 1994)

[96] Clifton, *Who Are These Salvationists?*, 62-63

such that reception of grace does not so much depend on the existence and valid practice of the sacraments as much as on the active faith of the individual believer, as part of a community of faith empowered by the Spirit. Grant Sandercock-Brown warns that 'we are in real danger of hardening our stance and formalising our own replacements for the two sacraments of Protestantism for no particularly valid reason'.[97] Gariepy's overview of the history of The Salvation Army similarly concludes that the Army has 'substituted its own rituals'.[98]

Yuill warns that

> To propose a denominational orthodoxy that denies us the right to use any legitimate material means—particularly those modelled by Jesus and hallowed by centuries of use by his church—of apprehending our Creator-Redeemer through our senses, and to make the adherence to that denial the very test of orthodoxy, to the point of even forbidding legitimate discussion of the subject, is at best a sad error and at worst a form of denominational totalitarianism.[99]

Where Army beliefs and practices are seen as neo-sacramental, it is held that

> Army theology is consistent in its belief that grace is available apart from any form of ritual, and is reliant on the action of God and the faith of the recipient. However… Army ceremonies are themselves a means of communicating grace for grace-based covenantal relationships between God and the participant.[100]

However, Chick Yuill again contends for a re-examination of the Army's position when he suggests that

> … if we agree that physical actions and material objects can be helpful symbols, if we agree that the use of such symbols in alerting us to the wonder of the gospel renders them more than "mere symbols" and allows them to be conduits of God's grace—if we accept all of that, why should we prohibit the use of those actions and elements which are hallowed by centuries of Christian practice and which many sincere and seeking souls believe have at least some warrant from the pages of scripture?[101]

General Arnold Brown wisely stressed the vitality of the Army's identity as a church as well a social services agency when he stated

---

[97] Sandercock-Brown, *21 Questions*
[98] Gariepy, *Christianity in Action*, 72
[99] Yuill, 'Sanctity and Sacraments'
[100] Adam Couchman, ''The neo-sacramental theology of The Salvation Army', (dissertation Charles Sturt University, Bathurst, NSW, Australia, 2007)
[101] Yuill, 'Sanctity and Sacraments'

> Under God, the Army was bequeathed a philosophy and a function that is the envy of many of the historic church bodies. The duality of structure which is the distinction and glory of the Army has proven its implicit strength and durability. On the one hand, the Army is a church, a denomination, a sect, if you like; on the other, it is the world's single largest welfare movement. The spiritual impulses of the one issue in the compassion of the other. But the two are indissolubly interrelated, interpenetrated. One without the other means far less than being half effective. One without the other means the end of The Salvation Army! [102]

We will now consider the Army's role in social services and humanitarian relief.

The Salvation Army as a social services provider

Taylor suggests that 'the postmillennial vision of the thousand year reign of Christ was a far more compelling priority for Booth than a theological reflection upon the nature of the church and the ecclesiology of his own movement' [103] and many contemporary evangelical revivalists were also working to usher in this reign of Christ; Booth's aggressive war metaphor was well suited to the postmillennial perspective, and salvation was two-fold – being saved from damnation in the next world and also from the miseries of the present world.

Booth himself, in the first edition of *The Salvationist*, states that

> We are a salvation people – this is our specialty – getting saved and keeping saved, and then getting somebody else saved, and then getting saved ourselves more and more, until full salvation on earth makes the heaven within, which his finally perfected by the full salvation without, on the other side of the river. [104]

Tim Keller asserts that 'the ministry of mercy is not just a means to the end of evangelism. Word and deed are equally necessary, mutually interdependent and inseparable ministries, each carried out with the single purpose of the spread of the kingdom of God'. [105] This is a perspective that Booth and his Army would share.

Karen Shakespeare correctly acknowledges that 'any discussion of The Salvation Army's commitment to social justice must begin from our

---

[102] http://armybarmyblog.blogspot.ca/2013_02_01_archive.html#!/2013_02_01_archive.htm (accessed 25 January 2013)
[103] Taylor, *Like a Mighty Army*
[104] William Booth, *Salvation Soldiery: A Series of Addresses on the Requirements of Jesus Christ's Service*, (London: Salvation Army, 1890), 15
[105] Tim Keller, *Ministries of Mercy, The Call of the Jericho Road*, (Phillipsburg, NJ: Presbyterian and Reformed Publ., 1997), 106

understanding of scripture and of the personal and corporate response that is required from the people of God'.[106] The nature of the Army's response to human need is therefore qualitatively different to that offered by secular agencies. While no undue pressure for a conversion response is applied, the goal is to offer the compassion of Christ in the midst of human suffering. [107]

The Army is, in some countries, better known as a social services provider than as a church. Indeed, in terms of its organisational skills in leadership and fund-raising, the movement has been hailed as 'the most effective organisation in the U.S.'[108] noting how the internal machinery and external relations contribute to the successful operation of a large, diverse organisation which 'is fuelled by the energy generated by [the] fundamental human drive for spiritual connection'.[109] Indeed, it was The Salvation Army which became a major beneficiary of the philanthropy of Ray (founder of the McDonald's chain) and Joan Kroc; in 1988, Mrs Kroc, then widowed, donated $90million to the Army to build a comprehensive community centre in San Diego, California, and on her own subsequent death in 2003, a further $1.5billion was left to the Army from her estate, by far the largest charitable gift ever given to the Army, and the largest single gift given to any charity at one time. Four additional Ray and Joan Kroc Corps Community Centres were built and the Army 'estimates that 28 centers in total will be built during the next several years ranging in size, services, location, and cost'.[110] Such was the answer to Joan Kroc's question 'if the right resources were available, what agency or organization could make the biggest difference in those neighborhoods?'[111]

Aspects of the Army's wide social services remit include accommodation and support for the homeless and vulnerable families, employment schemes, community centres and outreach, health services, education, and lobbying on social justice issues such as human trafficking, the liberation of women, non-discrimination, and the importance of due legal process. 'The Salvation Army, through this community engagement, is working towards the Millennium Development Goals. The Millennium Development Goals are eight specific goals to be met by 2015 that aim to combat extreme poverty across the world. The goals were created at the UN Millennium

---

[106] Karen Shakespeare, 'Fulfilling the Great Commission in the 21st Century. Outworking of the Response – Social Justice', a paper presented to the International Doctrine Council, February 2009, http://www1.salvationarmy.org/IHQ/www_ihq_isjc.nsf/vw-sublinks/B3DB4808441E738E802575EE0009F92F?openDocument (accessed 18 June 2012)

[107] Cf Matthew 25:35-36

[108] Robert A. Watson & Ben Brown, *The Most Effective Organization in the U.S. – Leadership Secrets of The Salvation Army*, (New York, NY: Crown Business, 2001)

[109] Watson & Brown, *The Most Effective Organization in the U.S.*, 13

[110] 'Ray and Joan Kroc Corps Community Centers', http://easternusa.salvationarmy.org/use/national-fact-sheet (accessed 7 March 2014)

[111] Watson & Brown, *The Most Effective Organization in the U.S.*, 85

Summit in New York in 2000'.[112] The Army also provides urgent response to emergencies (such as fires, explosions, natural disasters), and seeks to utilise the principles of 'integrated mission and community empowerment which have been evolved over recent years and particularly through involvement in complex emergencies'.[113] It also offers encouragement to armed services through both practical support and pastoral care.

Most Army territories have a Moral and Social Issues Council which helps formulate policy and responses. The International Moral and Social Issues Council 'advises the General on contemporary moral and social issues, and recommends statements of official positions on such issues. Its members are drawn from all around the world, and include both officers and soldiers of The Salvation Army. The council also calls upon expertise from outside the Movement when necessary'.[114]

An important aspect of coordinating the Army's international influence in this area is the International Social Justice Commission, based in New York; 'the director and staff are the Army's principle advocates and advisers on social, economic and political issues and events giving rise to the perpetuation of social injustice in the world'.[115] They liaise closely with the New York-based United Nations Organisation.

The Commission was inaugurated by General Shaw Clifton in 2008, noting 'a growing wave of concern and of fresh determination that we should speak out for the cause of right, regardless of the consequences'.[116] Clifton also outlined the responsibilities of the International Moral and Social Issues Council as 'monitor[ing] our ethical postures around the world as captured in formal positional statements... [remaining aware] that the Army is a collection of countless cultures and ethnicities'.[117] Their work was to be carried out in an ecumenical *milieu*, cognisant of the ethical positions formulated within other churches.

The Army's Positional Statements 'represent the consensus thinking of Salvationists on a given topic at a given moment in history... they can be changed...we must allow freedom of conscience since the topics are often contentious and subtly nuanced'.[118]

Dean Pallant writes of the challenges faced by the Army as it seeks to serve suffering humanity:

> It is a mistake to presume we are speaking the same language as our partners when we serve suffering humanity. In fact, we rarely share the

---

[112] http://www.salvationarmy.org/ihq/projaboutus, (accessed 15 March 2015)
[113] http://www.salvationarmy.org/ihq/iesmission (accessed 15 March 2015)
[114] http://www.salvationarmy.org/ihq/positionalstatements (accessed 15 March 2015)
[115] 'International Social Justice Commission', *The Salvation Army Year Book 2015*, 32
[116] Shaw Clifton, *Something Better...*, (London: Salvation Books, 2014), 318
[117] Clifton, *Writings II*, 123
[118] Clifton, *Writings II*, 170 – The Positional Statements can be accessed at http://www.salvationarmy.org/ihq/positionalstatements

same *telos* [our orientation, our goal, our purpose]. There are a number of *telos* being used by governments, corporate partners, NGOs [non-governmental organisations], even other FBOs [faith-based organisations]. There is a tendency for secular agencies to use fragments from lost moral traditions, fragments that have become abstracted from a shared notion of what constitutes the good life and human flourishing.[119]

Pallant also engages with the concept of 'healthy persons' as the *telos* for humankind in their relationships with one another, society, and with God. This also includes the importance of 'body-soul-in-relation'. He notes the previous dichotomy of Salvation Army service provision, where 'body' work was left to social services professionals while corps work focused on saving and sanctifying souls. There is now evidence of a more holistic approach, and Pallant observes that 'the integrated "body-soul" understanding of persons is also important in resisting the undervaluing of the body with a narrow evangelical priority to "go for souls"'.[120]

The Army has also developed the process of Faith-based Facilitation. This 'is a way of helping people think, talk, explore and respond to their issues in the light of faith. It results in the development of healthier people and communities who enjoy deeper relationships'.[121]

One of the calls of the International Spiritual Life Commission stated:

> The 'healing of a hurting world' and the need for 'prophetic witness in the face of social injustice'... must be seen as more than wishful thinking... We who have received complete love from Christ are called to give transparent witness to justice, peace, equality and holiness through actions which redeem and re-order the world.[122]

This is further evidenced in the *Handbook of Doctrine* which refers to The Salvation Army's social action and advocacy for social justice as a 'consequence of our salvation'.[123] Thus it is imperative for all Salvationists of whatever status to work as far as their influence will allow, to seek to love the poor and marginalised with divine compassion, and strive to effect social and political change for the betterment of all.

---

[119] Dean Pallant, 'What is The Salvation Army's Theology as we Serve Suffering Humanity?', paper presented at 2014 USA Salvation Army Conference for Social Work and Emergency Disaster Services, 25-28 March 2014, Orlando, Florida; http://www.salvationarmy.org/ihq/gt1c (accessed 27 March 2014)

[120] Dean Pallant, *Keeping Faith in Faith-Based Organizations: A Practical Theology of Salvation Army Health Ministry*, (Eugene, OR: Wipf & Stock Publishers, 2012), 157

[121] 'Faith-based Facilitation', http://www.salvationarmy.org/fbf/ (accessed 15 March 2015) - see also *Building Deeper Relationships using Faith-based Facilitation*, (London: The Salvation Army International Headquarters, 2010), http://s3.amazonaws.com/cache.salvationarmy.org/507a41d7-921f-42ac-8273-17b48b4bbab2_FBF-English.pdf (accessed 15 March 2015)

[122] Robert Street, *Called to be God's People*, 69-70

[123] *Handbook of Doctrine*, (London: Salvation Books, 2010), 176

The Salvation Army's legal foundation and identity

In this final section, it will be useful to note that the Army has a proper legal constitution and that it takes care to ensure that its international presence takes due regard of local legal requirements; the Army does its utmost to ensure that it is established according to such legal requirements, and also takes steps to ensure the highest level of freedom to operate according to its international regulations and preserve and protect its mission within the many different legal infrastructures encountered in the countries and regions where it operates.

The movement's name change from The Christian Mission to the Salvation Army, was confirmed by Deed Poll in 1878, and this also contained a statement of the Army's eleven doctrines (an amalgamation and clarification of the Wesleyan and holiness doctrinal positions held among the various incarnations of Booth's developing work).

This Deed Poll confirmed Booth's leadership of the organisation, the right of the leader to nominate his successor, and the sole trusteeship of the leader of all money and property. Importantly, the terms of the constitution could only be amended by an Act of the British Parliament. In 1904, a supplementary Deed provided for the convening of 'the High Council of The Salvation Army' as a safeguard for the potential removal from office of a General deemed unfit to continue. The High Council is currently constituted under provisions of the Salvation Army Act 1980 as amended by deeds of variation executed in 1995, 2005 and 2010. John Larsson provides a scholarly account of the Army's 1929 leadership crisis,[124] when William Booth's successor, Bramwell Booth, was ill and unable to provide effective oversight and leadership of the Army. A High Council was convened and this resulted in the Army's first elected leader, General Edward Higgins. The subsequent Salvation Army Act 1931, provided for: (i) the abolition of the General's right to nominate his or her successor, and the substitution of the election of every General by a High Council; (ii) the fixing of an age limit for the retirement of the General; (iii) the creation of a trustee company to hold the properties and other capital assets of the Army, in place of the sole trusteeship of the General.

The Army's International Headquarters staff includes the role of Legal Secretary (a role previously held as Legal and Parliamentary Secretary by Shaw Clifton, a trained lawyer). Priorities for this role include 'advising the General and the Chief of the Staff concerning the Army's legal status and constitutional machinery in every land where the Army was present... the interpretation and application of the Salvation Army Act 1980... be a resource to territorial leaders globally in any matter touching the fundamental legal status of the Army... to speak for the Army to the UK Government and to Parliament.'[125]

---

[124] John Larsson, *1929: A Crisis that shaped The Salvation Army's Future*, (London: Salvation Books, 2009); Larsson has also provided additional background to the role and functioning of the High Council: *Inside a High Council: How Salvation Army Generals are Elected*, (London: Salvation Books, 2013)
[125] Clifton, *Something Better...*, 182-183

Clifton provides a comprehensive guide to the legal complications in ensuring that the Army is correctly established constitutionally in each country or region where it operates and that its mission is adequately promoted and protected, while ensuring that – as far as practicable – The Salvation Army is indigenous to each country, and not perceived as a 'branch' of a British organisation on foreign soil. Legal documentation seeks to 'keep our constitutions as "Army" as possible as local laws will allow'.[126]

Of especial concern are issues such as confirmation of explicit and formal powers for the General, and a link between the Office of the General and the Army in the country concerned; being explicit about who the Army is and its mission, inclusion of a statement of its Articles of Faith; can the Army's international orders and regulations be made an explicit part of Army life in the place in question?

However, 'many of our constitutions take the form of an incorporation (a company) the form of whose Memorandum and Articles of Association will be closely circumscribed by local law so that on the face of the legal documents the only clue to our evangelical and spiritual purposes will be the name of the Army itself'.[127] A number of legal devices can be used for the Army's best interests in establishing its work internationally, and these include statute, incorporation, and trusts and foundations.

Clifton notes that the most complex constitutional arrangement is in the United Kingdom, where Booth had established his original Deed Polls. The Salvation Army Trustee Company had been set up on foot of The Salvation Army Act 1931 to safeguard Army property following the 1929 generalship crisis. Other Acts followed in 1963 and 1968, and a variety of trading companies established which undertake banking, insurance, travel, supplies, and housing activities. The Salvation Army Act 1980 primarily sought to free the General from undue involvement in the day-to-day operations and procedures of the Army in the United Kingdom; it also made the Trustee Company the sole trustee of Army assets which were previously vested solely in the General. The Act also defers to the Army's own internal regulations in matters such as the defining of territories, the tenure of office and retirement of the General.

Helen Cameron helpfully summarises this when she comments that

> In each country where The Salvation Army is at work a legal form must be adopted as we move gradually to registration as a church. In many democratic countries we are obliged to adopt the legal forms of both charity and company. They then become a taken-for-granted part of our identity, shaping what we do and how we do it.[128]

---

[126] Clifton, *Writings II*, 144
[127] Clifton, *Writings II*, 145
[128] Helen Cameron, 'A Household of Faith', *The Salvation Army Year Book 2015*, (London: Salvation Books, 2014), 4

Such formalities are designed to protect the Army's operations, and also affect the various relationships the organisation will have with local governments, ecumenically with other churches, interaction with Non-Governmental Organisations and Faith-based Organisations, as outlined in the section on social service work.

Conclusion

John Larsson has noted that

> The Army has tended to consider its theology as something that was settled once and for all by William Booth and that there is therefore nothing more to be said about it. But... unless that theology is made to come alive in each generation it loses its power to impel action.[129]

The aim of this chapter has been to provide an outline of The Salvation Army's origins, its self-understanding, and wider perceptions of it among other churches and society. It has not been possible to detail more than an introduction and further reading from the Bibliography may be helpful.

General Linda Bond, reflecting on John Gowans' mission statement, commented that 'we have one mission. Our mission is not three separate strands assigned to certain sections of the Army. It is one mission. No part of the Army can divorce itself from serving suffering humanity. Nor can any part ignore the imperative to bring people to Jesus and make disciples'.[130]

The following chapters address theological and practical issues arising from the Army's mission to Save Souls, Grow Saints, and Serve Suffering Humanity.

---

[129] John Larsson, 'Salvationist Theology & Ethics for the New Millennium'
[130] Linda Bond, 'International Vision Statement', *The Officer*, September - October 2011, 4

2. 'O Boundless Salvation'[1]

'Save Souls, Grow Saints, and Serve Suffering Humanity' – The Army's Holistic Vision

James E. Pedlar

One of The Salvation Army's great gifts to the broader Christian tradition is the holistic nature of Salvationist mission. When General John Gowans stated that the Army's mission was to 'save souls, grow saints, and serve suffering humanity', he immediately caught the imagination of Salvationists worldwide, because he so aptly captured the Salvationist story and ethos. These three aspects of Christian mission are integrally connected in Salvationist thinking. Evangelization is intended to lead to holy living, or 'full salvation', and both evangelization and holy living require the embodied demonstration of the gospel in service to the most vulnerable.

While this holistic vision was the intended basis of Salvationist mission from the early days of the movement, I will argue in this essay that the articulation of this mission in holistic terms was initially hindered by a dualistic conceptual framework, which bifurcated evangelism and holiness on the one hand, and the spiritual and social mission on the other. Thus, a two-stage view of Christian salvation undermined an integrated view of personal redemption, and a strong 'spiritual' vs. 'social' distinction undermined an integrated understanding of redemption in its corporate and social dimensions. Starting in the middle of the twentieth century, however, Salvationists began to move away from these dualistic conceptualizations, and to re-articulate their understanding of salvation, and therefore of their world-wide mission, in more holistic and integrated ways. This holistic theological perspective, which has emerged from the unique Salvationist history and ethos, offers the church catholic a compelling vision of salvation and Christian mission.

Toward the Reintegration of Sanctification and Salvation

While the early Salvation Army was primarily an evangelistic mission, the Booths had always maintained that "full salvation" was an essential aspect of the gospel they preached. Booth addressed the 1877 Conference of The Christian Mission with these words, which are well-known to students of Salvation Army history:

---

[1] William Booth, *The Song Book of The Salvation Army*, 298

Holiness to the Lord is to us a fundamental truth; it stands to the forefront of our doctrines. We write it on our banners. It is in now shape or form an open debatable question as to whether God can sanctify wholly, whether Jesus does save His people *from* their sins.[2]

The Booths associated themselves with a historic Wesleyan understanding of salvation, as interpreted by the transatlantic Holiness Movement. This meant that William Booth 'was sure that sanctification was a second, definite work of grace in the heart of the believer',[3] and that he stressed an instantaneous account of entire sanctification. In *Purity of Heart*, Booth outlined his understanding of entire sanctification in terms that echoed those of many other Wesleyan-Holiness preachers, clarifying that entire sanctification does not imply freedom from suffering, temptation, falling, or infirmities.[4] The 'pure heart' then, Booth states, is a heart that has been cleansed by the Holy Spirit from all sin, and enabled to please God in all it does; to love him with all its powers, and its neighbour as itself.[5] Catherine Booth likewise taught that believers could move from a justified state, where they had 'power over sin', to a 'platform where the believer abides so abides in Christ that he sins not, that he Loves God [sic] with all his heart, and soul, and mind, and strength'.[6]

Scholars have debated the extent to which various early Salvationist thinkers should be more closely identified with John Wesley's theology or Holiness Movement perspectives on entire sanctification. For example, John Read's recent book does an excellent job of teasing out various influences in Catherine Booth's holiness doctrine, noting that Palmer, Finney, Mahan, Broadman, and others had influence, but that she was most firmly rooted in the Wesleyan tradition as read through John Fletcher.[7] David Rightmire has argued that Samuel Logan Brengle brought Salvationist thinking back to a more authentically Wesleyan view, nuancing some of the more Holiness Movement-influenced articulations of the first generation of Salvationist

---

[2] William Booth, 'Holiness: An Address at the Conference', in *Boundless Salvation: The Shorter Writings of William Booth*, ed by. Andrew M. Eason and Roger J. Green (New York: Peter Lang, 2012), 81.

[3] Roger J. Green, *War on Two Fronts: The Redemptive Theology of William Booth* (Atlanta: Salvation Army Supplies, 1989), 35.

[4] For the original source of these common disclaimers, see John Wesley's Sermon 40, 'Christian Perfection', §§I.1-9, in Albert C. Outler, ed., *The Works of John Wesley*, vol. 2 (Nashville: Abingdon Press, 1985), 100–105.

[5] William Booth, *Purity of Heart*, Reprint. (London: Salvation Books, 2007), p. 14.

[6] Catherine Mumford Booth, *Papers on Godliness: Being Reports of a Series of Addresses Delivered at James's Hall, London, W., During 1881* (London: International Headquarters of the Salvation Army, 1896), 153.

[7] See chapters 3 and 4 of John Read, *Catherine Booth: Laying the Theological Foundations of a Radical Movement* (Eugene, Oregon: Pickwick Publications, 2013). Read insightfully notes that Catherine was closest to Palmer where Palmer was closest to Wesley. Ibid., 81.

leaders.[8]   Although there certainly are minor differences between the perspectives of the Booths and Brengle, they all display a Holiness Movement-influenced focus on the instantaneous character of sanctification – an idea which is present in Wesley, but not to the degree that it was taught by early Salvationists and their Holiness contemporaries.   As Brengle put it, the transformation of entire sanctification was "not to be a slow, evolutionary process, but an instantaneous work, wrought in the heart of the humble believer by the Holy Ghost."[9]   The instantaneous nature of the change was linked to another Holiness Movement-related characteristic of early Salvationist teaching on holiness: the idea that the sinful nature was 'destroyed' or 'removed' in the instantaneous work. 'Entire sanctification supposes *complete deliverance*', William Booth wrote. 'Sin is *destroyed* out of the soul, and all the powers, faculties, possessions, and influences of the soul are consecrated to the service and glory of God'.[10] While Wesley did write about inward sin being 'destroyed' in a few isolated places, it was neither his characteristic, nor his best way of explaining Christian perfection.[11]

    Further research and analysis regarding the degree to which the Booths and their early Salvationist contemporaries diverged from eighteenth-century Wesleyan theology is warranted and worthwhile. My reason for noting their particular emphasis on the instantaneous and eradicatory nature of sanctification as a second work of grace is not to enter into such a debate, so much as to underscore the way in which this focus on a second crisis led to a markedly two-tiered view of salvation.   In fact, it led to an unfortunate distinction between 'salvation' and sanctification, wherein conversion, new birth, and justification were identified with 'salvation', and sanctification was thereby conceived as something *additional to* salvation, rather than an *integral aspect of* salvation. This is a common issue in popular evangelical piety, wherein being 'saved' is equated with conversion. There is certainly a sense in which this is true – those who are justified *are* saved. And yet God's work of

---

[8] R. David Rightmire, *Sanctified Sanity: The Life and Teaching of Samuel Logan Brengle* (Alexandria, VA: Crest Books, 2003).

[9] Samuel Logan Brengle, *Heart Talks on Holiness* (London: Salvationist Publishing and Supplies, 1897), 4–5.

[10] William Booth, "Holiness," in *Boundless Salvation: The Shorter Writings of William Booth*, ed by. Andrew M. Eason and Roger J. Green (New York: Peter Lang, 2012), 88.

[11] The language of 'destruction' has been criticized by many twentieth-century Wesley scholars, who are keenly aware of its dangers, in part, because of the vigour with which this language was taken up by nineteenth century Wesleyans such as the Booths. As Randy Maddox has noted, Wesley's more helpful alternative was to speak of '"holy tempers" (i.e., enduring affections) *presently* reigning to the point of "driving out" opposing tempers (though these may return)'. Randy L. Maddox, *Responsible Grace: John Wesley's Practical Theology* (Nashville, Tenn.: Kingswood Books, 1994), 188. For example, see Q.12 in *Farther Thoughts Upon Christian Perfection* (1763), where Wesley writes of Christian Perfection as 'love filling the heart, expelling pride, anger, desire, self-will…' in Paul Wesley Chilcote and Kenneth J. Collins, eds., *The Works of John Wesley*, vol. 13 (Nashville: Abingdon Press, 2013), 100.

salvation is not yet complete, as Salvationists have always understood; salvation is a past, present, and future reality. The integral nature of the salvation experience, however, was subtly undermined by the markedly two-tiered soteriology of early Salvationism, in which "salvation" became equated with conversion, and sanctification was narrowly defined in terms of a subsequent instantaneous experience.

General Frederick Coutts is generally acknowledged as the driving force behind a shift in Salvationist soteriology in the mid-twentieth century. Coutts discussed holiness in a way which shifted the focus away from a strictly crisis-focused understanding of the second work of grace, and towards a more relative and process-oriented view. The characteristic of Coutts's approach to the question is his Christocentrism. He considered it 'one of the laws of spiritual life' that 'the experience of holiness is best understood in the light of the example of Jesus'.[12] Coutts still wrote of 'salvation' and 'sanctification' as if they were two different experiences,[13] but his focus on Christlikeness helped to move away from an overly static and dualistic framework.

Holiness is 'both a crisis and a process'," writes Coutts, describing the crisis as the beginning of holiness, for there "'can be no experience without a beginning, but no beginning can be maintained without growth'.[14] Though he discussed both process and crisis, he downplayed the crisis experience, and explained it a more anthropocentric manner than his predecessors. In early Salvationist literature, the crisis was primarily conceived as an act of the Holy Spirit that provided radical cleansing and empowerment, even if preceded by human 'conditions', and it was precisely because it was *God's* action that this experience was thought to enable 'instantaneous' sanctification. Coutts, on the other hand, while acknowledging that divine action is more important than human action, gives most of his attention to the 'act of full surrender' on the part of the believer.[15] He has much less to say than his forebears regarding what happens when the Spirit is received, and places his focus on what follows:

> The crisis must be followed by a process. In the initial act of surrender I receive of the fullness of the Spirit according to my capacity to receive. But that capacity grows with receiving – as a bandsman's facility to play grows with playing, or to speak with speaking or to follow his craft by practising it.[16]

While it would be accurate to over-state the relative difference on this point,

---

[12] Frederick Coutts, *The Call to Holiness* (London: Salvationist Publishing and Supplies, 1957), 15.

[13] For example, '...to pass from salvation to sanctification is for some like passing from clear sunshine into a damp and clinging sea mist which hides every landmark and blankets all sense of direction'. Ibid., 8.

[14] Coutts, *The Call to Holiness*, 34.

[15] Coutts, *The Call to Holiness*, 35.

[16] Coutts, *The Call to Holiness*, 36.

there is nevertheless in Coutts's theology of holiness a magnification of the process of sanctification, and a lessening of the priority on the crisis moment, which includes less focus on the effects of the Spirit's role in the crisis of sanctification. Thus, in his characteristic manner, Coutts writes, 'a full surrender is the beginning of the life of holy living; the end of the experience I do not – I cannot – see'.[17]

Coutts's thinking proved influential, in part because he went on to serve as General, and was able to oversee a radical revision of the Salvation Army's *Handbook of Doctrine*. The change in Salvation Army holiness thinking is thus dramatically illustrated in the differences between the 1955 and 1969 editions of the *Handbook*. In the 1955 edition, the bifurcation of sanctification and salvation is quite explicit and clear:

> *The chief difference between salvation and sanctification* is that: i. *Salvation* takes place when we are regenerated, and is deliverance from outward sin and the love of it. ii. *Sanctification* takes place usually some time after regeneration, and is deliverance from both inward and outward sin – from sin in disposition as well as in deed.[18]

The 1955 *Handbook* repeats many of the teachings of early Salvationism, often in very similar language, displaying all of the characteristics of early Salvationist thinking about salvation: a two-tiered perspective, in which sanctification is conceived primarily as an instantaneous experience which includes the destruction of inborn sin. In this model, as noted above, 'salvation' is basically equated with conversion (including regeneration and justification), and sanctification has been equated with instantaneous entire sanctification.[19]

While the 1969 *Handbook* does speak of the 'sanctified state',[20] and addresses the topic of 'full salvation' towards the end of the chapter,[21] its overall emphasis is a re-casting of Salvation Army holiness thinking around the category of 'Christlikeness'. The 'completeness' of sanctification here is defined, not in terms of a complete destruction of sin, but in the sense that sanctification "leaves no part of the personality untouched."[22] Jesus Christ is the Holy One, in whom 'this experience was both perfected and made available for every believer.'[23] As in Coutts's personal writings, an attempt is made to balance both crisis and process, but the crisis is here defined primarily in terms of 'the initial dedication when the commitment is made', rather than on a

---

[17] Coutts, *The Call to Holiness*, 37.
[18] *Handbook of Doctrine* (London: The Salvation Army, 1955), 118.
[19] Hence the following statement, intended as a clarification, is very telling: 'When in the Army we speak of sanctification we usually mean entire sanctification...' Ibid., 124. Indeed, the 1955 *Handbook* chapter on sanctification is entitled 'Entire Sanctification'.
[20] *Handbook of Doctrine* (London: The Salvation Army, 1969), 148.
[21] *Handbook of Doctrine*, 163.
[22] *Handbook of Doctrine*, 145.
[23] *Handbook of Doctrine*, 148.

radical work of the Spirit which destroys inbred sin.[24]

One can see, therefore, how Coutts's perspective brought fresh vision to Salvationist thinking about holiness, though he was not without his detractors.[25] Coutts was aware that many would receive this new approach as a 'watering down' of Army holiness teaching, but he insisted that the Christological focus actually made holiness 'more demanding', because it provided a 'sharply marked outline' and incarnate standard of holiness.[26] Regardless of how one might assess Coutts's perspective, it must be acknowledged that it is less dualistic, and more holistic, in its view of salvation. By softening the hard line of early Salvationist 'entire' and instantaneous sanctification, Coutts introduced a less rigid standard of holiness, one which is more easily integrated within the doctrine of salvation as a whole.

While the Couttsian shift in the mid-twentieth century helped move Salvationist thinking towards a more holistic viewpoint, it was the work of the International Doctrine Council at the turn of the twenty-first century that produced the next watershed moment in Salvationist holiness theology. The Doctrine Council's work on *Salvation Story* - another revision of the *Handbook of Doctrine* - brought the Army's soteriology to a more fully-integrated perspective.

This was accomplished, first, by beginning the discussion of 'full salvation' with reference to salvation as the work of creating us in 'the likeness of his Son, Jesus Christ', which is in fact a restoration of 'the true image of God'.[27] Conversion, therefore,

> inaugurates a journey during which we are being transformed into Christ's likeness. Thus salvation is neither a state to be preserved nor an insurance policy which requires no further investment. It is the beginning of a pilgrimage with Christ. This pilgrimage requires from us the obedience of separation from sin and consecration to the purposes of God. This is why 'obedient faith' is crucial: it makes pilgrimage possible.[28]

Thus sanctification is set more helpfully within the framework of salvation itself as a journey toward Christlikeness. The account still maintains the traditional stress on the need for redemption beyond the initial change of conversion, as 'the answer to this dilemma' of the Christian's frustration with their failure to live a holy life.[29] It is in this sense that *Salvation Story* addresses the crisis / process question, though the overall thrust of the text is

---

[24] *Handbook of Doctrine*, 159.
[25] See Glen O'Brien, 'Why Brengle? Why Coutts? Why Not?', *Word and Deed: A Journal of Salvation Army Theology and Ministry* 13, no. 1 (November 2010), 11–12.
[26] Coutts, *The Call to Holiness*, 24–25.
[27] *Salvation Story: Salvationist Handbook of Doctrine*. (London: Salvation Army International Headquarters, 1998), 85.
[28] *Salvation Story*, 86.
[29] *Salvation Story*, 87.

clearly more process-oriented. 'Experienced as a crisis, sanctification becomes a lifelong process', which has an 'already but not yet' quality, as we are 'becoming what we already are in Christ'.[30] *Salvation Story* stresses that this ongoing work of sanctification is 'not a new experience unrelated to saving faith and the experience of regeneration'. Rather,

> The same grace at work in our lives both saves and sanctifies. We advance towards the fulfilment of that which our conversion promises – victory over sin, the life of holiness made actual, and all of the graces of salvation imparted by the presence and action of the indwelling Holy Spirit and his sanctifying power.[31]

It is *Salvation Story's* framing of salvation as renewal according to the image of God which allows the text to avoid a problematic understanding of 'salvation' as simply the avoidance of eternal damnation. Thus holiness is not an add-on to a 'state' of salvation, but rather an intrinsic aspect of the gift of salvation, which has both past, present, and future dimensions. Holiness therefore is 'the work of God' which 'makes it possible to live according to the purpose for which we were created'.[32] This integrated soteriology is capped off by an affirmation of the category 'wholeness' as a way of talking about 'the comprehensiveness of God's saving work in Christ and of the Spirit's sanctification'.[33]

From Dual Mission to Integrated Mission

The other dualistic conceptual framework that existed within early Salvationism's comprehensive vision was the contrast between 'spiritual' and 'social' mission. The earliest Salvation Army did not did not engage in social ministries on a large scale, and generally considered these to be of secondary importance in relation to the work of converting sinners by the preaching of the gospel. Salvationists did engage with the poor and seek to alleviate various needs on a local basis, but there were no systematic social action programs.[34] In the 1880s this began to change through several grassroots initiatives. William Booth did not draw attention to these developments, however, and

---

[30] *Salvation Story*, 90.

[31] *Salvation Story*, 87.

[32] *Salvation Story*, 88.

[33] *Salvation Story*, 93.

[34] See, for example, the social ministries outlined in the first published report of The East London Christian Mission, issued September 1867, in Appendix I of Robert Sandall, *The History of The Salvation Army* (London: The Salvation Army, 1947), I: 265–266.

continued to speak of Salvationism as a purely evangelistic movement.[35] But Booth's thinking did shift around 1889 and 1890, as can be seen in his articulation of an expanded understanding of God's work of redemption, in his article 'Salvation for Both Worlds', and in the establishment of the Darkest *England* scheme.[36] I will not outline Booth's mature position on these questions in detail, since Roger Green has discussed this topic extensively in his chapter in this volume, as well as his previous writings.[37] For the purposes of my argument in this essay, it is sufficient to note that Booth believed that the disordering of human desires by sin and the rebellion against God which this disordering entailed were the cause of *both* eternal and temporal suffering. Thus he now believed that he had 'two gospels to preach – one for each world, or rather, one gospel which applied alike to both', and that the gospel 'came with the promise of salvation here and now, from hell and sin and vice and crime and idleness and extravagance, and consequently very largely from poverty and disease, and the majority of kindred woes'.[38] This new conception of Salvationist mission gave rise to the elaborate 'Scheme of Social Salvation' that Booth proposed in *Darkest England*.[39] Thus the concept of a 'dual mission' was established both theologically and institutionally at this time.

The challenge that Salvationists have faced from the very beginning is how they should conceptualize this 'dual mission'. Does evangelistic ministry remain the priority, or are the two to be kept in balance? Booth's own statements on this matter are not as clear as they might have been.[40] However, if we give him a charitable reading, it would seem that *Darkest England* retains an evangelistic priority. Booth claimed that his 'ultimate design' remained the conversion of sinners to the gospel, but that if the plan failed in this respect, 'I shall at least benefit the bodies, if not the souls, of men'.[41] So he maintained that 'if the inside remains unchanged you have wasted your labour. You must in some way or other graft upon the man's nature a new nature, which has in it the element of the Divine. All that I propose in this book is governed by that

---

[35] For an overview of these initiatives and Booth's response, see Roger J. Green, *The Life and Ministry of William Booth: Founder of the Salvation Army* (Nashville: Abingdon Press, 2005), 166–168.

[36] William Booth, 'Salvation for Both Worlds', in *Boundless Salvation: The Shorter Writings of William Booth*, ed by. Andrew M. Eason and Roger J. Green (New York: Peter Lang, 2012), 51–59; William Booth, *In Darkest England, and the Way Out* (London: Funk & Wagnalls, 1890).

[37] See Roger J. Green, 'An Historical Salvation Army Perspective', in *Creed and Deed: Toward a Christian Theology of Social Services in The Salvation Army* (Toronto: The Salvation Army, 1986), 45–81; Green, *War on Two Fronts*, 76–95; for a contrasting view, see Norman Murdoch, *Origins of The Salvation Army* (Knoxville: University of Tennessee Press, 1994), 146–167.

[38] Booth, 'Salvation for Both Worlds', 53–54.

[39] See Part II, which comprises the majority of the book, Booth, *Darkest England*, 85–285.

[40] See Green's comments, in 'An Historical Salvation Army Perspective', 69.

[41] Booth, *Darkest England*, Preface (no page number).

principle'.[42] We should also note that the shift in Salvationist missional practice was under-written by broadening of Booth's understanding of redemption itself, which led Booth to believe that the 'one gospel applied alike' to the present and future worlds.[43]   It was this expanded theological vision, along with his claim that personal conversion remained his ultimate priority, that allowed Booth to claim that the 'dual mission' was simply 'the plan to which the Spirit of God led me forty-four years ago' as a young preacher to the poor on the streets of Nottingham.[44]

Subsequent generations of Salvationists have continued to sense a tension in their movement in the relationship between the 'social' and 'spiritual' aspects of their mission. This spiritual-social tension is certainly evident during Bramwell Booth's time as General. He convened an International Social Council in 1921, and the papers from this event were published and circulated as an authoritative statement of the Army's position on these matters.[45] In the context of explaining 'The Relation of Social to Field Work', Bramwell Booth articulates a very broad vision for the Army's mission as 'a Movement designed to bring deliverance from evil to all classes'.

> We shall only maintain that broad-minded view – broad as the mercy of God, deep as His love, and high as His wisdom – if our purpose embraces the whole world...And just as we would deplore, and do deplore, a contraction of the purpose of The Army as a whole, so we ought to beware of such a contraction in our Departments or in ourselves.[46]

Bramwell is at pains to stress the unity of the worldwide movement, and that all its activities serve the purpose of spreading 'the Salvation of God' and 'the making of men and women into the disciples of His Son Jesus Christ'."[47] It is clear from the way that Bramwell proceeds with this argument that his ultimate aim is evangelical in the conversionist sense. He wants his officers to use 'every lawful means' to bring those who are helped by social work to the local

---

[42] *Darkest England*, 45. See also 'The Millennium; or, the Ultimate Triumph of Salvation Army Principles', in *Boundless Salvation: The Shorter Writings of William Booth*, ed. Andrew M. Eason and Roger J. Green (New York: Peter Lang, 2012), 68.
[43] Booth, 'Salvation for Both Worlds', 53.
[44] Booth, 'Salvation for Both Worlds', 59. It is surely an exaggeration on Booth's part to claim that he had the same 'plan' as a young man in Nottingham, but his point is that he was able to see it as an aspect of his calling as an evangelist.
[45] The book was prefaced with the following notice: 'GENERAL ORDER. Whilst the Notes and Addresses contained in this Volume are not to be taken as having quite the force of Orders and Regulations, they nevertheless are the considered expression of the General's judgment on the matters referred to'. *International Social Council, 1921* (London: International Headquarters of the Salvation Army, 1921), vi.
[46] Bramwell Booth, 'The Relation of Social to the Field Work', in *International Social Council, 1921* (London: International Headquarters of the Salvation Army, 1921), 29.
[47] Bramwell Booth, 'The Relation of Social to the Field Work', 30.

corps, and suggests that the 'ultimate success' of the social work 'must more and more be measured by the extent to which men and women and children are brought to the knowledge of Salvation, and passed on to The Army'. While stressing that social work that does not do this can still be considered a success in some sense, it is the move towards making disciples that 'distinguishes the Social Work of the Army' from other efforts.[48] Appealing to the revivalist origins of the movement, Bramwell stresses:

> We did not start out to take away from the Poor Law or from charitable societies their work. We started out to make men and women new by the power of the Spirit of God, and we have proved that it can be done. There may be a place for work which goes no further than the temporary alleviation of misery, and we have always been glad to see some work of that nature done. But, strictly speaking, *it is not our work, except so far as it opens the way for effective deliverance of the people.* The bread that perisheth can never do the much good, unless it brings them to the Bread of Life.[49]

The stress laid on this point seems to indicate a concern on Bramwell's part that The Salvation Army might be simply doing the social work of other agencies, without leading people to personal salvation in Christ. He closes by exhorting them to 'rise up in the power of the Spirit, and let us really make our Institutions what it was originally intended they should be [sic]', meaning that their success should be gauged by whether or not they produce Salvationists.[50]

In spite of this clear prioritization of 'spiritual' over 'social', Bramwell included a chapter in his 1925 revision of the *Orders and Regulations for Corps Officers* (1925) on 'Relationship to Social and Other Work' in which equality between the two branches of the Army was stressed. Here officers are advised to 'constantly bear in mind that the various branches of The Army comprise substantially one whole', since the 'ultimate object of both Corps and Social Work is the same'. Therefore officers are sternly warned that they should 'never, either in private or in public, utter anything which suggests that one side of the Work is superior or inferior to the other'.[51] The inclusion of such an explanation and warning suggests that some officers supported the superiority of one side or the other. Salvation Army social work continued to expand throughout the mid-twentieth century, and these tensions were certainly not eased as Salvationists became involved in health care,

---

[48] Bramwell Booth, 'The Relation of Social to the Field Work', 31–34.
[49] Bramwell Booth, 'The Relation of Social to the Field Work', 35. A similar account of the relation between social and 'spiritual' work is found in 'Brief Facts About The Salvation Army: What It Is'," in *The Salvation Army Year Book, 1925* (London: Salvationist Publishing and Supplies, 1925), 13–16.
[50] Booth, 'The Relation of Social to the Field Work', 36.
[51] Bramwell Booth and William Booth, *Orders and Regulations for Corps Officers of The Salvation Army* (London: The Salvation Army, 1925), 308.

education, and military chaplaincy.[52] The ongoing concern about a fragmentation of Salvationist mission along social/spiritual lines is evident by the fact that Bramwell's 1925 chapter on 'Relationship to Social and Other Work' was retained word-for-word in editions of the *Orders and Regulations for Corps Officers* through the 1970s.[53] The need to articulate a clear understanding of how Salvation Army social work was related to the gospel was a constant issue for each generation of Salvationist leaders.

Once again, General Frederick Coutts proved to be a pivotal thinker, crafting one of the most-quoted statements on this topic at the Army's centennial celebrations in 1965:

> ...the salvation of which the New Testament speaks had always to do with the healing of the whole man...If we ourselves, for want of a better way of speaking, refer to our evangelical work and also to our social work, it is not that these are two distinct entities which could operate one without the other. They are but two activities of the one and the same salvation which is concerned with the total redemption of man. Both rely upon the same divine grace. Both are inspired with the same motive. Both have the same end in mind. And as the gospel has joined them together we do not propose to put them asunder.[54]

Coutts was concerned to stress the unity of Salvation Army mission in part due to changes in public perception, as the movement sought increasing public support by emphasizing its social work, often without reference to its evangelistic mission. John Coutts's 1977 book *The Salvationists* acknowledged that 'the Army is often mistaken for a voluntary society like Oxfam or even the Red Cross: the Movement's own publicity does not always discourage this misunderstanding'.[55] But by this point in the movement's history even Salvationists, in articulating an apologetic for their social efforts, did not tend to prioritize the conversion of sinners over bodily assistance. Rather, as John Coutts puts it, 'the Salvationist's concern for man's present welfare is intended to be an expression of Christ's love'.[56] He notes that religious convictions are not forced on those who come to the Army's social services, but that the

---

[52] For the origins of Salvation Army involvement in these areas, see Frederick Coutts, *The Better Fight: The History of the Salvation Army, Vol. 6, 1914-1946* (London: The Salvation Army, 1976), 248–256; 267–277.

[53] See *Orders and Regulations for Corps Officers of The Salvation Army* (London: The Salvation Army, 1976), 94–95.

[54] Frederick Coutts, addressing centenary celebrations in Royal Albert Hall, 1965, quoted in Frederick Coutts, *The Weapons of Goodwill: The History of the Salvation Army, Vol. 7, 1946-1977* (London: The Salvation Army, 1986), 187. See also his account of Booth's original motivations in *Bread for my Neighbour: The Social Influence of William Booth* (London: Hodder and Stoughton, 1978), 20.

[55] John Coutts, *The Salvationists* (London: Mowbrays, 1977), 81.

[56] Coutts, *The Salvationists*, 82.

'Christian motivation' for such work 'is usually fairly obvious'.[57]

In the late twentieth century, Salvationists continued to attempt to re-frame their social ministries in such a way that they were not so clearly seen as inferior to evangelistic work, by moving towards a holistic understanding of the gospel. A major event in this regard was the symposium convened at Catherine Booth Bible College, Winnipeg, in the mid-1980s, to consider 'The Theology of Social Services'.[58] Of particular interest is the essay by Philip Needham, 'Toward a Re-integration of the Salvationist Mission', attempts to reframe the mission of the Army by drawing on the image of 'two arms' with 'one task', understood to be 'the redemption of human life'.[59] Needham discounts the idea of social service as 'charitable acts toward less fortunate people' in favour of a view that such ministry 'is to be understood as concrete steps toward realizing the new reality of social reconciliation which has come in Christ'.[60] Drawing on the idea of a boundless and comprehensive salvation, Needham argues,

> Social service is properly understood, interpreted, and practised only as a part of a total ministry based on the gospel of a thorough redemption – that is, a redemption of soul, mind, body, and relationships. As such, it neither stands alone as if it were its own justification, nor suffers the status of an unwanted but necessary stepchild, as if lacked true spirituality. It is the gospel speaking through human concern and concrete help.[61]

What this means is that Salvationists 'are never *only* interested in the social dimensions of a person's life – just as we are never *only* interested in the spiritual.[62] This integrated approach means that social service should not be separate from the life of the local congregation, but is properly understood as a ministry of fellowship – 'the overflow of Christian Caring'.[63]

Needham's argument is an excellent example of contemporary attempts by Salvationists to re-integrate 'social' and 'spiritual' mission on a theological level.   Movement towards integration remains the dominant

---

[57] Coutts, *The Salvationists*, 92.

[58] The papers from this conference were published in John D. Waldron, ed., *Creed and Deed: Toward a Christian Theology of Social Services in the Salvation Army* (Toronto: The Salvation Army, 1986).

[59] Phil Needham, 'Toward a Re-integration of The Salvationist Mission', in *Creed and Deed: Toward a Christian Theology of Social Services in The Salvation Army* (Toronto: The Salvation Army, 1986), 141–145.

[60] Needham, 'Toward a Re-integration of The Salvationist Mission', 129.

[61] Needham, 'Toward a Re-integration of The Salvationist Mission', 135.

[62] Needham, 'Toward a Re-integration of The Salvationist Mission', 144.

[63] Needham, 'Toward a Re-integration of The Salvationist Mission', 146. See also Needham's comments in *Community in Mission: A Salvationist Ecclesiology* (London: International Headquarters of the Salvation Army, 1987), 62–64.

theological trend in Salvation Army thinking about mission.[64] The practical re-integration of these two aspects of Salvation Army remains an ongoing challenge. Theologically, however, great strides have been made, in this more integrated perspective. It allows both types of activity to be seen as aspects of the ministry of evangelization, as both words and deeds serving testify to the good news of the gospel for the whole person.

A Vision for the Twenty-first Century

Salvationists have always been committed to a holistic vision, but their theological categories have sometimes subtly undermined that holism. Salvationist thinking over the past 150 years has been moving away from overly dualistic views of salvation and mission, and finding ways to reintegrate sanctification within salvation as a whole, while also reintegrating spiritual and social mission. These are very positive theological developments, which must be matched by holistic missional engagement at the grassroots level. In engaging these issues, Salvationists can offer an important perspective on struggles that the church as a whole must face as we move forward in the twenty-first century. Maintaining the integral connection between salvation and sanctification continues to be a challenge in the face of a prevailing popular understanding of salvation as simply 'going to heaven'. And while contemporary evangelicals are rediscovering the gospel's social implications, there is still a lively conversation taking place regarding the place of social action and social justice in relation to traditional evangelism. With their particular history and identity, Salvationists are perhaps uniquely positioned to wrestle with these very questions.

---

[64] See, for example, *Mission in Community: The Salvation Army's Integrated Mission* (The Salvation Army International Headquarters, 2006), http://www.saministryresources.ca/UserFiles/File/mission_in_community.pdf, (accessed May 28, 2014).

3. A Permanent Mission to the 'Whosoever'[1]

William Booth's Theology of Redemption

Roger J. Green

Introduction

Redemption was the controlling theme of William Booth's theology. All else revolved around the story of redemption.[2] He was convinced from the Bible and his own experience that human beings were created in God's image, but because sin had marred that image they were in need of atonement. And while there were many images of atonement embedded in the Bible and in the theological history of the Church, the image most clear to William Booth was that of redemption, which included images of rescue. He was personally aware that he himself had experienced such redemption, and any understanding of Booth's theology of redemption must begin with that experience.

William Booth was born into Anglicanism, but in his early teen years he was taken to the local Methodist church in Nottingham. And through the preaching of the ministers and the singing of the congregation Booth learned his theology. At the age of fifteen he experienced a rather dramatic conversion, conscious of his sin and guilt and conscious also of his need for a Savior. He became convinced that the step toward God could not be taken until his guilt was assuaged and a form of restitution made. "'In a boyish trading affair, I had managed to make a profit out of my companions, whilst giving them to suppose that what I did was all in the way of generous fellowship. As a testimony of their gratitude they had given me a silver pencil-case". This was the sin that withheld William Booth from grace. Nothing worse than this, which would have seemed to his father a sign of enviable astuteness, had defiled the boy's life. But it appeared to him the blackest of sins, nor could he comfort himself with the counsel of God until he had found the young fellow he had chiefly wronged and confessed his wickedness'. [3] Until Booth relinquished this secret sin and was free from his guilt, he could never know God or readily realize his personal redemption.

---

[1] Albert Orsborn, 'The World Council of Churches', *The Officer*, Vol. V, No.2, March – April 1954, 74
[2] See Roger J. Green, *War on Two Fronts: The Redemptive Theology of William Booth* (Atlanta, GA: The Salvation Army, 1989).
[3] St. John Ervine, *God's Soldier: General William Booth*, 2 Vols. (New York: The MacMillan Co., 1935), 1:34-35.

This was doubtless the advice and admonition of his Methodist class leader. Once the restitution was made to match William's repentance, he witnessed that the guilt of his heart was replaced by the peace of God, and he was resolved to serve God and his generation from that time forth. William Booth had decided for God. That was certain. Where this decision would take him was as yet, however, unclear. William Booth was as much driven to God as he was called by God. Nevertheless he firmly believed that he was a sinner in need of salvation, that God had graciously provided the way of salvation through sending His Son whose death on the cross was efficacious for all who believed, and that one had to decide for God in an active step of faith. William Booth acted on the theology that he had heard from the Methodist pulpit and in the class meetings at the Broad Street Wesleyan Chapel, and in doing so left behind his own ambitions. Now he would serve God and leave present circumstances, as well as his own future, in God's hands.[4]

The Shaping of Booth's Theology of Redemption

There were several people who shaped Booth's theology of redemption, the foremost being John Wesley. Wesley often visited Nottingham in the previous century and established a strong and enduring Methodism there—not in a denominational sense but in the form of a renewal movement within the Church.[5] Denominational Methodism, which had been established only after Wesley's death in 1791, was the place where Booth had experienced his own conversion. And later in life he would be ordained by New Connexion Methodism, a denomination founded to uphold the principles and theology of John Wesley.

During William Booth's day several itinerant Methodist preachers came to Nottingham seeking to restore the Scriptural way of salvation so often preached by the Wesleys. These included John Smith and David Greenbury, different in preaching styles, but effective in winning converts and raising up the saints in the way of holiness. It was evidently David Greenbury who urged William Booth to begin preaching, as he was 'struck by Booth's earnestness, by the vigour of his personality, and by his remarkable appearance and emphatic manner. He urged upon the young man that it was his duty to speak, that he owed it to God to conquer his timidity, which was a form of selfishness'.[6]

---

[4] See Roger J. Green, *The Life and Ministry of William Booth: Founder of The Salvation Army* (Nashville: Abingdon Press, 2005), chapter one for a fuller account of Booth's calling.
[5] Wesley recorded in his *Journal*, 'We went on in a lovely afternoon, and through a lovely country, to Nottingham. I preached to a numerous and well-behaved congregation. I love this people. There is something wonderfully pleasing, both in their spirit and in their behaviour'. Elizabeth Jay, ed. *The Journal of John Wesley: A Selection* (Oxford: Oxford University Press, 1987), 233
[6] Harold Begbie, *The Life of General William Booth*, 2 Vols. (New York: The Macmillan Co., 1920), 1:63.

However it is beyond doubt that the greatest influence upon William Booth at this time was the American Methodist preacher James Caughey. Booth first heard Caughey when he visited Nottingham in 1846, two years after Booth's conversion, and so he was not instrumental in Booth's conversion as some have assumed.[7]

Other American evangelists such as Charles Grandison Finney and Phoebe Palmer would be influential upon William Booth later in his life, but James Caughey was the first of the Americans to shape Booth's thinking and character, and to give Booth a vision both for the biblical understanding of redemption and also how to take that message of salvation to the whosoever. Norman Murdoch wrote the following:

> Booth was Caughey's heir. Caughey convinced Booth that converting the masses was possible through scientific, calculated means. Revivals which were planned, advertised, and prayed for would succeed. From the time they met in 1846 to his death in 1912, Booth was consumed with the idea of winning souls through mass meetings, house-to-house visitation, and personal witness. That was the legacy of James Caughey, who died in 1891 at age eighty-one, largely forgotten, despite his influence, not only on the Booths, but also on all British evangelicalism.[8]

As a result of his conversion and through his attraction to Methodists like James Caughey, William Booth was inextricably tied to Methodism. He had given his life to God, and as far as he was concerned that life would be lived out within Methodism. He was determined to allow God to help him overcome temptation and to turn his back on the allure of worldly pleasures and gains. Attention to the will of God and living in the Kingdom of God were now of first importance to his own vital piety. Redemption was at the heart of Booth's maturing theological vision at this point in his life, and of this he was sure—such redemption signified not only justification by faith but holiness as well. Furthermore, redemption in the life of the believer issued in good works motivated by obedience to God and love for one's neighbor. Such clarity of thought would not be deterred either by the apathy of the Church or the enormity of the problems that William encountered as he witnessed the daily pathetic struggle of the poor and impoverished. God in Christ had reached out to William Booth, and William Booth had turned to Christ in faith. The certainty of this conviction and the assurance that resulted would be the sure foundation of William Booth's life from now on. But to keep this to himself was impossible for this impetuous youth with his newly found faith. He had to share—he was called to preach!

---

[7] See 'Dr. Adam Clarke and the General's Spiritual Father', *The Conqueror* 5 (July 1896), 306.

[8] Norman Murdoch, *Origins of The Salvation Army* (Knoxville: The University of Tennessee Press, 1994), 12.

The greatest influence in his life was Catherine Mumford, the woman that he would marry in 1855.[9] Catherine shared Booth's Methodist background and understood theology much as Booth did, especially the theology of redemption. She would be a partner in marriage and eventually in ministry until her death in 1890. And Catherine encouraged Booth in his decision to enter into the Methodist ministry. His teacher, William Cooke, shaped Booth's theological thinking into a more systematic Wesleyan pattern, with the good news of redemption at the center of the theological story. He prepared Booth for ordination in 1858 as a New Connexion Methodist preacher.[10]

Aspects of Booth's Theology of Redemption

William Booth's theology of redemption matured as he studied the Bible and attempted to interpret his own life experiences. When he began his ministry as a New Connexion Methodist minister his preaching of redemption was largely to unconverted sinners, making them aware that due to their willful sinfulness and rebellion against God they were morally and spiritually depraved and justly exposed to the wrath of God. Unable to atone for their transgressions they could rely only on the sacrifice made for them by Christ on the cross to be reconciled to God and redeemed for the purposes for which God had created them. There was simply no other way. 'This Methodist and evangelical conviction, forged as a youth in Nottingham, proved to be the guiding passion of his life. Booth never tired of calling sinners to repentance, to faith in Jesus Christ. Few, if any, Victorians believed more strongly than the Army's founding father that redemption through Christ was the answer to the plight of humanity'.[11]

But here his preaching and teaching was principally to the individual. However, with the maturity of his theology as well as his enlarged vision of the work of the gospel came the realization that there was a corporate aspect to the

---

[9] See Roger J. Green, *Catherine Booth: A Biography of the Cofounder of The Salvation Army* (Grand Rapids, MI: Baker Books, 1996).
[10] For background on William Cooke see Henry Smith, *Sketches of Eminent New Connexion Methodist Ministers* (London: J. C. Watts, 1893), chapter five. And for an interesting article on the formation of New Connexion Methodism and William Booth's relationship to that denomination see Victor A. Shepherd, 'From New Connexion Methodism to William Booth', *Papers of the Canadian Methodist Historical Society*, Vol. 9 (1993), 91-107. William Booth resigned from New Connexion Methodism in 1861, the resignation taking effect a year later, over a dispute about keeping Booth in the pastoral ministry and not allowing him the evangelistic freedom that he desired. After leaving New Connexion Methodism William and Catherine Booth had an itinerant ministry until the founding of The Christian Mission in 1865 that evolved into The Salvation Army in 1878.
[11] Andrew M. Eason and Roger J. Green, *Boundless Salvation: The Shorter Writings of William Booth* (New York: Peter Lang Publishing, Inc., 2012), 41. See also William Booth, *The Doctrines and Disciplines of The Salvation Army, Prepared for the Training Homes* (1881; reprint, Toronto: Headquarters of The Salvation Army, 1885), 9-13.

biblical theology of redemption, demonstrated in three ways: redemption as sanctification, redemption as social ministry, and redemption as millennial theology.

Redemption as Sanctification

The doctrine of sanctification will be dealt with in other chapters in this book. However, here it is sufficient to say that understanding Booth's theology of redemption is incomplete without understanding it first as complete redemption for the individual, as purity of heart granted to the believer through the work of Christ ministered to through the Holy Spirit.[12] However, Booth's theology of sanctification evolved to include a corporate vision for sanctification—the sanctification of the whole Army for the purposes of winning the world for God. It becomes clear in his later theology precisely why he interpreted sanctification in this wider dimension. First, sanctification was the final answer to the problem of evil. By connecting sanctification with the ultimate conquest of the world and of evil--only a holy people could do a holy work-- Booth challenged any concept of the finality of evil.

Second his doctrine of sanctification gave legitimacy to the Army. He became convinced that God sanctified not only individuals, but groups as well. The doctrine of sanctification took on a new dimension for Booth as his Army grew and developed. Corporate sanctification, or institutional sanctification, became an important sign that The Salvation Army was of divine, and not merely human, origin. In a *War Cry* article in 1892 the Founder exhorted his readers in this way: 'Cast yourselves upon God. Keep on watching and praying and believing and expecting for me, for yourselves, for the whole Army at home and abroad, for the mighty baptism of burning fire!'[13] He reiterated this in one of his most important letters to his officers in 1909:

> The Salvation Army has known a great deal of this Divine inspiration. It is itself the creation of the Holy Spirit. All it knows of life and vitality, and all the power it possesses to bless the world, come from the Holy Spirit; and to this day waves of Divine influence, in a lesser or greater measure, are sweeping over it which proceed from Him alone.[14]

Third, Booth's wider understanding of sanctification became fundamental because this work of God in believers and in the Church was preparation for the final redemptive purpose of God—the establishment of the Kingdom of God. This aspect of sanctification prevented Booth's concept of holiness from being monastic—it was not a doctrine that called for separation from the evil world

---

[12] See William Booth, *Purity of Heart* (London: Salvation Army Book-Room, 1902).

[13] William Booth, 'Christianity on Fire, No. IV', *The War Cry* 13 (May 1892), 9-10.

[14] William Booth, *To My Officers: A Letter from the General on His Eightieth Birthday*, 33. The William Booth File. The Salvation Army International Heritage Centre, London, England.

until the work of redemption was completed by God Himself alone. As with the Wesleyan revivals in the previous century, people learned their theology not only by hearing the preacher, but also by singing the songs. One of Booth's songs clearly reflected his enlarged vision of sanctification for his Army:

> Thou Christ of burning, cleansing flame, Send the fire!
> Thy blood-bought gift today we claim, Send the fire!
> Look down and see this waiting host,
> Give us the promised Holy Ghost,
> We want another Pentecost, Send the fire!
>
> God of Elijah, hear our cry: Send the fire!
> To make us fit to live or die, Send the fire!
> To burn up every trace of sin,
> To bring the light and glory in,
> The revolution now begin, Send the fire!
>
> 'Tis fire we want, for fire we plead, Send the fire!
> The fire will meet our every need, Send the fire!
> For strength to ever do the right,
> For grace to conquer in the fight,
> For power to walk the world in white, Send the fire!
>
> To make our weak hearts strong and brave, Send the fire!
> To live a dying world to save, Send the fire!
> O see us on thy altar lay
> Our lives, our all, this very day,
> To crown the offering now we pray, Send the fire![15]

Redemption as Social Ministry

The Christian Mission, founded by William and Catherine Booth in 1865, had no organized social ministry, save the Food-for-the-Millions program, administered by Bramwell Booth and James Flawn, which ran from 1870 to 1874.[16] Each Mission Preaching Station tried to meet human need as much as possible, but no organized, centrally controlled ministry to the poor was undertaken in those days except for that Food-for-the-Millions program. What moved William and Catherine Booth as they surveyed Whitechapel Road in East London was that men and women were living in rebellion against God.

---

[15] William Booth, *The Salvation Army Song Book, 1899.*

[16] See Jenty Fairbank, *Booth's Boots: Social Service Beginnings in The Salvation Army* (London: International Headquarters of The Salvation Army, 1983). Bramwell Booth was the eldest son of William and Catherine Booth, would be instrumental in the formation of The Salvation Army in later years, and would succeed his father as the General of The Salvation Army. James Flawn, before his conversion in The Christian Mission, had been in the food catering business and provided various food services for The Salvation Army as a Salvationist until his death in 1917.

They were sinners who needed to be saved, and the preaching of both Booths called sinners to repentance and raised up saints in the life intended by God.

This was the controlling mission of The Christian Mission and The Salvation Army. The Booths were not unsympathetic to the lives of the poor, but that aspect of ministry would come later in their ministry. In explaining the change from The Christian Mission to The Salvation Army, Booth affirmed this single mission.

> We are a Salvation people—this is our specialty—getting saved and keeping saved, and then getting somebody else saved, and then getting saved ourselves more and more, until full salvation on earth makes the heaven within, which is finally perfected by the full salvation without, on the other side of the river....My brethren, my comrades, soul saving is our avocation, the great purpose and business of our lives. Let us seek first the kingdom of God, let us be SALVATIONISTS indeed.[17]

In defining the work of The Salvation Army to the Wesleyan Conference in August 1880, Booth stated 'we go on the three broad lines of Repentance, Faith, and Holiness of Heart'.[18] One would search in vain in this entire address in which he set forth the principles of The Salvation Army, and in many similar addresses during this period, to find any references to soup kitchens or lodging houses, let alone any biblical or theological justification for an extended vision of redemption. William Booth and his Salvation Army were still involved in the single mission of converting sinners. That, it was thought, was the highest service that could be rendered to the poor. 'This impulse was purely evangelical; it did not become what is called humanitarian or economic till ten years later. At its beginning, The Salvation Army was a society of men and women which existed only to preach the repentance of sins'.[19]

The magnitude of the social problems that The Salvation Army would eventually face head on in Great Britain came into sharp focus during the mid-1880s. Others in the movement began to recognize the complexity of their ministry, and there dawned an awareness in some of Booth's officers and soldiers that it was not enough to preach the gospel to the poor, but that preaching had to be complemented by taking care of the physical needs of the poor.

Booth's sensitivity to the poor, to whom he had been preaching for many years, was heightened through the experiences of his Army. A severe economic depression had taken its toll in England, and the effects of that depression manifested themselves in the places where Booth's Army was at work, '1873 being the date normally given for the beginning of the "great

---

[17] William Booth, 'Our New Name', *The Salvationist* (January 1, 1879), 1.
[18] William Booth, 'The General's Address at the Wesleyan Conference', *The War Cry* 1 (August 1880), 1.
[19] Begbie, *The Life of General William Booth*, 1:434.

depression" and 1874 as the beginning of the nineteenth century disaster to British agriculture'.[20]

The Army began a variety of social ministries to meet the needs of the poor not only in Great Britain, but also in Australia, the United States, India and other places around the world. And in 1890 Booth published *In Darkest England and the Way Out* to outline the social problems that the Army was encountering as well as the solutions to those problems. However, the book was also written to raise money for the ever-developing social ministries in The Salvation Army.

Finally it was decided that an office be created to coordinate the social reform operations of The Salvation Army. Therefore, by 1890 the tentative efforts of The Salvation Army at social reform were placed under the office of what became known as the Social Reform Wing of The Salvation Army, commanded by Commissioner Frank Smith, who played a significant role in moving General Booth's sympathies in the direction of social ministry.[21] And a 'Darkest England' Trust Deed was executed on January 30, 1891, in a public meeting in St. James's Hall, London.

It is critical here to understand that the inauguration of that ministry signaled both a turning point in the life of William Booth and his Salvation Army in 1890, as well as a maturing understanding of redemption on Booth's part. With the establishment of that Social Reform Wing, The Salvation Army entered into a new stage of its ministry under the direction of its General, which one biographer has characterized as 'an immense change in the direction of the Army'.[22] Booth and his Army finally recognized institutionally the importance of the second mission that had gradually gained acceptance. In 1889 and 1890 the commitment to social salvation became fixed. The timing was significant in the history of The Salvation Army. Hitherto its chief concern had been for personal salvation from sin, and social concerns were secondary, but increasing in importance. Now, however, the movement was engaged in redemption that manifested itself in two works—personal salvation and social salvation. It now had a dual mission.[23]

And so by 1890, Booth, convinced that it was theologically correct to address social redemption systematically, was willing to commit himself and his Army in a way that he wished for the Church. He was at times critical of the

---

[20] G. Kitson Clark, *The Making of Victorian England*, (Cambridge, MA: Harvard University Press, 1962), 32.

[21] Smith eventually resigned from The Salvation Army and channeled his energies into politics and journalism.

[22] Ervine, *God's Soldier: General William Booth*, 2:628.

[23] There is little evidence to substantiate John Kent's statement that "*Darkest England* appeared when the original religious basis of the Army was proving too weak to sustain the initial success" (John Kent, *Holding the Fort: Studies in Victorian Revivalism* [London: SCM Press, 1978], 335). In fact, it is altogether possible that the opposite is true—that *Darkest England* was written precisely because of the success and strength of the Army in many places in the world and because Booth had developed his understanding of redemption to include salvation for both worlds.

Church for not understanding either the necessity of or the nature of social redemption. "Why all this apparatus of temples and meeting-houses to save men from perdition in a world which is to come, while never a helping hand is stretched out to save them from the inferno of their present life?"[24]

This theological foundation was based on the great commandment of Jesus to love one's neighbor, a theological text that Booth referred to often in his later ministry. However, this foundation was not only biblical but also Wesleyan.[25] The Wesleyan theological option for the poor found expression in Booth's social ministry.

> There exist many parallels in the Army to the radical side of Methodist preaching. Booth remarks in his book *In Darkest England and the Way Out* that "The Scheme of Social Salvation is not worth discussing which is not as wide as the Scheme of Eternal Salvation set forth in the Gospel. The Glad Tidings must be to every creature, not merely to an elect few who are to be saved....It is now time to fling down the false idol, and proclaim a Temporal Salvation as full, free and universal, and with no other limitations that the 'Whosoever will' of the Gospel." Here one finds many of the Wesleyan themes of a personal "gospel egalitarianism" overflowing into a social vision for the poor, though perhaps not with the same theological sophistication but with the same anti-Calvinistic polemic.[26]

William Booth refused to make a distinction, as others had done, between the deserving poor and the undeserving poor. All must be offered the redemptive gospel message and the means to overcome their poverty. This became a vital aspect of the message of redemption.

By 1890 The Salvation Army was well launched on a second mission. It was now a movement that was committed to both spiritual and social redemption, and Booth's theology from this time forward reflected this dual mission. His public pronouncements attempted to maintain the tension of the dual mission. This developed theology of redemption still included personal salvation from sin for the individual who believes by faith. However, now Booth embraced a theology of redemption that included social salvation from the evils that beset people in this life. And just as there was the possibility of universal spiritual redemption in Booth's theology, reflecting his Wesleyan theology, so there was the possibility of universal social redemption, reflecting his postmillennial vision for the salvation of the world before the return of Christ.

---

[24] Booth, *In Darkest England and the Way Out*, 16.

[25] See Donald Burke, 'The Wesleyan View of Salvation and Social Involvement', 11-32 in John D. Waldron, ed., *Creed and Deed: Toward a Christian Theology of Social Services in The Salvation Army* (Toronto: The Salvation Army, 1986).

[26] Donald W. Dayton, '"Good News to the Poor": The Methodist Experience After Wesley', chapter 4, 87-88 in M. Douglas Meeks, ed., *The Portion of the Poor: Good News to the Poor in the Wesleyan Tradition* (Nashville, TN: Kingswood Books, 1995).

William Booth was nothing if not a military strategist for God. He knew that before launching this new ministry publicly, he had to bring his own people into line with his enlarged theological vision, and knew that it would not be possible to win the hearts and minds of all his soldiers and officers on this issue. Many would still hold that the salvation of the soul is the surest way to bring about social redemption. However, as part of his strategic plan Booth wrote one of his most important articles in 1889 appropriately entitled 'Salvation for Both Worlds' published in *All the World* in January 1889. In that article he explained that he had always been aware of the physical impoverishment of the people to whom he had preached, having experienced poverty himself. He nevertheless saw no remedy for such poverty and so was determined to save people's souls even if he could not help them in this world.

However, he noted that his own and his people's experience had taught him 'that the miseries from which I sought to save man in the next world were substantially the same as those from which I everywhere found him suffering in this'.[27] And Booth concluded that he now had two gospels to preach—a gospel of redemption from personal sin and a gospel of redemption from social evil. He broadened his theological language to take into account his changed theology. He added new meaning and a new dimension to the redemptive theological language that he had been expressing for years. Salvation now had social obligations and dimensions as well as spiritual ones.

Ten months after writing 'Salvation for Both Worlds', designed obviously to prepare his own people for a personal and institutional allegiance and commitment to a double mission, Booth wrote *In Darkest England and the Way Out to* explain his developed theology and thereby explain the evolution that had taken place in his own thinking and in the mission of the Army, which was increasingly placing itself in the public eye.

However, those who read and interpret Booth's book only in the light of its social analysis and constructive programs will seriously miss an important intention of the book, and in doing so will misunderstand William Booth at this critical juncture in his life and ministry. The book is also an expression of Booth's expanded view of redemption to include social redemption. He wanted to maintain the delicate balance between personal and social salvation. Doing so was important to Booth for at least two reasons. First, he feared that social salvation would break loose from its ties to spiritual salvation, thus rendering The Salvation Army merely an ineffectual social agency. Second, he wanted to respond to his critics on the one hand who denied the validity of his social work, and his critics on the other hand who denied the validity of his religious work.[28] Booth was not equally clear, however, in spelling out those intentions.

---

[27] William Booth, 'Salvation for Both Worlds', *All the World* (January 1889), 2.
[28] See Roger J. Green, 'Theological Roots of *In Darkest England and the Way Out*', *Wesleyan Theological Journal* 25:1 (Spring 1990), 83-105, and Norman H. Murdoch, 'William Booth's *In Darkest England and the Way Out:* A Reappraisal', *Wesleyan Theological Journal* 25:1 (Spring 1990), 106-16. The failure to connect the social ministry to Booth's theology is apparent in the biography by Roy Hattersley, *Blood and*

Nevertheless, it was important for Booth to explain that the social ministry of the Army was not an end in itself. The work of social redemption was preparatory, necessarily, to the work of spiritual or personal redemption. Experience had taught him that some people were so disastrously oppressed by their present physical circumstances that 'these multitudes will not be saved in their present circumstances'.[29] A similar theme is reiterated throughout his book. Booth was convinced that 'if these people are to believe in Jesus Christ, become the servants of God, and escape the miseries of the wrath to come, they must be helped out of their present social miseries'.[30] The clearest statement of Booth's intentions is found in his assertion that 'at the risk of being misunderstood and misrepresented, I must assert in the most unqualified way that it is primarily and mainly for the sake of saving the soul that I seek the salvation of the body'.[31] Years later that theological position is reiterated in a letter to his officers on the occasion of his eightieth birthday:

> But while you strive to deliver them from their temporal distresses, and endeavour to rescue them from the causes that have led to their unfortunate condition, you must seek, above all, to turn their miseries to good account by making them help the Salvation of their souls and their deliverance from the wrath to come. It will be a very small reward for all your toils if, after bringing them into condition of well-being here, they perish hereafter.[32]

Only when Booth's social mission is placed within the framework of his entire theological vision will it be completely understood. His newly formulated theology of redemption was sustained and supported by other aspects of his theology that he had articulated prior to 1889 and 1890. He had already conceived of his Army as a part of the universal church that was blessed by God and sanctified by the Holy Spirit. He had developed his imagery of Christ to include the conquering Christ who was the model for deliverance from the evils of this world as well as from the wrath of the next world. He believed that evil was not finally triumphant, but that universal redemption, both personal and social, was possible.[33] All people needed to be given the opportunity to

---

Fire: William and Catherine Booth and Their Salvation Army (New York: Doubleday, 2000). See Gertrude Himmelfarb's review of Hattersley's book, 'First Save the Body, Then the Soul', in *the New York Times Book Review* (July 9, 2000), 14-15.

[29] Booth, *In Darkest England and the Way Out*, 257.

[30] Booth, *In Darkest England and the Way Out*, 257. See also 35, 205, 264, 268.

[31] Booth, *In Darkest England and the Way Out*, 45. See also 104, 110, 218. Begbie, who did not understand Booth's theology, claimed that 'his social work was chiefly an excuse for getting at the souls of men' (Begbie, "Booth, William [1829-1912], *Dictionary of National Biography*, 51.

[32] William Booth, *To My Officers*, 44.

[33] This should not be confused with universalism. Salvation is universal for Booth only insofar as God offers his redemption to all people, but only those who respond by faith will realize that redemption.

respond to the gospel message by faith. He believed in an ultimate eschatological goal—a goal that would embrace both spiritual and social redemption, and he held out that goal as hope for ultimate redemptive victory for his Army of salvation. It is interesting and not inconsequential that his most important article dealing with this eschatological goal was written in August 1890, the same time that he was completing the writing of *In Darkest England and the Way Out.*[34]

Redemption as a Millennial Vision

A third aspect of Booth's vision of redemption was his postmillennial vision for winning the world for God, and for Booth there was a natural transition from the doctrine of sanctification as a means of preparation for redemption, and the doctrine of the kingdom of God as a result of the work of redemption by God's holy people here on earth. And until that full redemption in the kingdom comes, the people of God demonstrate their lives in Christ by loving God and loving their neighbors. But sanctification and the winning of the world for God cannot be treated separately. 'If you are a holy man or woman' Booth wrote, 'you will help forward the War, and spread the glory of Christ's name far more effectively than you will if you are not fully saved. Holy people are the great need of the world. I am sure they are one of the great wants of the Army'.[35] Those who shared the organizational and institutional power with Booth espoused the same theology that they believed was both biblically based and socially functional in giving legitimacy to the organization. They, too, were convinced of these doctrinal principles: the nature of institutional holiness, and the ultimate redemptive purposes of that holiness—the conquest of the world."[36]

---

[34] William Booth, "The Millennium; or the Ultimate Triumph of Salvation Army Principles," *All The World* 6 (August 1890), 337-343.
[35] William Booth, *Purity of Heart*, 70-71.
[36] The evidence is overwhelming that those around Booth also shared much of his theology, including his postmillennial theology. There are innumerable examples of this, but the following with suffice: For Catherine Booth see the following: Catherine Booth, "The Holy Ghost," *All The World* 16 (June 1900), 339-342; Catherine Booth, "The Kingdom of Christ," *All The World* 1 (August 1885), 183-184; and Catherine Booth, *Popular Christianity,* (London: Salvation Army Book Depot, 1887), 197; for Bramwell Booth see Bramwell Booth, "Salvation Army," *Encyclopedia of Religion and Ethics*, 12 Vols. , James Hastings, ed. (New York: Charles Scribner's Sons, 1921), 11:151; for Evangeline Booth see Evangeline Booth, *Toward a Better World* (Garden City: Doubleday, Doran and Company, 1928), 241. Evangeline Booth wrote a song entitled "The World for God"; for Arthur Booth-Clibborn see Arthur Booth-Clibborn, "The Pentecostal Programme," *All The World* 11 (June 1895), 401-405; for John Lawley see John Lawley, "Down with the Gates!" *The War Cry* 14 (November 1893), 12. For Elijah Cadman see Elijah Cadman, "The New Kingdom," *All The World* 11 (July 1895), 3-4. Roland Robertson's observation is correct—that during the history of The Salvation Army in Booth's lifetime, millennial teachings were important, and "from

William Booth's vision of the kingdom of God was shaped by his postmillennialism. Postmillennialism 'holds that the millennium will come first, usually "as the fruit of the present Christian agencies now at work in the world", and that the Second Coming or the delivering agency will occur at the end of the process'.[37] A clearer and more succinct definition of postmillennialism, and one that relates postmillennialism to the social reform work of the Army and other movements, is found in Donald Dayton's *Discovering an Evangelical Heritage*. Postmillennialism is the expectation of 'Christ to return in judgment *after* a millennial reign of one thousand years'.[38] Dayton goes on to affirm that 'reform activity was in part to prepare the way for the millennium, which was in turn a reflection of the vision of the "state of the perfect society" that drew Evangelicals into reform'.[39]

Millennial themes of various stripes had been the subject of countless books, articles, discussions and movements from the period of the New Testament to the nineteenth century. Neither Booth's concepts nor his practical application of those concepts were new. However, his distinctive contribution and focus was in the relationship of the Army and his theology to the establishment of the kingdom. His postmillennialism provided a grand triumphant vision for an Army on the march, and the constant growth of the Army likewise sustained that postmillennial vision.

Booth's millennial thinking, therefore, became part of the fabric of the working theology of redemption of The Salvation Army in his day, although no millennial statement or position was ever included in the official doctrinal statements of the Army. However, Booth's millennialism, in the context of Booth's total theological system, in the context of The Salvation Army and its ministry and social concern, and in the context of other millennial visions was neither strange nor insignificant. Rather, it provided both justification for the existence of the Army as well as hope for the primary work of the Army.

William Booth was convinced, and in his international travels he was constantly persuading his people, that this work of redemption was the will of God. He reasoned that just as God willed that an individual be saved, so God extended that will to the whole world, and God wanted the entire world to be saved. 'We must increase the speed if we are to keep pace with the yearnings of the Almighty Heart of Love that would have all men to be saved'.[40] Given

---

time to time the question of the millennium was viewed with some degree of urgency" (Roland Robertson, "The Salvation Army: The Persistence of Sectarianism," 71 in Bryan R. Wilson, ed. *Patterns of Sectarianism* (London: Heinemann Educational Books, 1967), 49-105.

[37] James Black, *New Forms of Old Faith* (London, 1948), quoted in George Shepperson, "The Comparative Study of Millenarian Movements," *Millennial Dreams in Action*, Sylvia R. Thrupp, ed. (The Hague: Mouton, 1962), 44.

[38] Dayton, *Discovering an Evangelical Heritage*, 125.

[39] Dayton, *Discovering an Evangelical Heritage*, 126.

[40] William Booth, *The General's Letters*, 99. To understand the consistency of this message in Booth's ministry see the following as examples: William Booth, 'Hints to

that fact, Booth was equally convinced that God's people on earth were the agencies of that redemption, and none were better suited or qualified for that than Salvationists.[41]

Here William Booth's single-mindedness and his inextricable relationship with The Salvation Army came to his service as an international evangelist and religious figure. He became increasingly convinced that he and his people were to have a significant part to play in the establishment of such a kingdom. Setting some sort of time frame for the establishment of the kingdom of God by reading the nineteenth and twentieth centuries back into the books of Daniel and Revelation was of no interest to Booth. He was concerned, however, that his people understand their place in God's redemptive activity, and that they be well motivated, realizing all along that there was a divine organizational goal to which they were marching—the kingdom of God. It was that goal that Booth was constantly preaching and that, in turn, gave such significance in the lives of his followers. 'When God's people wake up to the importance of this great War, and go forth to engage in it after this fashion, the millennium will not be very far away'.[42] On that practical, pastoral level rested the chief concern of William Booth for his Salvationists. On May 30, 1885 he wrote:

> I want to see a new translation of the Bible into the hearts and conduct of living men and women. I want an improved translation—or transference it might be called—of the commandments and promises and teachings and influences of this Book to the minds and feelings and words and activities of the men and women who hold on to it and swear by it and declare it to be an inspired Book and the only authorized rule of life. . . .It is of no use making correct translations of words if we cannot get the *words translated into life*. . . .Wayfaring men, though fools, can make this translation, and fifteen years' perseverance in it will, I have not the shadow of a doubt, go a long way towards bringing in the millennium.[43]

Soul Winners', *The Christian Mission Magazine* (May 1875), 124-126; William Booth, 'Go!' *All The World* 1 (November 1884), 1-4; William Booth, 'Memorial Challenge!' *The War Cry* 32 (May 1911), 9; and William Booth, 'Fifty Years' Salvation Service: Some of Its Lessons and Results. Interview with the General,' *All The World* 14 (July 1894), 7.
[41] See William Booth, *The General's Letters, 1885*, 60.
[42] Booth, *The General's Letters*, 22.
[43] Booth, *The General's Letters*, 142-145. Booth 'believed that it was possible to bring men and women of every degree and temperament into the fold of The Salvation Army, and he even dared, in certain moments of enthusiasm, to think that he himself might live to accomplish this consummation' (Begbie, *The Life of General William Booth*, 2:252). See also 251, 359, 402, 403. Shortly before his death in 1912 Booth said, 'I am more confident than ever that Salvation is the only hope for the world. Were it not for Salvation and the Salvation of The Salvation Army, I should think that the probability was that the world was on its way to universal suicide' (Begbie, *The Life of General William Booth*,.2:417).

Such hopeful relationship of The Salvation Army and the establishment of the kingdom of God would prevail in Booth's thinking throughout the remainder of his life. His single-mindedness continued unabated, and The Salvation Army was the agency best suited for the work of universal redemption. Booth believed that, as did thousands of his followers.

As Booth's ministry expanded so did this vision of the kingdom of God. And this was happening at the same time as Booth developed his view of salvation to include social as well as personal salvation. In fact, his clearest expression of the millennium was written in 1890 in an article entitled 'The Millennium; or the Ultimate Triumph of Salvation Army Principles'.[44] And only two months after the publication of that article Booth published his *In Darkest England and the Way Out*. And so, with the publication of 'The Millennium', followed almost immediately by the publication of *In Darkest England and the Way Out*, 1890 proved to be a critical juncture in both the theology and ministry of the Founder of The Salvation Army. His Salvationists would understand that the dual mission of the Army, undergirded by a theology of redemption that was both personal and social, was preparatory to the establishment of the millennial kingdom on earth, and thereby a harbinger of the Second Advent of Christ and of full redemption. Likewise, Booth's increased emphasis on the possibility of a millennium provided a final eschatological vision of the conquest of God over the forces of evil as well as of the work of universal redemption. And in Booth's mind, he and his Army were the center of that redemptive story. His article on the millennium, therefore, is important because Booth spells out the various characteristics of the millennium, and thereby provides goals to be obtained by his Salvationists. To reiterate Booth's vision was a shared vision, and the more he preached around the world and saw a growing Salvation Army, the more convinced he was of the biblical justification for such a vision.

This motivation for the mission of the Army was not taken particularly from a Wesleyan theology, but more from the cultural and social context of Booth's day. Booth's postmillennial expression was not derived specifically from a doctrine of creation that would lead toward the redemption of creation. Rather it was more of an expression of the perceived natural result of the methods of revival coupled with an English version of ruling the world.

Here Booth reached beyond his spiritual mentor, John Wesley. The Wesleyan revivals as well as the revolutionary activities of Europe in Wesley's days 'induced in him a touch of "post-millennialism"—an expectation of a notable out pouring of gospel grace and progress on earth. Rank-and-file Methodist attitudes varied'.[45] But basically millennial speculation did not concern either Wesley or his Methodists. Such matters 'were not of central concern to him. What did matter was doctrine concerned with personal

---

[44] See William Booth, "The Millennium; or the Ultimate Triumph of Salvation Army Principles," *All The World* 6 (August 1890), 337-343.
[45] Rack, *Reasonable Enthusiast*, 491.

salvation as the achievement of holiness to the point of perfection'.[46] And the same could be said of Charles Grandison Finney. While Finney was a postmillennialist early in his ministry, the Civil War inevitably dampened his proclivities toward postmillennialism.[47]

Conclusion

Redemption was at the heart of William Booth's theology. As far as he was concerned, the message of redemption was central to the Scriptures, to the life of the Church, and to the ministry of The Christian Mission and the Army. That redemptive theology was fully developed by Booth in three ways: as central to the doctrine of sanctification, as foundational to the social ministry of the Army, and as the fulfillment of the promises of God to establish his kingdom fully on earth. Booth was certain of these three aspects, and his theology simply cannot be understood without coming to terms with them. His vision for boundless salvation demanded a full-fledged doctrine of redemption.

---

[46] Rack, *Reasonable Enthusiast*, 382.
[47] See the mentions of postmillennialism in Finney's theology in Hardman, *Charles Grandison Finney (1792-1875): Revivalist and Reformer*.

Part Two: Growing Saints

4. 'Draw me close to Thee in deeper consecration'[1]

Reflections on The Salvation Army's spiritual life

Denis Metrustery

As part of the Christian Church, The Salvation Army stands in a long heritage of Christian spirituality. This chapter will explore the distinctive elements that comprise a specifically Salvation Army expression of spirituality, and I will seek to place the Army within the wider context of Protestant and Evangelical spirituality. We will also note the influence of other Christian spiritualities within the Army's spiritual life, and suggest that these can only enhance and strengthen the Army's pursuit of Christlikeness as it seeks to reach upward to God and outward to humanity. Importantly, as the Army is an international movement, we note that it is possible to live an authentically Christian life in any culture, and that each culture can bring a fresh understanding of Christianity, just as the church brings the gift of the message of Christ to each culture. Indeed, Christianity has crossed cultural boundaries from the Day of Pentecost to the present.

We will recognise the work of the Army's International Spiritual Life Commission, and the Calls made to the worldwide Salvation Army as the outcome of its evaluation of the history, current position, and future needs of the Army's spiritual life.

St. Paul encourages the Galatians that 'since we live by the Spirit, let us keep in step with the Spirit'[2] or 'walk by the Spirit'. Spirituality is a way of describing a particular style of Christian discipleship, a way of portraying a style of walking in the Spirit.

Catholic theology has utilised the term *spirituality* in similar ways to the usage in wider Christianity in the present day, developing 'mystical theology' and 'ascetical theology' and various 'schools' of spirituality were recognised, such as Ignatian spirituality and Franciscan spirituality. Spiritual theology seeks to understand and evaluate the spiritualities within differing Christian traditions. Contextualisation 'is the process in which Christianity speaks to a group of people in language and symbols with which they are at home, and they in turn express their Christian faith within their culture'.[3] As we discuss the spirituality of the evangelical tradition, we will begin to identify a style of walking in the Spirit with which Salvationists are 'at home'.

---

[1] 'In the depths of my soul's greatest longing' *The Song Book of The Salvation Army*, 493 (chorus), Margaret MacMillan
[2] Gal. 5:25
[3] Bradley, P. Holt, *A Brief History of Christian Spirituality*, (Oxford: Lion Pub., 1993, 1997), 25

If we are comfortable that holiness, sanctification, is a lifelong process[4] of transforming us into the likeness of Christ, then it has been suggested that the area of 'spiritual formation within evangelicalism is simply the Protestant doctrine of sanctification *in a new key.*'[5] Thus, a consideration of Christian spirituality is nothing less than an appreciation of how the Holy Spirit works in the lives of particular believers (and faith communities), in order to effect the transformation to Christlikeness. It is a journey, or pilgrimage, which can be intensely personal as well as rewardingly corporate, as the Church, Christ's Bride, is prepared for him.

A brief survey of Christian spirituality

Alister McGrath suggests that 'spirituality is not something that is deduced totally from theological presuppositions, nor is it something which is inferred totally from our experience. It arises from a creative and dynamic synthesis of faith and life, forged in the crucible of the desire to live out the Christian faith authentically, responsibly, effectively, and fully'.[6]

It can be proper to speak of 'Christian spiritualities' for the distinct emphases found in differing theological traditions allow for differentiation in the approach of denominations, and indeed individual believers, to living out the Christian life and exploring various 'means of grace'. The issues of personality, sociology and economics can inform how Christians relate to the outworking of the gospel message. Similarly, attitudes to the world, culture, and history can have implications for the outworking of living an authentically Christian life.

In the first century, Christianity became recognised as a distinct sect to Judaism - the Nazareans or people of 'the Way' - and developed from being a sect within a particular ethnic group, to being a transcultural religion, though frequently misunderstood and persecuted. Through its first six centuries, significant themes developed in Christian spirituality which form the basis of an engagement with the divine and a means whereby genuine personal transformation is possible. Many of the basic elements carried on from Judaistic roots, such as prayers, psalms, preaching, and singing. The Eucharist increased in importance to become the central feature of Christian worship, where the 'Bread of life' was accessed and Christ's victorious sacrifice celebrated. Holt concludes that 'Christian spirituality in the early centuries was communal spirituality, originating in baptism, rooted in the worship of the

---

[4] cf John Gowans, 'It's the work of a moment', *Glory! A Musical*, (London, Salvationist Publishing & Supplies Ltd. 1977), Song 34 – 'It's the work of a moment, it's the work of a lifetime, it begins in an instant, it may take eternity…'

[5] Steve L. Porter, 'Sanctification in a New Key: Relieving Evangelical Anxieties over Spiritual Formation', *Journal of Spiritual Formation and Soul Care*, Vol. 1, No 2, (2008) (Institute of Spiritual Formation, Biola University), 129

[6] Alister E. McGrath, *Christian Spirituality*, (Oxford, Blackwell Publ., 1999), 9

congregation, and nourished by weekly celebrations of the Supper instituted by Jesus'.[7]

McGrath summarises three traditions within Christianity:[8] (i) Catholicism, which is a complex movement, but tends to stress a 'strongly corporate conception of the Christian life and of the authority within the church'; it is strongly liturgical in its forms of worship reflecting the concept of *lex orandi, lex credendi*; Catholicism is also strongly sacramental, the benefits of Christ's death and resurrection are communicated to the church through the sacraments; Catholic spirituality also emphasises the role of the saints and of the Virgin Mary, though insisting that such *veneration* does not equate to the *worship* that is due to God alone; the use of the Rosary allows prayerful contemplation of key gospel stories, and incorporates the recitation of the Creed, the Lord's Prayer, and the invocation of Mary and the saints; (ii) Greek and Russian Orthodoxy hold a strong sense of the value of church tradition (*paradosis*) as 'a resource for the present'; it also holds a distinctive understanding of salvation as *theosis* (deification) whereby Christ's sacrifice in becoming human allows humans to participate in the divine nature; Icons (pictures of Jesus, Mary, or other saints) are understood as 'windows of perception' through which the believer 'may catch a glimpse of the divine reality'; Orthodoxy places great value on the importance of stillness (*hesychasm*), and the repetitive use of the 'Jesus Prayer' allows the believer to enter a tranquil state where they can reflect and meditate; (iii) the Protestant churches, originating in the European Reformation of the sixteenth century also seek to stress their historical and theological continuity with the early church; the Protestant tradition is reflected in the development of a number of different denominations which have particular theological emphases; the tradition places emphasis on the public and private reading of Scripture, and often values personal 'quiet time' set aside during the day for Bible reading and prayer; a number of the Reformation churches are known as 'broad churches' and permit allegiance to varying approaches, such as Anglo-Catholicism and evangelicalism.

Certain disciplines developed through church history as aids to living an authentic Christian life in the particular circumstances, and many of these remain as part of the armoury of Christian spirituality, adapted over time. Richard Foster proposes that 'God has given us the Disciplines of the spiritual life as a means of receiving his grace. The Disciplines allow us to place ourselves before God so that he can transform us'.[9] Due to the reliance on the transforming power of the Spirit, practice of the spiritual disciplines cannot be equated with use of willpower alone. Foster, again, warns that 'by themselves

---

[7] Holt, *A Brief History of Christian Spirituality*, 39

[8] McGrath, *Christian Spirituality*, 14-19

[9] Richard Foster, *Celebration of Discipline*, (London: Hodder & Stoughton, 1978, 1980), 6

the Spiritual Disciplines can do nothing; they can only get us to the place where something can be done. They are God's means of grace'.[10]

Of interest are two specific practices – asceticism and monasticism – which reflect the desire to live in ways pleasing to God.

The Apostle Paul compares the Christian life to a race, and the responsibility of believers as similar to those of committed athletes: 'Do you not know that in a race all the runners run, but only one gets the prize? Run in such a way as to get the prize. Everyone who competes in the games goes into strict training. They do it to get a crown that will not last; but we do it to get a crown that will last forever'.[11] The Christian life can be seen as the exercise of virtue and the avoidance of vice; thus the practice of *asceticism* grew, whereby believers were required to conduct their lives – with the Holy Spirit's help – to avoid the lure of sin and to engage in beneficial activities from a pure conscience. Three early Christian writers who agreed on the importance of ascetic disciplines for the Christian life were Origen (Alexandria), Tertullian (Carthage), and Ephrem (Asia). While certain aspects of the practice of asceticism can be helpful, a potential danger is the living of a morally upright life in one's own strength, something which can equally be achieved in a non-Christian context, and which may be perceived as an attempt to merit God's favour or to continue to punish ourselves for something that God has already forgiven.

Asceticism was taken a step further when certain believers began to withdraw from society in order to focus on the practice of spiritual discipline. While this initially centred on individual hermits in the desert, it is best portrayed in the rise of communal monasticism. Early monastics were the Cappadocian Fathers,[12] Evagrius of Pontus, and John Cassian. The latter adopted teaching of Evagrius from Egypt and established a monastery in Marseilles. His writings, specifically, the *Institutes* and *Conferences*;[13] Benedict incorporated Cassian's thought into his monastic Rule, and recommended that his monks read Cassian's works. Since the Rule of St Benedict is still used by Benedictine, Cistercian, and Trappist monastics, the thought of John Cassian, and the desert tradition behind him, still guides the spiritual lives of thousands of men and women in the Catholic Church. Holt notes that 'the rhythm of prayers seven times each day interspersed with physical labour, eating and sleeping in moderation, became the norm for Western monks up to the present day'.[14] Benedict also prescribed *lectio divina* whereby monks committed to read the Scriptures and early Christian writers for four hours a day.

One of the forms of earlier Christian spirituality seeing renewed interest today is represented by Celtic spirituality. The Celtic tradition appears

[10] Foster, *Celebration of Discipline*, 6
[11] 1 Cor. 9:24-25
[12] Basil of Caesarea, Gregory of Nyssa, Gregory of Nazianzus
[13] In these books he not only transmitted his Egyptian experience but he also gave Christian monasticism a profound evangelical and theological basis
[14] Holt, *A Brief History of Christian Spirituality*, 57

to have been influenced by the Coptic monks; a particular feature of Celtic spirituality became the concept of *anamchara* ('soul friend') where a close companion was found for the Christian journey with a view to counsel, confession, and support. Furthermore, the Celtic tradition embraced a self-imposed exile of leaving one's own immediate circumstances and surroundings as part of the journey of faith, hence the widespread influence of many Irish monks spreading Christianity throughout Europe where they travelled.

In understanding mysticism in the Christian tradition, it is important to appreciate the link between *being* and *doing*. While mystics are often represented as living in a perpetual state of spiritual ecstasy,[15] we should remember that an important element of developing one's personal relationship with God is that God can be shared with others through our lives (whether through prayer or activity). One definition of a mystic is 'a person who is deeply aware of the powerful presence of the divine Spirit; someone who seeks, above all, knowledge and love of God and who experiences to an extraordinary degree the profoundly personal encounter with the energy of divine life'.[16] Holt presses this further when he suggests that mystics 'tend to see the whole world as charged with divine glory, and sometimes actively change the world by their vision of justice and love'.[17] Mystics must not be disconnected from the world, and can express themselves in '... two ways largely determined by personality and context: outwardly in the world through specific roles or tasks; or, more inwardly in an inner searching often finding expression in a change of lifestyle, writing, and/or the arts. Usually both are present; it is a matter of emphasis'.[18] The spiritual disciplines, therefore, are routes to Christlikeness, participation in his character and mission.

Richard Foster categorises a number of disciplines as follows:[19]
- Inward disciplines
  - Meditation
  - Prayer
  - Fasting
  - Study
- Outward disciplines
  - Simplicity
  - Solitude
  - Submission
  - Service
- Corporate disciplines
  - Confession

---

[15] Often referred to as 'being so heavenly-minded as to be no earthly use...'
[16] Ursula King, *Christian Mystics, Their Lives and Legacies Throughout the Ages* (Mahwah, New Jersey: Hidden Spring, 2001), 3
[17] Holt, *A Brief History of Christian Spirituality*, 64
[18] James Hurley, "Mysticism - Some Notes for Reflection," in *Mysticism, Psychoanalytic Thinking and Spiritual Direction*: The Wellspring Centre, 2008)
[19] Foster, *Celebration of Discipline*

o Worship
o Guidance
o Celebration

Space does not permit a detailed explication of each, but further information on these disciplines can be found
in the appropriate literature. The use of such exercises emphasises the concept of *journey*, further to the traditional evangelical stress on the moment of conversion. Luther's approach, for example, called for a 'spirituality of the cross' as well as a 'theology of the cross'. Such a spirituality is particularly conscious of the need to follow Christ through suffering and pain, but stops short of embracing healing, transformation and resurrection. The later Reformer, Calvin, held to a mystical union of the believer with Christ through baptism, and subsequent lifelong growth in that union. For him 'this mystical union is given to all Christians by faith, not as the end of a long road with progressive stages of growth. Thus every Christian is a "mystic", living in union with Christ'.[20] The metaphor of life as a journey is a rich one, later also adopted by the Puritans who understood that Christianity demanded the commitment of the whole of personal and social life. John Bunyan's *Pilgrim's Progress* echoes the mysticism of Teresa of Avila[21] and John of the Cross[22] as it outlines the confusion and drought that can often be part of the spiritual path. Alister McGrath includes the concept of journey as one of a number of biblical images which influence approaches within spirituality; he also lists the feast, exile, struggle, purification, the desert, the concept of ascent, darkness and light, and silence.[23]

The Evangelical tradition

David Gillett proposes that 'evangelicalism represents one of the important spiritualities, or more accurately, *groups* of spiritualities, within the Church'[24] while it has also been asserted that, traditionally, evangelicals 'are suspicious of scholastic and mystical spirituality and fear that the Carmel we are bidden to ascend may be the Sinai of bondage, and all our asceticism dead works'.[25] There remains a creative tension between the liberty of the Spirit and our access to God, and the utilisation of processes or systems (disciplines) that may assist in personal and corporate spiritual development.

---

[20] Holt, *A Brief History of Christian Spirituality*, 94
[21] *Interior Castle*
[22] *The Dark Night of the Soul*
[23] McGrath, *Christian Spirituality*, 88-109
[24] David Gillett, *Trust and Obey: Explorations in Evangelical Spirituality*, (London: Darton, Longman & Todd, 1993), 3
[25] 'Spirituality' in Gordon Wakefield (ed), *A Dictionary of Christian Spirituality*, (London: SCM Press, 1983), 362

Evangelicalism, as a general movement, is usually defined following Bebbington's four characteristics: conversionism, activism, biblicism, and crucicentrism[26] and Shaw Clifton confirms that 'these four pillars characterize and sustain Salvationist evangelicalism as we enter the twenty-first century'.[27] Activism, in particular, pervades The Salvation Army, so careful consideration must be given to intentional development of its spiritual life. In order to keep pouring out (the water of life), the vessel must continually be refilled.

Since the centrality of personal encounter with Christ is seen as more important than commitment to particular ecclesial structures, 'evangelical spirituality is difficult to locate because it is continually evolving'.[28] While no spiritual experience is self-authenticating and must be subject to Scriptural testing, evangelicalism has (since the 1960's) been enriched by the pervasive charismatic renewal, and challenged in respect of a cross-fertilisation from different streams of Christianity, the excess of cerebralism and legalism in its spirituality, and the relationships between the intellectual and emotional, the ordinary and the miraculous, Word and Spirit. Indeed, 'in remoulding many aspects of evangelical spirituality, charismatic renewal has been one of the most obvious factors in encouraging evangelicalism to broaden its sympathies and develop a fuller appreciation of the spiritual emphases of other traditions within the Church'.[29] Ian Randall notes the different expressions of evangelical spirituality through time and concludes that 'those who look to the past for some kind of pristine model of evangelical spirituality are destined to be disappointed. Change has been a constant characteristic of the expressions of evangelical experience and this is set to continue'.[30]

Roger Green proposes that The Salvation Army 'in its history, theology, and practice, is inextricably linked with Protestant evangelicalism in general, and with the historic Wesleyan expression of evangelicalism specifically'.[31] He notes the importance of both appreciating the value of other traditions while also continuing to emphasise the Army's own distinctives as an important contribution to the mosaic of evangelical culture – 'the Army's contribution to the broader evangelical community will be valuable only if the

---

[26] David Bebbington, *Evangelicalism in Modern Britain*, (London: Unwin Hyman, 1989), pp. 5-17; to these, McGrath adds the lordship of the Holy Spirit and the importance of the Christian community Christian for spiritual nourishment, fellowship and growth – see Alister McGrath, *Evangelicalism & the Future of Christianity* (Downers Grove, IL: InterVarsity Press, 1995), 55–56

[27] Clifton, *Who Are These Salvationists?,* 45

[28] Gillett, *Trust and Obey*, 9

[29] Gillett, *Trust and Obey*, 11

[30] Ian Randall, *What a Friend we have in Jesus: The Evangelical Tradition*, (London: Darton, Longman & Todd, 2005), 186

[31] Roger J. Green, 'The Salvation Army and the Evangelical Tradition', Word & Deed, Vol. 5, No. 2 (May 2003), p. 53; see also *Salvation Story: Salvationist Handbook of Doctrine* (London: The Salvation Army International Headquarters, 1998), xiii–xiv

Army identifies itself clearly as an intentional community framed by the military metaphor and all that implies'.[32]

Ursula King astutely observes that 'much of the genius of Protestantism is expressed in hymns, creatively combining the art of music with religion in a way that powerfully underscores a deeply mystical Protestant piety and a great yearning for God's love and intimate presence. This is especially true of the two Wesleys',[33] and consequently also of The Salvation Army in its collections of hymns and songs, and its home-grown hymnody and musical repertoire.

While located within the wider spiritual traditions of the Church, McGrath observes that evangelicalism has become 'spiritually derivative', borrowing the spirituality of other traditions instead of paying attention to its own spiritual heritage, and suggests that 'evangelicalism is seen to lack a spirituality to give its theology staying power in the modern period.'[34] He cautions that in adopting the spiritualities of other traditions, we may also begin to be swept along by their theological distinctives and lose sight of our own. However, Gillett rightly proposes that a 'cross-fertilisation' between varied spiritualities can lead to the discovery of wealth in such traditions.[35]

D.A. Carson warns against the wholesale adoption of 'spiritual disciplines', suggesting that while some of these practices may be beneficial, the only certain way to achieve spiritual maturity is to be guided by the Holy Spirit and the Scriptures, and that the notion of utilising a 'discipline' connotes a measure of meritocracy. He suggests that 'the truly transformative element is not the discipline itself, but the worthiness of the task undertaken: the value of prayer, the value of reading God's Word'.[36] However, as weak and fallible humans, such concrete activities encapsulated within the range of spiritual disciplines perhaps help to keep us both motivated and moving along the right path. This is perhaps also why the use of such disciplines can often seem an optional specialism within the church, and account for the comparatively low levels of actualised sanctification among those called to be disciples. After all, the Greek word for 'disciple' connotes a learner or apprentice; we are called to be taught by the Spirit and guided by him into the fullness of Christ. Similarly, 'discipline' and 'disciple' share the same Latin root, so we can suggest that following discipline leads to the goal of discipleship – being transformed into the likeness of Jesus[37] - '...until Christ is formed in you'.[38] While we must

---

[32] Green, 'The Salvation Army and the Evangelical Tradition'

[33] King, *Christian Mystics,* 175

[34] McGrath, A E 'Evangelical Spirituality: Past Glories, Present Hopes, Future Possibilities', St Antholin's Lectureship Charity Lecture, 11-12
http://latimertrust.org/jdownloads/Publication%20Downloads/PDF%20books/sal1993m cgrath.pdf (accessed 30 April 2015)

[35] Gillett, *Trust and Obey,* 182

[36] D.A. Carson, 'Spiritual Disciplines', *Themelios*, Vol. 36, Issue 3, (November 2011), http://thegospelcoalition.org/themelios/article/spiritual_disciplines (accessed 31 March 2014)

[37] cf 2 Cor. 3:18

remember that we cannot *earn* grace, we still need to *receive* grace, and that from every means which God's Spirit will offer to bring this to us. Our exercise of the disciplines cannot, of course, coerce God to reveal himself to us, but 'if we habitually neglect solitude and silence… we must not be surprised if eventually we make ourselves deaf to God's voice when it does come to us'. [39]

There has also been a recovery of the concept of *spiritual formation* beyond what may have traditionally been required in training for ordained ministry, to recognise that if Christ is to be formed in us, this necessitates an intentional movement along that trajectory, with the use of appropriate disciplines or practices, and the involvement of some level of mentoring, spiritual direction, or mutual accountability.

Influences on Salvationist spirituality

Glen Shepherd, noted that 'in a most positive sense, our identity is a tangle of threads – threads of theological emphasis, threads of identity, threads of mission priority, These threads reflect the richness of the church'.[40] He refers to the range of 'streams' within the Christian church, and concludes that 'I am struck by the number of traditions in which I see names which have exercised an influence on the Salvation Army. The mosaic of our identity is extremely rich. We have roots in every tradition'.[41] It has also been noted that 'these broader traditions and writers of the Church were known to our early Army leaders and in fact many were held up as examples of Christian faith and practice'.[42]

Margaret Wickings has carried out insightful research into Salvationist spirituality,[43] reflecting theologically on the issue and assessing perspectives of UK-based cadets (ministry trainees), training college staff, and Salvation Army national leadership. Prior to becoming a member of the faculty at William Booth Memorial College in London, she had served in a training capacity in Africa for over 14 years; on her return to the UK she observed that Salvationism had 'changed dramatically' and set out to research current attitudes to spirituality. Her research is welcome in helping to identify trends and perspectives in Salvationist practice.

---

[38] Gal. 4:19

[39] Chris J. H. Hingley, 'Evangelicals and Spirituality'. *Themelios*, 15.3 (April 1990), 86-91

[40] Glen Shepherd, 'Spiritual Identity', *The Officer*, May/June 2002, 13

[41] Shepherd, 'Spiritual Identity'

[42] 'Salvationists and the Spiritual Disciplines', https://www.sarmy.org.au/en/Ministry/Spiritual-Life-Development/Spiritual-Disciplines/ (accessed 26 September 2014)

[43] Margaret M. Wickings, 'Salvationist Spiritualities: An Examination of the Spirituality and Underlying Theology of The Salvation Army in the United Kingdom with Particular Reference to the William Booth Memorial Training College', MTh dissertation, Westminster College, Oxford, 1998

Heavily influenced by the Holiness and Revivalist movements, the Salvation Army identified 'the world' as an evil which must be conquered in Christ's name, both in personal and social contexts; only wholehearted submission and self-sacrifice would allow holiness of life to be achieved through the indwelling Holy Spirit. Thus, the Army developed a spirituality of personal consecration, abstention from worldly desires and affectations, and evangelistic mission. Wickings suggests that 'the keystone to original Salvationist spirituality was the experience of salvation itself, the relationship with God that it brought, and the holiness experience to which it led'.[44]

In Salvationist theology, 'holiness' was an integral part of 'salvation', though the multiplicity of terminology for this experience indicates its intensely personal nature; this demanded a further submission to Christ after initial repentance, and required continual submission and consecration of one's life to his service. For William Booth, holiness meant 'cleansing and victory', for Catherine Booth it connoted 'restoration', while for Samuel Logan Brengle it offered the opportunity for 'Christlikeness'. However, an assessment of holiness based on abstention from worldly concerns often led to a culture of legalism. Brengle's articulation of the doctrine offered a joyful experience that was accessible to all believers, and although the intervening years have seen a decline in the teaching of a traditional holiness doctrine, 'Brengle Institutes' (conferences), held internationally, have re-emerged to offer teaching in practical holiness to both officers and soldiers. Maintaining holiness required resistance of personal temptation in order to avoid 'backsliding' whereby one's salvation could be lost, although regained through further repentance. The inner struggle with temptation was reflected in outward spiritual warfare through evangelism and social action – 'evangelical mission is the inevitable result of the infilling of the Holy Spirit in holiness'.[45]

Early Salvationists also engendered an ethos of culturally-relevant worship, utilising the musical idiom of the masses, and meeting in establishments normally associated with entertainment, harnessing popular melodies and introducing spontaneity in worship with lively singing and brass bands. Personal testimony – a feature of earlier revivals – was maintained, the Booths noting its value in both private and corporate spiritual growth. The disuse of the sacraments highlighted the importance the consecrated life.

Wickings concludes that early Salvationist spirituality was 'heavily prescriptive' and that 'where salvation-holiness experience was lacking, or defective, salvationist spirituality could become an oppressive burden; when experience was alive and real, no aspect of the battle was too hard'.[46] From her research findings she raises issues for further exploration:

> Is there then one Salvationist spirituality, or many? Secondly, early Salvationism encouraged introspection; is that helping or hindering the

---

[44] Wickings, 'Salvationist Spiritualities', chapter 2
[45] Wickings, 'Salvationist Spiritualities', chapter 2
[46] Wickings, 'Salvationist Spiritualities', chapter 2

spiritual pilgrimages of Salvationists today? Thirdly, do Salvationists really comprehend the nature of worship, or does a lack of understanding dilute Salvationist spirituality? Fourthly, does the officer-training system enable cadets to explore and develop their spirituality freely, in preparation for ministry? [47]

Wesleyanism bequeathed the importance of conversion and holiness of life to the early Salvationists, who were also influenced by the call to public consecration found in the contemporary renewal and revivalist movement; these had an important impact on Salvation Army spirituality. Indeed, the revivalism of the Christian Mission was ecumenical in character and drew the engagement of 'Quakers, Anglicans, and member of many other denominations [who] joined the movement and left their mark upon its emerging spirituality'.[48] John Read identifies four characteristics of Salvationist spirituality: (i) they recognise the possibility of spirituality 'before and after conversion to Christ' in that the heart's hunger for spirituality 'is evidence of God's prevenient grace'; (ii) though not practising the traditional sacraments of the church, the Salvationist can know the immediacy of God's presence through the Holy Spirit; (iii) an integration of inner spiritual life and evangelistic outreach, 'the first is often characterised as an inward journey of self-discovery, the second as a self-forgetting venture toward a needy world';, (iv) an openness to the supernatural activity of the Holy Spirit, influenced by the charismatic renewal, but with Pentecostal experiences in the expectations and experience of the Founders.[49]

Openness in Salvation Army attitudes is evidenced, for example, by its commitment to the 24/7 Prayer movement, its adoption of spiritual formation in relation to officer training,[50] and its acknowledgement of a contemplative tradition within the Army: 'For while we (Salvationists) express ourselves primarily in the language of evangelicalism, we know ourselves to be called to deep, personal and loving relationships with God, expressed in compassionate ministry and in a growing, lived out, personal and social holiness. This is about interior transformation'.[51]

It has been proposed that three historical phases can be identified in Salvationist spirituality: (i) the early innovation and experimentation; (ii) achievement and implementation of methods discovered in the first phase within an expanding international movement; (iii) a time identified by some as change and confusion and by others as renewal and exploration, in an attempt

---

[47] Wickings, 'Salvationist Spiritualities', chapter 5
[48] John Read, 'Spirituality and Spiritual Formation', in John G. Merritt (Ed), *The A to Z of The Salvation Army*, (Lanham, MD: Scarecrow Press Inc., 2006), 555
[49] Read, 'Spirituality', 555-556
[50] Julie Slous, 'Spiritual Formation Mentoring Blueprint'. MA dissertation, Queen's College, Memorial University, St. John's, Newfoundland, Canada, 19; Christine Faragher, *Other Voices: Exploring the contemplative in Salvationist spirituality,* (Melbourne, Australia: Salvo Publishing, 2010, 162-163
[51] Faragher, *Other Voices*, 47-48

to 'rediscover and reinterpret... the vision and values of the movement's founders'.[52]

The reflections of the International Spiritual Life Commission

In commending the work of the International Spiritual Life Commission (ISLC) and its recommendations on the Army's spiritual life, prayer, and worship, General John Larsson reminded us that 'the Army is a spiritual movement, or it is nothing. The cleverest plans cannot make up for the absence of spiritual power'.[53]

Addressing the ISLC at its first meeting in July 1996, General Paul Rader insisted that 'it is time for us to take more seriously issues related to our inner life. We owe it to our people. It is essential to maintaining the engine of commitment and passion. Our mission is energised by our spirituality'.[54] The Commission was to examine 'cultivating and sustaining of the spiritual life' of Salvationists, and 'ensure that we are not denying our people necessary means of grace and that their participation in the life of the Army through their corps affords them every available advantage in living the Christian life.' The inclusion of the term 'means of grace' highlights that the Army continually looks beyond the traditional sacraments of the Church (which are not used in Army worship) to seek immediate encounter with God in all aspects of everyday life, a stance that informs its spirituality and interest in exploring wider streams of spirituality within the Christian tradition. Especially important in this spiritual quest is Scripture reading and prayer, which both require direct fellowship with the Holy Spirit to allow God's guidance and comfort to be known. In preparation for the 2015 *Boundless* International Congress[55] in London (celebrating the Army's 150th anniversary), a global Bible reading initiative was launched (*Boundless* – the Whole World Reading) to encourage personal and community interaction with the Scriptures. The Army has also instituted a regular Worldwide Prayer Meeting on Thursdays for corps centres and individuals, and its themes can be also followed by interaction on social media. In conjunction with the Congress, *Boundless* – the Whole World Praying sought to involve the international Army in prayer for this significant occasion and its outcomes.

Following its discussions, the Commission issued a series of 12 Calls to Salvationists[56] structured so as to invite the Army to revisit aspects of its devotional life and communal fellowship in order to ensure a strengthening of

---

[52] Read, 'Spirituality', 556-557
[53] John Larsson, 'More About Renewal', *The Officer*, January/February 2003, 3
[54] Robert Street, *Called to be God's People: The International Spiritual Life Commission: Its report, implications and challenges* (London: Salvation Books, 1999), x
[55] The *Boundless* theme echoes William Booth's song 'O Boundless Salvation', *The Song Book of the Salvation Army*, 298
[56] See Appendix E

the movement's inner life which would be evidenced in increased personal and corporate holiness (defined as growing in Christlikeness) and increased power in its outreach programmes and evangelistic mission.

The report suggested that

> Christ says 'Come to me' before he says 'Go into the world'. These two movements are in relation to each other, like breathing in and breathing out... [57]

This expresses well the inherent tension within evangelicalism, where it is tempting to emphasise personal faith at the expense of community life and engagement with the world, and *vice versa*. With the Spirit's guidance, and experience of existing spiritual traditions, a *via media* can be determined which integrates the two, recognising that without the love that develops from personal spiritual growth (holiness/sanctification), outward action can be like a 'clanging cymbal'.[58] Similarly, an intense personal devotional life which does not reach out with Christ's compassion and love is equally incomplete.

Karen Shakespeare summarises that within the ISLC's Calls 'personal spiritual experience, corporate spiritual disciplines, theological understanding and the historical self-understanding of the movement are interwoven to form a statement of belief, purpose and aspiration, which gives shape to Salvationist spiritual experience'.[59] Robert Street's book[60] highlights the calls, affirmations, statements, and thinking of the ISLC; the Commission recognises the difficulty of providing guidelines to suit all countries and cultures where the Army is at work, and 'the diversity of cultures, methods, and resources was seen as both a strength and a blessing'.[61]

While it is difficult to assess the global impact of response to the ISLC's Calls, each Territory now has a Secretary for Spiritual Life Development with a remit to address the Army's spirituality in local contexts. The Army's international website also hosts a Centre for Spiritual Life Development section,[62] which provides relevant material and resources for prayer, Bible reading, and engagement with spiritual development programmes.

The ISLC concludes that 'the vitality of our spiritual life as a movement will be seen and tested in our turning to the world in evangelism and service, but the springs of our spiritual life are to be found in our turning to God

---

[57] Robert Street, *Called to be God's People*, 7

[58] cf 1 Cor. 13:1

[59] Karen Shakespeare, 'Knowing, Being, and Doing: The Spiritual Life Development of Salvation Army Officers',
Doctorate in Practical Theology Thesis, Anglia Ruskin University, 2011,
http://angliaruskin.openrepository.com/arro/bitstream/10540/211700/1/ShakespeareK_Thesis_2011.pdf (accessed May 9, 2012), 52

[60] *Called to be God's People*

[61] Robert Street, 'International Spiritual Life Commission' in Merritt, *A to Z of The Salvation Army*, 298

[62] http://www.salvationarmyspirituallife.org/

in worship, in the disciplines of life in the Spirit, and in the study of God's word'.[63] A formula that reflects an evangelical, holiness tradition determined to engage with its Christian heritage while facilitating an integrated mission of worship and service to God with active compassionate outreach to the world.

---

[63] Street, *Called to be God's People,* 7

5. 'And the Holy Spirit fell on them...'[1]

Transitions in Salvation Army Holiness Theology: A Historical Assessment

R. David Rightmire

Introduction

From the time of its inception, the Salvation Army has maintained a commitment to the doctrine of holiness, by the inclusion of this theological emphasis in its official doctrinal statements through the years. What is also clear, however, is the fact that the Army's understanding of the doctrine and experience of holiness has gone through certain modifications over time. This chapter explores the development of Salvation Army holiness theology from its beginnings to the present, evaluating the shifts of pneumatological emphases evident in its official doctrinal statements and literature.

Early Salvation Army Holiness Theology

William and Catherine Booth

William Booth's understanding of holiness was based on the theology of John Wesley, as mediated by his mentor in the Methodist New Connexion, William Cooke in 1854. However, William and Catherine Booth were even more significantly influenced in their understanding and experience of entire sanctification by the American holiness movement through Walter and Phoebe Palmer's holiness revivals and earlier campaigns by James Caughey in England.[2] The latter not only influenced William Booth's decision to enter into the ministry and his use of revivalistic methods, but above all, Caughey's teaching of the Wesleyan doctrine of holiness made a lasting theological impact on William. Caughey's influence is further substantiated by the fact that, from an early date, the Army included selections from his works in their publications.[3] Likewise, the devotional works of Phoebe Palmer were

---

[1] Acts 10:44

[2] Andrew Eason and Roger Green (editors), *Boundless Salvation: The Shorter Writings of William Booth* (New York: Peter Lang, 2012), 72-80; R. David Rightmire, *Sacraments and the Salvation Army: Pneumatological Foundations* (Metuchen, NJ: Scarecrow Press, 1990), 134-35, 167-69; John Kent, *Holding the Fort: Studies in Victorian Revivalism* (London: Epworth Press, 1978), 325-28.

[3] E.g., James Caughey, 'Holiness: Your Remedy', *War Cry* [London] (March 6, 1880). For Caughey's influence on the Booths, see Roger Green, *The Life and Ministry of*

republished by the Army press, but often without any mention of her name, thus leading some Army historians to miss the vital interrelationship between this prominent American holiness revivalist and the Booths' fledgling movement.

Catherine and William Booth's hunger for holiness reached back to their youth.[4] Although the Booths did not claim the experience of holiness until 1861, they both earnestly sought for the 'blessing' through the 1850s. Catherine's assurance of heart cleansing was based on Phoebe Palmer's altar phraseology, as mediated to her through William Boardman's *The Higher Christian Life*.[5] Catherine's familiarity with the holiness teaching of John Wesley, John Fletcher, Charles Finney, Phoebe Palmer, William Boardman, Thomas Upham, and others, had an impact on her husband's holiness experience and theology.

From the beginning, the Salvation Army had a holiness theology, although such was shaped not only by William and Catherine Booth, but also by their son Bramwell, George Scott Railton, and later, Samuel Logan Brengle. Although holiness thought influenced their theology and experience earlier, the explication of holiness doctrine by these leaders did not appear until the 1870s. In the first Conference of the Christian Mission (1870), the doctrines of the Christian Revival Society were revised and to them was added an article on entire sanctification: 'We believe it is the privilege of all believers to be "wholly sanctified" and that 'their whole spirit and soul and body may be preserved blameless unto the coming of our Lord Jesus Christ' (1 Thessalonians 5:23)'.[6]

In 1876, the doctrine of entire sanctification was further defined by Railton and agreed upon by the Conference:

> We believe that after conversion there remain in the heart of the believer inclinations to evil or roots of bitterness, which unless overpowered by Divine Grace, produce actual sin, but that these evil tendencies can be entirely taken away by the Spirit of God, and the whole heart thus cleansed from everything contrary to the will of God, or entirely

---

William Booth, Founder of The Salvation Army (Nashville: Abingdon Press, 2005), note 36, 237-38. Cf. Richard Carwardine, *Transatlantic Revivalism: Popular Evangelicalism in Britain and America 1790-1865* (London: Greenwood Press, 1978), 102 ff.; Melvin E. Dieter, *The Holiness Revival of the Nineteenth Century* (Metuchen, NJ: Scarecrow Press, 1980), 60-61.

[4] W. T. Stead, *Life of Mrs. Booth: The Founder of the Salvation Army* (New York: Fleming H. Revell Co., 1900), 180; George Scott Railton, *The Authoritative Life of General William Booth, Founder of the Salvation Army* (New York: Reliance Trading Co., 1912), 9.

[5] See Catherine's letter to her parents, dated February 11, 1861, as quoted in Frederick St. George de Latour Booth-Tucker, *Catherine Booth*, 2 vols. (New York: Fleming Revell, 1892), Vol. 1, 263-64.

[6] Doctrine number ten, quoted in Robert Sandall, *The History of the Salvation Army*, Vol. 1: 1865-1878 (London: Thomas Nelson, 1947), 289.

sanctified, will then produce the fruits of the Spirit only. And we believe that persons thus entirely sanctified may by the power of God be kept unblamable and unreprovable before Him.[7]

At the January Conference of the Christian Mission in 1877, William Booth placed great emphasis on holiness doctrine, following on the heels of the visit of Asa Mahan to a conference sponsored by the Mission in December of 1876. In an address on 'Holiness' given by Booth at the 1877 conference, the doctrine of entire sanctification is not only presented as central and essential to the essence of the Salvation Army, but is also stated categorically and dogmatically, indicating the crystallization of doctrinal formulation:

> Holiness to the Lord is to us a fundamental truth; it stands in the front rank with our doctrines. We inscribe it upon our banners. It is with us in no shape or form an open debatable question as to whether God can sanctify *wholly*, or whether Jesus does save His people *from* their sins. In the estimation of the Salvation Army that is settled forever; and any officer who did not hold and proclaim the ability of Jesus Christ to save His people to the uttermost from sin and from sinning, I should consider out of place among us.[8]

With the institutionalization of the Salvation Army and its accompanying theological development in the late 1870s and early 1880s, holiness is not only more fully explicated, but also promulgated as the 'cardinal doctrine' of the movement, the 'secret of its conquering power'.[9] Thus, as the 1880s progressed, holiness doctrine was not only more explicitly affirmed, but also was viewed as the means of perpetuating the spiritual gains of the movement. For William Booth, holiness was not optional for Salvationists, but signified Christ indwelling human 'vessels', purifying and equipping them for greater usefulness. God commands holiness. The believer is required to consecrate him/herself to obeying this command, depending on the Holy Spirit to bring it about.[10]

In a holiness sermon preached by General Booth in May of 1880, God's grace is said to be sufficient to purify the heart entirely. Faith is the instrument, the Holy Spirit the agent in entire sanctification. The object of faith in this purification is the blood of Christ. Booth describes this cleansing as a

---

[7] Sandall, *History of the Salvation Army*, Vol. 1, 263-64.

[8] William Booth, 'Holiness: An Address at the Conference', *Christian Mission Magazine* 9 (August 1877): 193-98.

[9] Catherine Mumford Booth, *Aggressive Christianity* (Boston: McDonald and Gill, 1883), 11

[10] William Booth, 'A Higher Up Religion', Series in *War Cry* (March 13, May 29, June 26, July 31, 1880), Reprinted in *Holiness Readings: A Selection of Papers on the Doctrine, Experience, and Practice of Holiness* (Atlanta: Salvation Army, n.d.), 16, 21-25, 27-28, 35-37.

grace event claimed by faith. 'You have not to struggle to purify and save yourself, but to bring yourself to God and trust Him to do it'. The faith that purifies requires three 'unalterable conditions' to be met: first, the renunciation of sin; second, consecration to God; and third, trust in the sufficiency and efficacy of God's grace. Subsequent years would evidence similar emphases by William Booth on heart purity and holy living, grounded in the atonement of Christ, and 'sustained by direct union with him'.[11]

For Catherine Booth, holiness was the experience of a 'perfect heart', a heart renewed and kept right by the Holy Spirit. As 'the central idea, end, and purpose of the gospel of Jesus Christ', purity of heart is restored and maintained by the power of the Holy Spirit. If a 'real, practical transformation...accomplished *in us* is not possible, then the gospel is useless, for "the whole end purpose of redemption is this – that He will restore us to purity [and] keep you purged to serve the Living God'.[12] Thus, salvation is more than forgiveness of sins, but involves the purification of the heart of those within whom Christ dwells, enabling love for God and neighbor, evidenced in lives of sacrificial service.[13]

Catherine speaks of entire sanctification as being 'filled with the Holy Spirit', or being baptized by the Holy Spirit. This is not an optional 'higher life', but the 'privilege of all believers', to be experienced once the prerequisites of faith, renunciation of sin, and consecration to God, are met.[14] She presses the analogy between Pentecost and the transforming power of the Holy Spirit at work in the Salvation Army, emphasizing continuity with the faithfulness of God in the promised baptism of the Holy Spirit.[15] Catherine maintained that the 'blessing of a clean heart' involves an 'all-embracing confidence in God', and a daily 'renouncing of my right to choose in anything apart from Him'. This radical dependence on God in sanctification results in direct communion with him.[16]

George Scott Railton and Bramwell Booth

The influence of George Scott Railton on Army holiness doctrine has already been indicated in his definition of sanctification accepted at the 1876

---

[11] William Booth, *Purity of Heart* (London: Salvation Army, 1902), 40-55, 88-96, 108-118; William Booth, *The Seven Spirits: Or, What I Teach My Officers* (London: Salvation Army, 1907), 14, 30.

[12] Catherine Booth, *Papers on Godliness* (London: Salvation Army, 1890), 94-99, 148, 149-50, 166.

[13] Catherine Booth, 'A Mock Salvation and a Real Deliverance from Sin', Lecture 2 in *Practical Christianity* (London: Salvation Army, 1907), 29-53.

[14] Catherine Booth, *Aggressive Christianity*, p. 135; Catherine Booth, *War Cry* (Feb. 24, 1881), in *Holiness Readings*, 109-12.

[15] Catherine Booth, *Aggressive Christianity*, 168-69.

[16] Catherine Mumford Booth, *Messages to the Messengers* (London: Salvation Army, 1921), 110-11.

Conference of the Christian Mission. An even earlier witness to his holiness teaching is found in the February 1873 issue of the *Christian Mission Magazine*, in an article entitled 'Can Anybody Live the Holy Life?' In this defense of the possibility of experiencing entire sanctification, Railton points to the moral perfection of God as the basis of holiness, the blood of Christ as the means by which such cleansing is made possible, and the presence of Christ as the source of holy living.[17] Railton's *Heathen England* (1879) points to the priority of teaching converts how to be holy as a practical means of ensuring the vitality and purity of salvation warfare.[18] In an article for the *War Cry* (August 28, 1880), he further defined holiness as a necessary separation unto God and a partial realization of the eschatological hope.[19]

Bramwell Booth, more than any other individual in early Army leadership, helped to institutionalize holiness theology within the movement. Although his parents espoused holiness doctrine since their ministry in Gateshead, and although Railton exercised a tremendous influence on William and Catherine Booth as an exponent of Wesleyan perfectionism, it was Bramwell who became the 'teacher of holiness'. He began a regular series of mid-week holiness meetings that served as prototypes for the Sunday morning holiness meetings in the 1880s. For many officers, the Army's "now clearly-defined doctrine of holiness was to a great extent new ground." The experience of entire sanctification was no longer optional, and officers needed both to enter into it and teach others about it. Bramwell played a chief role in overcoming opposition within the movement to an institutionalized understanding of holiness. Meetings to promote holiness teaching were organized and sporadically led by Bramwell from 1876 onward. He began a weekly holiness meeting in Whitechapel Hall in 1879 in which he declared that 'salvation through Jesus Christ included salvation from all sin for all time.'[20] By 1882, morning worship services officially became known as 'holiness meetings'.[21]

In the *War Cry* of July 24, 1880, Bramwell characterized entire sanctification as 'deliverance from all outward and indwelling sin, from unbelief, from the very *roots* – pride, anger, love of the world....the filling of the heart with all the graces and fruits of the Spirit. The being perfected in love'.[22] In the same article, Bramwell states the promise of sanctification is dependent on the faith response of the believer to the command "be ye holy":

---

[17] George Scott Railton, quoted in *The Privilege of All Believers*, edited by John Waldron (Toronto: Salvation Army, 1981), 121, 125.
[18] George Scott Railton, *Heathen England*, 3rd ed. (London: S. W. Partridge and Co., 1879), 145-46.
[19] Railton, in *Holiness Readings*, 45; cf. 41-42, 44.
[20] Catherine Bramwell Booth, *Bramwell Booth* (London: Rich and Cowan, 1933), 141, 144.
[21] The practice, begun at Coventry in September, 1882, spread rapidly and became official policy for all corps soon thereafter. This had definite theological implications for the Army's sacramental self-understanding and practice. Rightmire, *Sacraments and the Salvation Army*, 187-97.
[22] Bramwell Booth, in *Holiness Readings*, 73-74.

'Believe that He is able and willing to do this; that He is able and willing to do it now, not tomorrow; that if you have faith He will now do it'.[23]

Bramwell preferred the phrase 'full salvation' as the most appropriate designation for the experience of holiness. This term expressed for him not only the soteriological significance of holiness, but also the eschatological union of the soul with God. Deliverance from the power of and the disposition to sin made possible such divine communion. Full salvation for Bramwell included elements of soul cleansing, transformation of the preferences of the soul, and divine power, enabling the believer to walk in purity and submissiveness to God. The conditions for such sanctification were a 'full surrender to the will of God' and a 'full consecration to His service'. Bramwell insisted that the doctrine and experience of full salvation were absolutely essential to the ongoing work of the Salvation Army. The neglect of holiness teaching, he believed, would render the Army's ministry ineffective.[24]

Brengle's Theological Influence

The development of Salvation Army holiness doctrine was dramatically influenced by Samuel Logan Brengle.[25] As a convert of the late nineteenth century American holiness revival, he became the major exponent of holiness theology in the Salvation Army. Although developed and espoused as central to the 'discipline, devotion, and dynamic' of the Salvation Army from the beginning,[26] holiness doctrine was even further explicated by Brengle in the 1890s and early decades of the twentieth century. More than any other individual, Brengle provided a theological foundation for Salvation Army holiness thought. Joining the Booths' movement in 1887, this American Methodist advocate of Christian perfection helped further the influence of the American holiness movement on the Army. Brengle's ministry served to perpetuate the holiness emphases of the early Army leaders.

Brengle's books sought to promote holiness teaching and further institutionalise perfectionist theology within the Salvation Army. His *Helps to Holiness* (1896), *Heart-Talks On Holiness* (1897), *The Way of Holiness* (1902), *The Soul Winner's Secret* (1903), *When the Holy Ghost Is Come* (1909), *Love Slaves* (1923), *Resurrection Life and Power* (1925), *Ancient Prophets: With a Series of Occasional Papers on Modern Problems* (1929), and *The Guest of the*

---

[23] Bramwell Booth, in *Holiness Readings*, 79-80. Cf. Bramwell's own sanctification experience as witnessed to in the September 11, 1880 issue of the *War Cry*.
[24] Bramwell Booth, 'Full Salvation', in *Privilege of All Believers*, 85-86, 90-91; Bramwell Booth, 'Consecration', *War Cry* (December 29, 1881) in *Holiness Readings*, 147.
[25] For the most recent biographical and theological treatment of this holiness 'prophet', see: R. David Rightmire, *Sanctified Sanity: The Life and Teaching of Samuel Logan Brengle* (Alexandria, VA: Crest Publications, 2003).
[26] Paul A. Rader, 'Holiness, Revival, and Mission in the Nineteenth Century', in *Heritage of Holiness* (New York: Salvation Army, 1977), 85.

Soul (1934), had a far reaching effect within the Army, as did his numerous articles and addresses.[27] His reasoned defense of holiness theology ('sanctified sanity') reflects the rational, analytical religious mood of the late Victorian era.

Brengle's holiness theology must be understood in the light of his personal experience of entire sanctification. Throughout his life, he constantly referred back to January 9, 1885, not only as his 'day of days' but also as his entry into a dynamic life of spiritual blessing, characterized by purity, power, and above all, love. Of this experience he wrote: 'One wondrous morning He sanctified my soul. He purified my affections; He cleansed my heart; He bent my will into loving harmony with His will. He captured and held my whole being until I adored and wondered and worshiped, and wept for love and joy. Glory to God!'[28]

One of Brengle's favorite phrases to describe the experience of entire sanctification was 'full salvation' – salvation in all its fullness.[29] The purpose of Christ's death on the cross was to reconcile sinners to God and to make them holy. The work of Christ, thus, provides the basis for Brengle's understanding of entire sanctification. He maintained that holiness is an essential part of Christ's soteriological work.

> One of the Army's central doctrines and most valued and precious experiences is that of heart holiness. The bridge which the Army throws across the impassible gulf that separates the sinner from the Savior – who pardons that He may purify, who saves that He may sanctify – rests on these two abutments – the forgiveness of sins through simple, penitent, obedient faith in a crucified Redeemer, and the purifying of the heart and empowering of the soul through the anointing of the Holy Spirit, given by its risen and ascended Lord, and received not by works, but by faith. Remove either of these abutments and the bridge falls.... [30]

Thus, the critical experience of holiness, involving the death of the 'old man' and the impartation of the fullness of the Holy Spirit, is made possible solely through the work of Jesus Christ in his life, death, and resurrection.[31]

Union with Christ is by the baptism of the Holy Spirit, equipping the believer for effective service. In fact, mission requires this experience for power and purity. Christ, as Savior and Sanctifier, pardons that he might purify

---

[27] For a comprehensive bibliography of Brengle's writings see: Rightmire, *Sanctified Sanity*, 205-206, 210-24.

[28] Samuel Logan Brengle, 'After Twenty-Nine Years: A Personal Testimony', *Officer* 21:11 (November 1913), 545-46. For a more in-depth treatment of Brengle's holiness experience see: Rightmire, *Sanctified Sanity*, 9-10, 85-88.

[29] John Larsson, *Spiritual Breakthrough: The Holy Spirit and Ourselves* (London: Salvation Army, 1983), 87.

[30] Samuel Logan Brengle, *Love Slaves* (Atlanta: Salvation Army, 1960), 68-69.

[31] Samuel Logan Brengle, *Heart Talks On Holiness* (New York: Salvation Army, 1897), 1-2, 19-21.

and empower for service.[32] The Army's motto, 'saved to serve,', finds expression in Brengle's holiness doctrine. A clean heart is required not only for personal growth, but also for a zeal for souls and perfected love for others.[33] 'Holiness, for you and for me, is not maturity, but purity: a clean heart in which the Holy Spirit dwells, filling it with pure, tender and constant love to God and man'.[34] This emphasis on purity is evident in Brengle's definition of holiness as 'nothing more nor less than perfect love, for God and man, in a clean heart'.[35]

Heart purity is a result of Christ's divine nature imparted to humanity.[36] 'Holiness is the state of our moral and spiritual nature which makes us like Jesus in His moral and spiritual nature'.[37] Brengle insists on the necessity of intimate knowledge of and union with the person of Jesus Christ in sanctification. Intimate fellowship with Christ is thus the basis for Brengle's understanding of holiness.[38] The relational nature of holiness, however, must not only take in a person's relationship with God, but also with other persons. This is especially true within the Body of Christ. 'The religion of Jesus is social. It is inclusive, not exclusive. We have the glory only as we are united'.[39] The basis for this unity is the indwelling presence of Christ's Spirit.

When describing the work of God in entire sanctification, Brengle preferred the use of ethical terms, emphasizing heart purity, relational transformation, and Christlikeness.[40] What God desires most for his children is perfect love. In *Helps To Holiness*, he defines holiness as 'pure love'. The baptism of the Holy Spirit is a 'baptism of love'. As 'perfect deliverance from sin', holiness is a state free from intentional sin, free from doubt or fear, 'in which God is loved and trusted with a perfect heart'. Christian perfection is not absolute, angelic, or Adamic perfection; rather, it is relative to a person's natural limitations as a fallen creature. The 'second work of grace' is available to all believers in this life. It is the uprooting of the sin nature and the instantaneous implanting of the divine nature, not to be equated with growth in

---

[32] Brengle, *Heart Talks On Holiness*, 37-44.
[33] Samuel Logan Brengle, *The Way of Holiness* (New York: Salvation Army, 1911), 77-82.
[34] John Waldron (ed.), *Wait On the Lord: Selections from the Writings of Commissioner Samuel L. Brengle*, revised edition (New York: Salvation Army, 1960), 24.
[35] Brengle, *Way of Holiness*, 15.
[36] Samuel Logan Brengle, *Resurrection Life and Power* (London: Salvation Army, 1925), 184.
[37] Brengle, *Heart Talks On Holiness*, 17.
[38] Samuel Logan Brengle, 'A Man in Christ: The Sons of God Unveiled', *Officer* 25:2 (February 1917), 124; Samuel Logan Brengle, *Helps to Holiness* [1896] (Atlanta: Salvation Army, 1984), 99; Brengle, *Heart Talks On Holiness*, 96-101; Samuel Logan Brengle, *Guest of the Soul* [1934] (Atlanta: Salvation Army, 1992), 53, 76.
[39] Samuel Logan Brengle, *At the Center of the Circle: Selections From the Published and Unpublished Writings of S. L. Brengle*, edited by John Waldron (Kansas City: Beacon Hill Press, 1976), 38, 42.
[40] For further exploration of this emphasis, see chapter 8: 'Ethical Dimensions of Holiness', in Rightmire, *Sanctified Sanity*, 99-108.

grace. Although growth is essential in order to maintain the 'blessing', the once-and-for-all nature of entire sanctification is emphasized.[41]

Holiness, as the work of God, is dependent on his sovereign grace. Thus, it is received by faith, not works. 'He [God] will do it today – now – this moment, if you will but believe'.[42] When Brengle urges his readers to appropriate the second blessing 'now', he is stressing the need to expect it at a definite point in time, and to desire it in the present.[43] Those who trust God 'for present cleansing from all sin' must 'keep steadily looking to Him for...the filling of their hearts with the fire of perfect love'.[44] Although entire 'sanctification is an instantaneous act',[45] it requires a process of 'diligently seeking'[46] and waiting on God. The wait does not have to be long, but the seeker must nonetheless wait on God by faith.[47] The period of 'patient waiting' can be 'shortened by mutual consent'.[48] Consecration and faith are the conditions that need to be met and 'maintained against all contrary feelings' for God to 'suddenly come into His holy temple, filling the soul with His presence and power'.[49]

One crucial point of investigation in discussing Brengle's influence on Salvation Army holiness theology in relation to the nineteenth-century holiness movement is at the point of sanctifying faith. In contrast to John Wesley's emphasis on the witness of the Holy Spirit testifying with our spirits to provide assurance of entire sanctification, early Salvation Army holiness theology (as mediated to the Booths by Caughey and Palmer) opted for a 'naked faith' approach.[50] Once one has fulfilled the conditions of entire sanctification (consecration and faith), holiness can be claimed as complete.

In the Army's early years, people were encouraged to ask for the assurance, but the 'blessing' was accepted by naked faith prior to any assurance.[51] Representative of such a position was J. A. Wood, whose book, *Perfect Love*, influenced early Salvation Army holiness thought. He believed

---

[41] Brengle, *Helps To Holiness*, 2, 5 ff., 103-104.

[42] Samuel Logan Brengle, 'A Perfect-Hearted People', *Officer* 44:3 (March 1927), 190.

[43] Brengle, *Helps To Holiness*, 112-13.

[44] Samuel Logan Brengle, 'How to Get People Sanctified Wholly', *Officer* 6:8 (August 1898), 238.

[45] Samuel Logan Brengle, *Fifty Years Before and After: 1885–January Ninth–1935* [pamphlet] (N.p.: National Association For the Promotion of Holiness, n.d.), 18.

[46] Samuel Logan Brengle, 'Officers Who Burn and Shine!' *Officer* 38:2 (February 1924), 139.

[47] Brengle, *Helps To Holiness*, 113; Samuel Logan Brengle, *When the Holy Ghost Is Come* (Atlanta: Salvation Army, 1982), 16-17; cf. Brengle, *Resurrection Life and Power*, 6-8.

[48] Samuel Logan Brengle, 'Is the Baptism With the Holy Ghost a Third Blessing?' *Officer* 49:4 (October 1929), 273.

[49] Brengle, *Heart Talks On Holiness*, 94.

[50] Cf. James Caughey, *Earnest Christianity Illustrated* (Boston: J. Magee, 1855), 198-99, 202; John Kent, *Holding the Fort*, 323.

[51] See 'Subject Notes', *Officer* 1:3 (March 1893), 88.

that in order for faith to be 'pure', it must be 'naked' (i.e., faith prior to the witness of the Spirit).[52] William Booth concurred: 'Remember, the most naked faith is the most efficacious'.[53] This emphasis is reflected not only in Booth's teaching, but also in other early Army literature, much of which is heavily dependent on the holiness theology of Phoebe Palmer.[54]

The tension between the immediacy of expectation and the waiting upon God for the assurance of sanctification, as found in Wesley's holiness theology, however, is not dealt with in early Salvation Army theology. Before the advent of Brengle, the immediacy of the experience of entire sanctification, appropriated by simple faith, was the predominant teaching within the movement.[55] Although Brengle would concur with the receiving of the second blessing by faith alone, he viewed the witness of the Spirit as essential for one to know that the blessing had been given. His writings, especially *Helps to Holiness* and *Heart Talks on Holiness*, both written prior to the turn of the century, are more in line with Wesley, in that they emphasize the need to wait on the Lord for his witness and assurance. Thus, it was Brengle's role to direct the Salvation Army away from the emphases of Phoebe Palmer and the misuse of her 'altar theology' in popular piety to a more orthodox Wesleyan expression. The corrective that Brengle's theology presented served to moderate earlier American holiness emphases within the movement, and to center Salvation Army holiness theology in the tradition of Wesley, maintaining a balanced tension between active faith and patient waiting in the experience of entire sanctification.[56]

This is all the more important in light of the fact that Brengle became the Army's *de facto* holiness theologian. Implicit support for this claim can be found not only in the official approval of his books and articles, which became the Army's definitive statement on sanctification, but also in his thirty-five year appointment as 'Spiritual Special', promotion to the rank of Commissioner, and his receiving the Order of the Founder for a lifetime of holiness evangelism. Explicit evidence for this claim is based on the incorporation of Brengle's

---

[52] J .A. Wood, *Perfect Love; Or Plain Things For Those Who Need Them*, 36th edition (London: Salvation Army, 1902), 64, 75.

[53] William Booth, 'Letter from William Booth to the the the Brethren and Sisters Laboring for Jesus in Connection with the Dunedin Hall Mission, Edinburgh', *The East London Evangelist*, 1 (April 1, 1869), 105.

[54] See 'Sanctification', *The Christian Mission Magazine*, 8 (February 1876), 35-36; cf. Phoebe Palmer, *Entire Devotion to God* (London: Salvation Army, n.d.), which was used as a primer for the teaching of entire sanctification within the Army.

[55] See Wood, *Perfect Love*, 62; Palmer, *Entire Devotion*, 38, 153, 176-77; W. Bramwell Booth, 'The Sheffield Council of War', *The Salvationist*, 11 (April 1879), 89; W. Bramwell Booth, "What Must I Do?" *War Cry* 31 (July 24, 1880), n.p. Cf. John Rhemick, 'The Theology of a Movement: The Salvation Army In Its Formative Years' (Ph.D. dissertation, Northwestern University, 1984), 82-87.

[56] For further treatment of Brengle's theological influence, see: R. David Rightmire, 'Samuel Brengle and the Development of Salvation Army Pneumatology', *Word and Deed* 1:1 (Fall 1998): 29-48; Rightmire, *Sanctified Sanity*, 150-56.

interpretation of holiness into the 1925 *Orders and Regulations for Officers of the Salvation Army*. His articulation of entire sanctification thus served as the basis for Salvation Army holiness self-understanding for several decades. Although other official explications of the doctrine of entire sanctification emerged in the first half of the twentieth-century, doctrinal continuity with Brengle's theology was maintained throughout.[57] In fact, Brengle's understanding of holiness held sway within the Army until the 1969 *Handbook of Doctrine*, when a revised interpretation of sanctification was officially set forth by General Frederick Coutts.

Further Modifications to the Army's Official Position

During the 1960s, the foundations of Salvation Army holiness doctrine underwent further modification. The chief protagonist in this development was Frederick Coutts, whose *Call to Holiness* (1957) sought to re-articulate the doctrine of entire sanctification. According to his son, John Coutts, Brengle's holiness theology was antiquated and in need of re-balancing in the light of other emphases: 'Among Salvationists of the 1950s, to...whom the idea of a "second blessing" was...outdated, some new interpretation was called for'.[58] In seeking to answer the question of whether the experience of holiness is gained instantly or gradually, Frederick Coutts maintained that the life of holiness involves both a crisis and a process: 'In the initial act of surrender I receive of the fulness of the Spirit according to my capacity to receive. But that capacity grows with receiving'.[59] Such a dynamic view of holiness actually differs little from Brengle's own teaching, although the caricature of Brengle's position as 'all crisis and no process' has been perpetuated by those who use him as a foil for a more processive understanding of sanctification.[60]

In fact, Coutts borrowed Brengle's definition of holiness as 'Christ in you', and developed the progressive implications of the resulting communion between God and man. He explicated his doctrine of holiness in terms of Christlikeness, expounding such in the Pauline categories of love, joy, peace,

---

[57] Cf. T. H. Howard, *Standards of Life and Service* (London: Salvation Army Book Department, 1909), 8-14, 28-29, 40-48, 71-72, 98, 100, 102, 104, 113-22, 123, 126, 152, 154; Frederick St. George de Latour Booth-Tucker, ed., *The Successful Soul-Winner: A Summary of Finney's Revival Lectures* (London: Salvationist Publishing and Supplies, 1926), 22-23, 26, 35,63, 68, 85, 110; *Orders and Regulations For Officers of the Salvation Army* (London: International Headquarters, 1936), 8-9, 10-11; and, *The Salvation Army Handbook of Doctrine* (London: Salvation Army, 1927), 103-106, 124-26, 128-38, 145-47.
[58] John Coutts, *The Salvationists* (London: Salvation Army, 1977), 58-59.
[59] Frederick L. Coutts, *The Call to Holiness* (London: Salvation Army, 1957), 36.
[60] For more on this almost exclusive emphasis on process by the 'Coutts camp', see: Glen O'Brien, 'Why Brengle? Why Coutts? Why Not?' *Word and Deed* (November 2010), 11.

longsuffering, goodness, truthfulness, meekness, and temperance.[61] One significant point of contrast, however, is that although both Brengle and Coutts emphasize the holiness experience, Coutts, instead of talking of the elimination of the sin nature, preferred to speak of the redirection of the will towards the good. What needs sanctifying is the will. Holiness involves the 'redirection and control' of 'normal human appetites' by the Holy Spirit, as Christ is formed within.[62] The experience of holiness is the possession of the 'same Holy Spirit who was in Jesus'.[63] What is emphasized is the ongoing relationship that such communion entails, not the crisis experience. According to some, Coutts' expression of 'a more nuanced balance between crisis and process in the life of holiness has blunted the blade of the "second blessing" understanding of sanctification in The Salvation Army', resulting in a reconfiguration of holiness teaching 'that has made the crisis dimension either foreign to or unnecessary for many Salvationists' understanding of the maturing Christian life'.[64]

Although Frederick Coutts' interpretation emphasizes both crisis and process,[65] the crisis is seen as only a 'gateway experience to growth in holiness'. John Larsson comments that 'whether the interpretation of the crisis as simply the gateway to the mountain trail of holiness fully accounts for the kind of experience Samuel Brengle knew on 9 January 1885 needs consideration'. Larsson views the increased emphasis on process as signaling a major shift in Salvation Army holiness theology, as illustrated in more recent editions of the Army's official *Handbook of Doctrine*. 'Until 1969 the editions devoted about 7,000 words to the crisis experience and only about 200 words to the process. But in the handbook published in 1969, a different pattern emerges. The chapter heading changes from "Entire Sanctification" to simply "Sanctification," and the proportion of words dealing with the crisis and process is reversed'.[66]

The shift in emphasis is particularly evident in the transition between the 1927 and 1969 editions of the *Salvation Army Handbook of Doctrine*. In the 1927 edition, regeneration is portrayed as partial sanctification, to be completed in entire sanctification. Regeneration is deliverance from outward sin, while

---

[61] Strong Christological emphases are to be found in the holiness teaching of both Brengle and Coutts, despite claims to the contrary by those who would characterize the teaching of the former as 'pneumatological holiness' and that of the latter as 'Christological holiness'. See: Philip Cairns, 'Personal Perspectives of the Holiness Experience', *Word and Deed* 13:2 (May 2011), 53, 57.

[62] Frederick Coutts, *Call to Holiness*, 103, 109.

[63] Frederick L. Coutts, *Essentials in Christian Experience* (London: Salvation Army, 1969), 13-14.

[64] Brian Tuck, 'Wesleyan/Wesleyan Holiness Movement', in John Merritt (editor), *Historical Dictionary of the Salvation Army* (Lanham, MD: Scarecrow Press, 2006), 632.

[65] Whether or not one views Coutts as maintaining a balanced emphasis on both crisis and process, it is clear that those who followed in his footsteps emphasized process almost exclusively.

[66] Larsson, *Spiritual Breakthrough*, 57-58.

entire sanctification usually occurs subsequent to regeneration, and brings deliverance from both inward and outward sin. The unregenerate are referred to as 'under sin', the regenerate are 'over sin', and the entirely sanctified are 'without sin'. As the 'dwelling-place of God himself', the entirely sanctified have divine communion.[67]

In contrast to this presentation of 'Entire Sanctification', the 1969 edition of the *Salvation Army Handbook of Doctrine* sees 'Sanctification' as including regeneration, adoption, and sanctification. All three involve the work of the Holy Spirit, 'who makes men the children of God both in name and in likeness of His holy nature'. Absent is any terminological distinction between 'partial' and 'entire' sanctification. In setting forth the tenth doctrine ('Sanctification'), the writers emphasize 'God's provision for sanctification' in the atonement of Christ. More emphasis is placed on the process following the crisis of holiness. The result of this growth in grace is increasing and 'continual fellowship with the risen Saviour'. The call to holiness necessarily involves a call to communion with Christ.[68]

Similar shifts in emphasis are evident in other writings through the 1970s. Instead of emphasizing the experience of holiness in entire sanctification, greater stress is placed on the relationship of the believer to Jesus as Lord. Frederick Coutts, in an article on 'Mission and Method' (1975), describes holiness as a relational growth process and a means of fully appropriating God's grace.[69] In the 1977 orders and regulations for soldiers, holiness is defined as 'Christ in you', emphasizing a living relationship.[70]

In a 1982 abridgment of Army doctrine, instantaneous aspects of holiness are seen primarily in relation to 'the response God requires', namely, our consecration. Although there is mention of the gift of the Holy Spirit as a 'life-changing power', characterized by the 'grace of love', the divine work of heart purification is muted.[71] Continued reflection on holiness concerns in the early 1980s led Army writers to de-emphasize the ontological change wrought in the believer by the Holy Spirit in the experience of entire sanctification, and to stress the importance of growth in grace. One Army leader wrote: 'Heart holiness is...simply a matter of human will consciously and deliberately accepting the control of the Holy Spirit'.[72] Although Spirit baptism is still

---

[67] *Salvation Army Handbook of Doctrine* (1927), 103-106, 124-26, 128-29.

[68] *The Salvation Army Handbook of Doctrine* (London: The Salvation Army, 1969), 128-30, 151-54, 159-62.

[69] *Another Harvest of Years: An Anthology of Salvation Army Year Book Articles, 1957-1975* (London: Salvationist Publishing and Supplies, 1975), 21. Other works on holiness in the 1970s include: Edward Read, *Studies in Sanctification* (1975), and Clarence Wiseman, *Living the Holy Life* (1978).

[70] *Chosen To Be a Soldier: Orders and Regulations For Soldiers of the Salvation Army* (London: Salvation Army, 1977), 28-29.

[71] *The Doctrine We Adorn: An Abridged Study of Salvation Army Doctrines* (London: Salvation Army, 1982), 98-103.

[72] Hubert Scotney, 'Heart Holiness', *Officer* 31 (June 1980): 262-66.

stressed as the only baptism that confers grace,[73] it serves as the basis for a continual and increasing knowledge of Christ, as the Holy Spirit 'interpret[s] Jesus to us in contemporary terms...bringing Him into our time'.[74]

Another important source for assessing the Army's theological self-understanding is found in its official song book, since the movement's doctrinal commitments find expression in its worship. When examining the 1953 and 1987 editions of *The Song Book of The Salvation Army*, one notices that a shift in emphasis takes place in the time period between these two editions. In the earlier edition, there are many more songs that emphasize entire sanctification as an instantaneous experience of divine grace. In the later edition, not only is there a 15% drop in the total number of songs devoted to holiness (174 in 1953 as compared to 148 in 1987), but of the 47 songs dropped from the 'Life of Holiness' section, 23 were by Charles or John Wesley (hymns, many of which emphasize both critical and progressive dimensions of entire sanctification).[75]

Further expressions of the Army's holiness theology surfaced in the 1990s. Shaw Clifton presents the experience of sanctification as a learning process whereby Christians become 'saints' in reality, and not only in status. Growth in grace is seen as a narrowing the gap between imputed and imparted righteousness.[76] Emphasis on holy living, in terms of its 'personal, relational, social and political' dimensions is the focus of the report from the International Spiritual Life Commission (1996-1998), with allowance for a 'diversity of experience and expression' regarding the holy life.[77]

An official restatement of Salvation Army theology appeared in 1998. *Salvation Story: Salvationist Handbook of Doctrine* presents holiness as progressive growth in grace in the larger 'faith journey' of salvation. As with Brengle and Coutts, *Salvation Story* defines holiness as 'Christlikeness' and characterises such as the 'realization of the Christ-life within' by the power of the Holy Spirit. Although recognizing the 'life-changing' dimensions of sanctification, such changes are made synergistically, as the Christian is 'empowered to make radical changes of direction', leading to 'spiritual breakthrough and new levels of relationship with...God, with others, and with

---

[73] Milton S. Agnew, 'The Wesleyan Doctrine of the Holy Spirit', *Officer* 34 (December 1983): 542-46.
[74] William Burrows, 'Spirit of Truth and Grace: The Holy Spirit as Contemporary', *Officer* 32 (April 1981): 177-78. For works on holiness from the late 1980s see: Arthur Pitcher, *Holiness in the Traffic* (London: Salvation Army, 1987); Chick Yuill, *We Need Saints: A Fresh Look at Christian Holiness* (London: Salvation Army, 1988).
[75] *The Song Book of The Salvation Army* (New York: Salvation Army, 1953); *The Song Book of The Salvation Army* (New York: Salvation Army, 1987). It should also be noted, that although there were 19 'Holiness' songs added in 1987 edition, the majority of these appear in the 'Consecration and Service' or 'Praise and Thanksgiving' sections.
[76] Shaw Clifton, *Never the Same Again* (Alexandria, VA: Crest Books, 1997), 114.
[77] 'The Report of the International Spiritual Life Commission', Unpublished report (London: Salvation Army, 1998), Appendix 4. Cf. Robert Street, *Called to Be God's People: The International Spiritual Life Commission, Its Report, Implications and Challenges*, Revised Edition (London: Salvation Army, 2008), 79-86.

ourselves'. So, although recognizing the importance of experiencing critical moments in the continuum of sanctification, the emphasis is on 'life-long process', sustained by the believer's 'obedience of separation from sin and consecration to the purposes of God', rather than on the sovereign work of God.[78]

The 2010 edition of *The Salvation Army Handbook of Doctrine* follows the same trajectory of treating the experience of holiness in terms of 'a journey which should be characterized by growth and development'. Under the chapter title of 'Full Salvation: The Doctrine of Holiness', sanctification is described as 'mature Christian living... Christlikeness....the realization of the Christ-life within'. Holiness, as 'a life-long process', is discussed with regard to its covenantal, ethical, therapeutic, and missional implications. Although allowing for the experience of a 'moment of grace that leads to spiritual breakthrough', such experiences are characterized as the exception rather than the rule. In fact, 'such life-changing moments...are not always a feature of our growth in holiness'. As further evidence of the downplaying of the critical dimension of entire sanctification, the handbook's historical sketch of the development of holiness doctrine within the movement dramatically understates the importance of the Army's commitment to an instantaneous work of grace in entire sanctification (a position that was staunchly maintained for nearly one hundred years within the movement).[79]

The 2010 *Handbook of Doctrine* also mentions the need for the Army to continue exploring the individual and communal implications of holiness in the twenty-first century. In line with an increased emphasis on the social and relational dimensions of the Christian life, the writers find in the doctrine of the Trinity (understood as a 'community in relationship'), a fruitful model for focusing on the communal nature of holiness. Philip Needham's concept of a 'singular and plural' holiness can be seen as an example of this increased emphasis on the corporate nature of sanctification.[80] Similar emphases on social and relational dimensions of holiness can be found in a Robert Street's 2011 article, 'Personal Holiness: Holiness For a New Generation'. Allowance for variety in personal experience of holiness is encouraged, but such must find expression in relation to other believers.[81]

[78] *Salvation Story: Salvationist Handbook of Doctrine* (London: Salvation Army, 1998), 86, 88-90.
[79] *The Salvation Army Handbook of Doctrine* (London: Salvation Books, 2010), 191-94, 196-98.
[80] Philip Needham, 'Integrating Holiness and Community: The Task of an Evolving Salvation Army', *Word and Deed* 3:1 (November 2000), 11.
[81] Robert Street, 'Personal Holiness: Holiness For a New Generation', *Officer* (May-June, 2011), 11, 12. Cf. Robert Street, *Holiness Unwrapped: To Be Like Jesus* (London: Salvation Army, 2005).

Conclusion: Shifts in Salvation Army Holiness Theology

As has been indicated in the above historical sketch, Salvation Army holiness self-understanding has undergone some modifications over the years. Although its commitment to the doctrine of holiness has been maintained throughout its history, the balance of emphasis on the crisis and process of entire sanctification has been displaced by a view of holiness as progressive growth in grace.[82]

Such theological transitions in the understanding of holiness are not unique to the Salvation Army. In fact, shifts in emphasis are to be found throughout the Wesleyan-holiness movement. What has been a gradual development over the last several decades has resulted in a 'theological identity crisis that many holiness scholars and Salvationist writers are seeking to resolve in a way that is consistent with Scripture and connected with the historical roots from which they grew'.[83] It is hoped that by making clear the transitions in Salvation Army holiness theology over time, this study will lead to further reflection on the importance of this doctrine to the movement's identity and mission.

---

[82] For the theological implications of such pneumatological shifts in relation to the Army's sacramental self-understanding, see: Rightmire, *Sacraments and the Salvation Army*, 257-72.
[83] Tuck, 'Wesleyan/Wesleyan Holiness Movement', *Historical Dictionary*, 633.

6: 'To be Wholly Sanctified'[1]

Wesleyan Holiness as Prerequisite for Salvation Army Mission

Paul A. Rader

The Salvation Army is a real army in a real war that cannot afford to engage the enemy of our souls with anything less than the fullness of the blessing of the Gospel of peace. To the Army, the Wesleyan understanding of full salvation is not an arcane sectarian dogma, but a strategic necessity and condition for victory in the Great Salvation War. The doctrine of Sanctification is a vital element in the wider conviction affirming a positive, open-ended, victory-oriented theology of possibility and power.

The Wesleyan Imperative

Wesley's delineation of Prevenient Grace offered a salvation available to all, opening wide the door to the Wesleyan *ordo salutis*: conviction, repentance, saving faith, regeneration, consecration, sanctification and glorification. The goal of redemption is transformation into likeness to Christ expressed in disciplined and godly lives of Christ-like virtue, purity, compassionate action, commitment to mission, submission and integrity. In a word, holiness. Sanctification is that heart-cleansing, empowering and engracing work of the Spirit, through the merits of the shed blood of the Savior and the power of his risen life that makes such a transformation possible.

Salvationists believe that Scripture teaches all can be saved through and through and for all-time (Hebrews 7:25). We believe it is possible to live above the power of sin as we are transformed into Christ-likeness from one degree of glory to another. Our founders, William and Catherine Booth required a salvation from sin and sinning for the sin-enslaved, addicted and depraved among whom they were called to pursue their mission. With a mandate to 'Go for souls and go for the worst!' they required a Gospel of Hope. Their Gospel was one of 'Apostolic Optimism' proffering a life of victory and faithfulness. It included a call to arms for every redeemed person, enlisting them in the conflict that they believed would end in final victory and the millennial reign of Christ.

---

[1] See Appendix B, Doctrine 10

Verdict Theology

There were a number of influences that contributed to the positive nature of the Gospel they embraced. William and Catherine Booth came out of a Wesleyan heritage, finally settling into ministry within the Methodist New Connexion until their call to launch out on their own. William Booth was a convinced Wesleyan, as was his more theologically astute companion in arms, the redoubtable Catherine Booth. Their commitment to Wesleyanism was forged in the fires of the mid-century awakening in which they established themselves as effective evangelists. They preached for results. The adoption of the Mercy Seat was an expression of the conviction that God can and would meet saving faith with soul-transforming power and do it now. Under the influence of the American Revivalist and erstwhile trial lawyer, Charles G. Finney, they adopted a 'verdict theology' that drove their hearers toward decision.

Finney may not have been the first or only evangelist to introduce the 'Anxious Seat,' the Penitent Form, or Mercy Seat, but it was entirely consistent with his style of evangelism. Finney's *Lectures on Revivals of Religion* were 'gospel' for William and Catherine, and commended by them to the early Army. The Mercy Seat eventually became a central focus for all Salvation Army worship. Major Nigel Bovey has traced the evolution of its usage in the contemporary Army toward a more diverse range of applications.[2] Still, it remains the focus for the call to saving and sanctifying surrender and faith that anticipates an instantaneous work of grace. Indeed, the founders were adamant that preaching should move to that end. In Salvation Army worship 'all roads lead to the Mercy Seat.' Some see it as a 'place of prayer.' Certainly, the Mercy Seat has become a place of intercession, communion, renewal, rededication, and more. But essential to maintaining the uniqueness of the Army's mission is the centrality of the Mercy Seat, not only as furniture (and sad is the day when it no longer has a visible presence in a Salvation Army Hall!), as a metaphor, or program item, but as a focal point of saving and sanctifying grace.

Holiness Then or Now

The Booths proclaimed a 'transactional Gospel.' Army meetings have long been reprised in terms of 'results.' Logs are kept of seekers after salvation and sanctification. Seekers were helped to 'pray through' at the Mercy Seat, to the assurance that the work was done as faith laid hold on the promises of God and the Holy Spirit did his saving and sanctifying work. As the Army has come more and more to terms with its ecclesial identity a pastoral drift is identifiable toward a gradualism that supersedes the call to a transactional and experiential emphasis to which a positive witness can be borne. The Army's 'Apostle of Holiness', Commissioner Samuel Logan Brengle and his presentation of the Holiness message have often been contrasted with the extensive Holiness

---

[2] Nigel Bovey, *The Mercy Seat* (London: The Salvation Army, UK Territory 1996)

teaching of General Frederick Coutts.[3] Brengle has been identified with a theology of crisis, more consistent, it must be acknowledged with the preaching of the early Salvationists and reflecting the influence of the American Holiness Movement. General Coutts has been identified with a view of sanctification that emphasized a more gradual growth toward Christ-likeness. Setting the one against the other in absolute terms is clearly a mistake. Brengle taught the need for a gradual maturity toward Christ-likeness with the crisis of sanctification as the door to such growth in holiness. And Coutts accepted the need for decisive surrender of the self in the pursuit of godliness. Major Geoff Webb observes: "The 'neo-Coutttsian' tendency was something that was probably not part of Coutts' agenda at all – the effective collapsing of crisis into process at the point of conversion."[4] General John Larsson summarizes the relationship between these differing perspectives in this way: "Whether the interpretation of the crisis as simply the gateway to the mountain trail of holiness [as Coutts seems to maintain] fully accounts for the kind of experience that Samuel Brengle knew on 9 January 1885 needs consideration. Moving the state of being perfect before God into the future as an ideal always beckoning us on, is a positive step. But on the other hand we must also guard against the error of minimizing the epochal nature and transforming power of a crisis experience such as Brengle experienced." [5]

Would it be fair to suggest that Brengle was more the evangelist than the pastor, inclined by vocation and gifting to expect immediate results? And that Coutts was more the pastor than the evangelist, inclined by experience and reflection to deal with the struggles of the faithful in quest of a holy heart and life? In fact Brengle had only a few short years in corps work. The bulk of his ministry was as a traveling evangelist or Spiritual Special. Doubtless, General Coutts was faithful to his covenant to seek the salvation of the lost with evangelistic purpose. And Commissioner Brengle would not have been cheered by a charge of being indifferent to the pastoral realities with which seekers after holiness might struggle. Indeed his books, beginning with *Helps to Holiness*, are concerned with the practical implications of holy living in the aftermath of a crisis of sanctification. Still, one suspects that insofar as the teaching of the one can be set against the other, the particular gifts and ministries of these two advocates of the holy life may account for the emphases for which they have become known. The Army has learned from and benefited immeasurably from the approaches of both Brengle and Coutts.

Having said that, as Major John Merritt has shown, there has been a widespread abandonment of a crisis theology of sanctification in much of the contemporary Army in favor of a gradualism that is not far afield from a

---

[3] See articles by David Rightmire and Wayne Pritchett in the initial issue of *Word & Deed*, Fall 1998.
[4] Geoff Webb with Kalie Webb, *Authentic 'fair dinkum' Holiness for Ordinary Christians* (The Salvation Army Australian Southern Territory, 2007), 210
[5] John Larsson, *Spiritual Breakthrough: The Holy Spirit and Ourselves* (London: The Salvation Army International Headquarters, 1983), 58

Reformed understanding of the pursuit of godliness.[6] Fairly or unfairly, he finds this drift reflected in *Salvation Story,* the Salvationist Handbook of Doctrine published in 1998, despite what he deems a rather too oblique reference to crisis. Larsson observes that "until 1969 the editions [of the Handbook] devoted about 7,000 words to the crisis experience and only about 200 to the process. But in the handbook published in 1969 a different pattern emerges. The chapter heading changes from *Entire Sanctification* to simply *Sanctification,* and the proportion of words dealing with the crisis and the process are reversed."[7]

For the Booths and the early Salvationists, the biblical call to holiness (1 Peter 1:15-16) lay at the heart of the Gospel. Their aggressiveness in mission derived from a conviction regarding the provision of the Cross and the power of the Spirit to break the power of canceled sin and set the captive free. They were convinced the invitation to freedom in Christ made possible living godly in Christ Jesus in this present age (Titus 2:12). Nothing less would do. Catherine declares: "[The Deceiver] has got the Church, nearly as a whole, to receive what I call an 'Oh, wretched man that I am' religion! He has got them to lower the standard which Jesus Christ himself established in this Book -- a standard, not only to be aimed at, but to be attained unto -- a standard of victory over sin, the world, the flesh, and the Devil, real, living, reigning, triumphing Christianity!"[8] She called for a salvation full and freeing realized in the experience of saving and sanctifying power available to every earnest believer. The notion of living above sin and the inevitability of sinning was as counter-intuitive then as it is now. But William Booth was not inclined to accept the backsliding experience of others as a standard for his people. "Now I affirm on the authority of the Bible that Jesus Christ your Saviour is able and willing to keep you from doing wrong. His name was called Jesus, that is, Saviour, because He should 'save his people from their sins.' You may make mistakes; you may have temptations; you may have perplexity in your mind and anguish in your heart . . . and yet, in spite of all this and all else of the same kind, you can be kept from sin. In the name of my dear Lord, I assert that it is possible for you to have and to keep a pure heart."[9]

The Wesleyan message fit the founders' commitment to a salvation that saves from sin and sinning, aggressive evangelism and a concern for the plight of the poor and exploited masses. It extended to their broader concerns for human welfare. In their view, God was not accepting the sufferings of the poor and oppressed and neither would they. There was a 'sanctified pragmatism' at work here. In the openness and breadth of their vision, physical as well as spiritual redemption were embraced in an integrated Gospel of

---

[6] John G. Merritt, 'Emerging Patterns: A "Literary History" of the Doctrine of Holiness in The Salvation Army' (unpublished paper), 38
[7] Larsson, *Spiritual Breakthrough,* 57
[8] Catherine Booth, *Aggressive Christianity* (London: International Headquarters, 1891) 6
[9] Cyril Barnes (ed.), *The Founder Speaks* (London: Salvationist Publishing and Supplies, Ltd., 1960), 27-28

wholeness and *shalom*. It was a Gospel calculated to gain the results that were wanted in the battle for souls. It offered hope of a steadfast and durable faith. It was a message of hope to those hopelessly enslaved by their own heart's bondage and the soul-destroying circumstances of poverty, powerlessness and exploitation in which they were ensnared.

Holiness is not only a possibility for all in Salvationist understanding, it is the purpose of God, the provision of Christ and the standard of Scripture for every believer. "We believe that it is the privilege of all believers to be wholly sanctified and that their whole spirit and soul and body may be preserved blameless unto the coming of our Lord Jesus Christ." Earlier iterations of the 10th Doctrine were more explicit regarding the nature and extent of the sanctifying work of the Spirit in regard to heart cleansing and a decisive dealing with the nature of inbred sin. The explication, ostensibly attributable to the influence of George Scott Railton, was later reduced to a footnote and then removed with the 1969 edition of the Handbook of Doctrine. John Merritt observes: "The ultimate removal of the footnote on the basis of the obvious interpretive misuse and creedal misappropriation of Hebrews 12:15 reflects, in my judgment, what I consider to be a gradually weakening emphasis on the Wesleyan understanding of entire sanctification as a radical crisis of cleansing from indwelling sin subsequent to regeneration."[10] Whatever one's understanding of the nature and extent of the heart cleansing work of the Spirit in the crisis of sanctification, the Army remains firmly committed to the possibility and priority of holiness to be experienced and lived as essential to its mission.

The Way into the Blessing

Holiness was not intended to create a spiritual elite or special class of Christian whose standards remained 'counsels of perfection' for ordinary believers, ever beyond the reach of all but super saints. In speaking of sanctification as a 'privilege' it was never intended to suggest that the pursuit of godliness was optional for Christ followers in general or Salvation soldiers in particular. Nor can it be presumed that progress toward a crisis of sanctifying grace and the growth in Christ-likeness that makes it possible is pain-free or inevitable. Although in the event Catherine Booth herself claimed the blessing of a clean heart at her husband's urging on the basis of what came to be known as the 'altar theology' propounded by Phoebe Palmer. That is, the faith that the altar sanctifies the gift and that if all is on the altar then the heart is made clean. It was not without a long period of struggle that she made bold to claim the blessing by 'clean faith.' Yet, there was for Catherine a definite moment of entering into the assurance of sanctification. It was not what some have called "the Longer Way" of sanctification experienced only after a long journey of dying to self. Her experience is perhaps best characterized as the 'Middle Way'

---

[10] Merritt, "Emerging Patterns," 18

of earnest seeking until one receives the gift of faith to claim the blessing.[11] It may, indeed, be an arduous way of anguish over the blackness of one's heart in the light of Christ's purity, renouncing one's idols and dying to self. It is the way of the Cross which affords no 'Calvary by-pass.' There may be a seeking, knocking and asking until the door is opened. The Booths called for a patient and persistent waiting on God until the work is done. Significantly, William and Catherine appeared to move toward advocating the 'Shorter Way' in their later preaching in the quest for definite results, emphasizing the instantaneous experience of heart cleansing. True, they acknowledged that for most the path to a heart-cleansing crisis of sanctifying grace was steeper and more beset by obstacles than this would suggest. But the ideal was there: the possibility and the privilege for all who meet the conditions. Ultimately, entering in is a matter of faith's hand reaching out to claim the promised Gift.

> God's great, free, full salvation
> Is offered here and now;
> Complete blood-bought redemption
> Can be obtained by you.
> Reach out faith's hand, now claiming,
> The cleansing flood will flow.
> Look up just now, believing.
> His fullness you will know.
>
> To the uttermost he saves.
> To the uttermost he saves.
> Dare you now believe
> And his love receive
> To the uttermost he saves.

(Commissioner John Lawley)[12]

In all of this the Spirit of Holiness is seen as the active agent: convicting, illuminating, strengthening faith, cleansing, empowering, freeing and flooding the heart with boundless love poured out (Romans 5:5).

---

[11] Chris Bounds has helpfully explained these classic approaches to experiencing sanctifying grace in his paper presented to a Doctrinal Symposium sponsored by the Wesleyan Church in 2005 entitled 'Spiritual Transformation: What is the range of current teaching on Sanctification and what ought a Wesleyan to believe on this doctrine?'

[12] *Song Book of The Salvation Army* (London: The Salvation Army, 1986) 413:2. (Hereafter, SASB.)

'Fighting Holiness' – A Strategy of Grace

Oswald Chambers writes of 'Missionary Munitions', in referring to what it takes to survive and thrive in the line of fire as we pursue our mission in a world that is no friend to grace. We live out our particular calling as Salvationists in a world yet in the grip of the Evil One – it is a world in which we are silently and subversively drawn toward a comfortable mediocrity devoid of a passion for holiness that neutralizes the believer as a fighting unit. Satan is an active agent set against all those who presume to live godly in Christ Jesus. Yet Scripture assures us that "His divine power has given us everything we need for life and godliness through the knowledge of him who calls us by his own glory and goodness." Through the promises given us we may "participate in the divine nature and escape the corruption in the world caused by evil desires" (2 Peter 1:3-4). The Army ethos calls for just such a life beyond though never apart from conversion, regeneration and the assurance of salvation. It demands a Cross-bearing, sin-denying, devil-driving, total dedication to the fight of faith and the tough and costly business of opposing evil, while snatching brands from the burning and advancing the cause of our Blood and Fire banner. The early day Holiness teacher, and regular preacher at Thursday night Holiness Meetings in the London of the Founder's day, called for a "Fighting Holiness." Not a "hot-house emotionalism or glass-case sanctity, but a vigorous, daring, aggressive religion on the lines of the Saviour's words, 'The Kingdom of Heaven suffereth violence, and the violent take it by force.'"[13]

True Salvationism calls for a purity of desire, a disciplined devotion, and a resilient and durable faith under fire. It requires a humble submission to those over one in the Lord and a joyful, confident experience of grace that issues in a winsome life in the beauty of holiness. Nothing less will do. This is the standard toward which every Salvationist is called to aspire. And it is possible. The successes of the Army throughout its history may be traced to the soldiers and officers who epitomized these qualities of holiness lived out amid the cut and thrust of our engagement in mission. As such, it is a strategic necessity.

Only a holy heart can sustain an acceptance of discipline and submission to authority that the Army requires, particularly in this generation. Holiness produces a unique capacity for self-sacrifice and sustainability in soldierly obedience. Only a costly, molten love poured through the channels of a holy heart suffices. "The fierce heat of pure love, created and maintained by the Holy Spirit, makes the Salvationist watch and pray, toil and talk and suffer, careless of what it costs him in doing so, if he can only gain the blessed object on which his heart is set . . . . If you are resolved to spend your life in blessing

---

[13] T.H. Howard, *Standards of Life and Service* (London: The Salvation Army Book Department, 1909), 123.

and saving men and fighting for your Lord, you must have a pure heart."[14] In reflecting on the great success of her ministry in pioneering the Army's work in France, Catherine, the eldest daughter of William and Catherine Booth, who to the end of her long life was known in France as The Maréchale, declared: "If I am asked what was the secret of our power in France, I answer: First, love; second, love, third, love. And if you ask how to get it, I answer: First, by sacrifice; second, by sacrifice; third, by sacrifice. Christ loves us passionately, and loves to be loved passionately. He gives Himself to those who love Him passionately. And the world has yet to see what can be done on these lines."[15] If John Wesley preferred to view Holiness as Perfect Love, then it is just such love, pure and passionate, that powered the early advances of the Army, not only in France, but around the world. Such suffering, self-sacrificing love is not incidental to missional effectiveness. It was, and is, the essential dynamic for mission.

The autocratic system of governance that took hold of the early Army under the dominant leadership of the Founder was not incidental. Perhaps it was inevitable, given the personality of the man himself and the urgent demands of the rapidly advancing movement under his direction. His legal counsel suggested that he wanted to be made a pope. Booth did not deny it. He was convinced that centering authority in himself (under God) was the most strategically efficient structure for an active Army. The exigencies of the war demanded it. The first generation of warriors acceded to it gladly. But it wasn't long after the General 'laid down his sword' in 1912, that there began to be pushback -- beginning even earlier with the promotion to Glory of Catherine who seemed to be the glue that held the family together by the very strength of her personality. Indeed, she had a presentiment that her own children might not stay the course under the autocratic control of their father. She was right. There were early and distressing cracks in the dyke of unquestioning devotion.

At this point, Commissioner Railton, a central figure in the leadership team at the beginning, who found himself side-lined because of his resistance to the direction he perceived the Army to be taking away from a primary and consuming commitment to evangelism, opined that without a sanctifying experience Salvationists would not over time accept the discipline. The very system of governance demanded holy hearts, not only on the part of the governed, but evidenced in the life and leadership of the movement. A holiness that set aside one's own will and ambitions and was prepared to joyfully accept the will of the Army as the will of God was required. Without it, the Army system simply would not work, in Railton's view.[16] Defections were inevitable. To a great extent, he was right. And we are now understanding more than ever that this standard of holy love and Christ-like humility must extend to the

[14] Barnes, *The Founder Speaks Again*, 23-24.
[15] James Strachan, *The Maréchale* (Minneapolis, MN: Bethany Fellowship, Inc., 1966) 46-47
[16] G.S. Railton, *The Authoritative Life of General William Booth* (New York, NY: The Reliance Trading Company, 1912), 70-71

structures and functioning of the institution and the confidence of the led in the character of those who lead.

Covenantal Commitment

The renaming of the Articles of War, signed by every new soldier at their swearing in under the flag, as The Soldier's Covenant, was wholly appropriate. The relationship of every soldier to the movement is covenantal in nature. It assumes a calling to be a Salvationist and an unconditional acceptance of the ethical demands which are set out in some detail, as well as a missional commitment to the cause. By their very nature, covenants imply an enduring commitment. They are intended to be lifelong. Commissioner T.H. Howard, referencing Jeremiah 50:5 writes of the Salvationist's "perpetual covenant." The earlier versions of the Articles of War ended with the words: "till I die!" No doubt the leaders who moderated the expectation of faithfulness by removing those words had their reasons for doing so. It is a 'hard sell' in a day of 'open options.' But one cannot help but feel that their inclusion was more in keeping with the ethos of the Army, the expectation of our founders and the very nature of covenant itself.

Does the heart holiness which the Army commends to its people and proclaims as God's purpose and provision require unquestioning submission to authority and life-long allegiance to the movement, not only as a spiritual movement raised up by God but as a sometimes all too human enterprise? In time, the Booth siblings, all of whom were charismatic exponents of the Holiness message, reacted against the authority imposed by their elder brother, Bramwell. Perhaps it had to do more with their relationship with their brother than any quarrel with the system or its demands. Who can doubt the sincerity of Herbert Booth, whose moving holiness songs and ringing call to arms enrich and inspire in Army worship to this day?

> To the front! The cry is ringing;
> To the front! Your place is there;
> In the conflict men are wanted,
> Men of hope and faith and prayer.
> Selfish ends shall claim no right
> From the battle's post to take us;
> Fear shall vanish in the fight,
> But triumphant God will make us.
>
> No retreating. Hell defeating,
> Shoulder to shoulder we stand
> .... (SASB 702:1)
>
> or
>
> Let me love thee, thou art claiming
> Every feeling of my soul;
> Let that love in power prevailing,

Render thee my life, my all.
. . . .
Love will soften every sorrow,
Love will lighten every care.
Love unquestioning will follow.
Love will triumph, love will dare.
(SASB 503:1, 3)

Given the expectations of the time and the high visibility of Herbert and his wife, Cornelie, it is perhaps not surprising that they were virtually excommunicated when they left the work in February 1902. The Maréchale, Catherine, was forbidden to speak to her father as he lay dying.[17] She had followed her husband, Arthur Booth-Clibborn out of the work in January 1902 when her husband became enamored with the cultic views of one John Alexander Dowie.

If the founders' own children could let the old flag fall, for whatever reason, what might be expected of soldiers in the ranks. Yet the extraordinary level of continued loyalty in the years that followed were a tribute to the covenantal commitment of ordinary Salvationists. They had promised to be faithful "till I die!"

We will follow our conquering Saviour,
From before him Hell's legions shall fly;
Our battalions never shall waver,
They're determined to conquer or die.
From holiness and Heaven
We never will be driven;
We will stand our ground forever,
For we never will give in.

Such was the sentiment of Captain William James Pearson (SASB 800:2).[18]

Holiness unto the Lord

For Salvationists, 'Holiness unto the Lord' is more than our watchword and song, or a motto embroidered on the covering of the Holiness table in an Army hall. It is at the heart of the movement. Commissioner Brengle famously affirmed its centrality to the Army's life and witness.

The bridge the Army throws across the impassable gulf which separates the sinner from the Savior, who pardons that He may purify, who saved

---

[17] Roger J. Green, *The Life and Ministry of William Booth: Founder of The Salvation Army* (Nashville, TN: Abingdon Press, 2005), 191-192

[18] Pearson (1832-1892) was author of 21 songs in the current song book. He was one of the company of early song writers who were gifted to the Army to express its spirit and ethos

that He may sanctify, rests upon two abutments: the forgiveness of sins through simple, penitent, obedient faith in a crucified Redeemer, and the purifying of the heart and empowering of the soul through the anointing of the Holy Spirit, given by its risen and ascended Lord, and received not by works, but by faith. Remove either of these abutments and the bridge falls; preserve them in strength and a world of lost and despairing sinners can be confidently invited and urged to come and be gloriously saved![19]

The Optimism of Holiness

The Spirit of the Army is a spirit of 'Holy Optimism.' Our God is a God of unfailing love who wills all to be saved and 'to come to the knowledge of the truth' (1 Timothy 2:4). In keeping with our Wesleyan heritage we proclaim that all can be saved through the merit of the shed blood of the Savior. And all who come to God through him can be saved to the uttermost (Hebrews 7:25 AV; TNIV 'completely': 'through and through' 1 Thessalonians 5:23). As has been seen, our founders insisted that salvation is a salvation from sin and sinning, or it is no salvation at all. Every believer is privileged to enter by full consecration and faith into the blessing of a clean heart through the sanctifying work of the Spirit. This confidence in the full possibilities of grace for holy living in this present world is wholly consistent with our founders' commitment to a positive gospel of possibility and power. The result is a fighting force prepared and empowered to engage the evil and suffering of our world. Given such confidence, William Booth could not help but believe that the forces of righteousness would prevail. The battle is the Lord's and his Army would march steadily on towards final victory. Our Army flag is not just a symbol, but a banner trumpeting the inner dynamic of a fighting and prevailing Army made holy by Blood and Fire. It leads the way toward final victory when every knee shall bow and tongue confess that Jesus Christ is Lord to the glory of God the Father.

---

[19] Samuel L. Brengle, 'The Holiness Standard of The Salvation Army in Teaching and Practice' in John D. Waldron (ed.), *The Privilege of All Believers* (Atlanta, GA: The Salvation Army Supplies and Purchasing Department, 1987), 109

7. 'To love and serve Him supremely all my days'[1]

Vocational Ministry in the Salvation Army: Perspectives on Officership & Leadership

Harold Hill

Christian ministry is participation in Christ's ministry, and all such ministry is "vocational" because it is in response to Christ's calling. However, for the purposes of this paper, *Vocational* ministry is that of people who do not have the further responsibility of having to earn their living at the same time. Indeed, that is fundamentally how the Salvation Army differentiates the ministry of its officers from that of its soldiers. Its *Orders and Regulations for Officers* says that "Officers of The Salvation Army are soldiers who have relinquished secular employment in response to a spiritual calling, so as to devote all their time and energies to the service of God and the people..." Or, as has been put more succinctly by Commissioner Wesley Harris, "Officership is availability,"[2] alternatively expressed as "Officership is *appointability*". This also underlines that this commitment is within the framework of organisational obedience. Such conditions of service, expressed in an Officers' "Covenant" and "Undertakings", are intended to help express and facilitate Christ's ministry in the world today.

Of course friends, supporters, employees and attendees at Salvation Army meetings, as well as Adherent Members, may all participate in the Army's, and Christ's, ministry. More narrowly, the basic constituent unit of the Salvation Army and therefore of its ministry, is the Soldier. A Soldier has signed the Soldier's Covenant, affirming Salvationist beliefs and committing to Salvationist lifestyle and disciplines, including "the dedication of my life to His service for the Salvation of the whole world". This encapsulates the Salvation Army's theology of ministry. Officers are in fact soldiers first; it is not just officers but all soldiers who are expected "to love and serve Him supremely all my days", even though that phrase is drawn from the Officer's Covenant. The words do not support a theology of ministry distinct from that of any *non-officer* Salvationist. The distinction is administrative, not theological; the Salvation Army does not have a priesthood distinct from that of all believers.

The situation is not so simple however, because sociology tends to trump theology in the evolution of ecclesiology. The ways we behave in practice are sometimes at variance with what we think we believe. We might assume that we believe, and then act accordingly; that our theology shapes our practice. That is not necessarily so. As anthropologist Michael Jackson argues, "Beliefs

---

[1] The Officer's Covenant – see Appendix D
[2] Wesley Harris in *The Officer*, June 1979, 243-5.

shadow practice rather than produce it."[3] Ray Anderson in his "Theology of Ministry" proposes the same principle: "Ministry precedes and produces theology, not the reverse".[4] Theology is not simply "faith seeking understanding"; it is the product of an on-going action-reflection process. A description of vocational ministry in the Salvation Army therefore involves telling its story as well as exploring the ways in which it might involve participation in Christ's ministry. This essay attempts just the first of these tasks.

Ministry in the Salvation Army compares to other churches

The institutional structure within which Salvation Army ministry is offered bears a superficial resemblance to that of the churches. The church has members; the Army has soldiers. Both the Army and the church have office-holders with pastoral and leadership roles. Both have units of corporate life; parishes or congregations or corps at the local level and most have collectives such as synods or dioceses and provinces or Divisions and Territories to facilitate supervision.

However, the correspondence between these church and Salvation Army terms is not exact, because of differing histories and the theologies arising from them. The Scriptural call to share Christ's ministry is made to the whole people of God but inevitably the emergence of differing roles has led to gradations of status within the church. In the Catholic tradition, the calling to a separate vocational ministerial priesthood, essentially different from that of the laity, is believed to derive from the command of Christ himself. The Salvation Army, arising no earlier than 1865, holds no such doctrine of priestly character but its officership has also come to assume a similarly clerical ethos.

The theological underpinnings are different. For example, in the Catholic tradition the presidency of the Eucharist is central to the clerical role (or in the Reformed tradition, the ministry of both Word and Sacrament), rather than the "appointability" of the officer. Again, officers are still soldiers whereas clergy in the church are by definition *not* laity. Clearly, the essence of officership as distinct from soldiership derives not from any theological rationale but lies in its practical convenience to the performance of the Army's mission. It arises from praxis; theologising has followed. Of course the Salvationist would argue that the same is true of Catholic priesthood or Reformed ministry. A different route has been taken to a similar destination: a clericalised vocational ministry.

Whereas the early Army used to rejoice that it differed from the churches, more recently it has asserted its similarity, both formally (as by the introduction of the term "ordination") and informally (as in corps being described as

---

[3] Michael Jackson, *The Accidental Anthropologist: a memoir* (Dunedin: Longacre, 2006) 150.
[4] Ray S. Anderson, "A Theology of Ministry", in Ray. S. Anderson (Ed.), *Theological Foundations for Ministry* (Edinburgh: T&T Clark, 1979) 7.

churches and officers as pastors). Such claims obscure theological distinctions and promote an apparent convergence. This essay explores the course of these developments, and the subsequent theologising which has invested an originally functional role with a gloss of clerical identity.

The Salvation Army began as a "non-denominational" mission, the Christian Mission. It was not a "church" and its operatives were not clergy. William Booth, having been ordained in the Methodist New Connexion, always maintained his clerical distinction, but his associates in the new enterprise from the mid-1860s were always *lay* evangelists. Their assumption of military-style ranks from 1878 was not seen as a departure from that principle.

Nevertheless, the Salvation Army inherited Methodism's ambiguity about ministry – its officers were "lay", but like Wesley's lay-preachers before them, they increasingly adopted a clerical identity. Originally simply itinerant evangelists, with, in Wesley's words, "nothing to do but save souls", Salvation Army officers soon came to perform such Clerical tasks as administration of sacraments, pastoring, preaching/teaching and government.[5] In practice they soon became "clergy", even if it took several generations for the Army to make this claim. Reflection on this practical development has led to a changed form of belief. Doctrine has eventually followed praxis. Let us trace the process by which this came about.

On the one hand, William Booth wrote:

> I have lived, thank God, to witness the separation between layman and cleric become more and more obscured... [6]

> [There is]...no "exclusive order of preachers" nor ministry confined to a particular class of individuals who constitute a sacred order specially raised up and qualified... authorised to communicate the same power to their successors, who are, they again contend, empowered to pass on some special virtues to those who listen to their teaching... I honour the Order of Preachers; I belong to it myself... but as to his possessing any particular grace because of his having gone through any form of Ordination, or any other ceremonial whatever, I think that idea is a great mistake.
> And I want to say here, once and for all, that no such notion is taught in any authorised statement of Salvation Army doctrine or affirmed by any responsible officer in the organisation... As Soldiers of Christ, the same duty places us all on one level. [7]

---

[5] Including offering the sacraments of baptism and the Lord's Supper until a change of policy in 1883, and thereafter to be responsible for such quasi-sacramental equivalents as the Army devised.
[6] George Scott Railton, *General Booth* (London: Hodder and Stoughton, 1912) 17.
[7] William Booth, in *The Officer* (June 1899) 202-3.

Not only were officers *not* "clergy" but soldiers in effect *were*. Booth in 1898 hoped that soldiers would not shirk their duty "by any talk of not being an officer."

> You cannot say you are not ordained. You were ordained when you signed Articles of War, under the blessed Flag. If not, I ordain every man, woman and child here present that has received the new life. ... I ordain you with the breath of my mouth. I tell you what your true business in the world is, and in the name of the living God I authorise you to go and do it. Go into all the world and preach the gospel to every creature! [8]

But contemporaneously with claims that the Army made no distinction between the 'ordination' of officers and that of soldiers, we find a growing emphasis on the distinctive role of officers. Booth wrote in 1900:

> Indeed, the fact is ever before us – like Priest, like People; like Captain, like Corps.[9]

And in 1903:

> ... it is the Officer upon whom all depends. It has always been so. If Moses had not made a priesthood, there would have been no Jewish nation. It was the priesthood of the Levites which kept them *alive*, saved them from their inherent rottenness... and perpetuated the law which made them.[10]

Regarding this statement, St. John Ervine considered that Booth's own views changing:

> This was a far different note from any that he had hitherto sounded. Priests had never previously been much esteemed by him who was more ready to admire prophets than priests... The Soldier-Prophet was about to leave his command to a Lawyer-Priest. A younger William Booth would have known that this was dangerous, but Booth was old and solitary and tired, and old men want priests more than they want warriors.[11]

---

[8] *The War Cry* (22 January 1898) 9, col. 3.
[9] William Booth, *Letter to Commissioners and Territorial Commanders* (London: Salvation Army, 1900) 15.
[10] Harold Begbie, *Life of William Booth* (London: Macmillan, 1920) II, 306.
[11] St. John Ervine, *God's Soldier, General William Booth* (London: Heinemann, 1934) II, 777-8.

Roland Robertson commented that Booth had come "to the conclusion that the priesthood of all believers, although already effectively dropped in practice, had to be attenuated as an ideal."[12]

Bramwell Booth wrote in 1925:

> In this, we humbly but firmly claim that we are in no way inferior... We, no less than they, are called and chosen to sanctification of the Spirit and to the inheritance of eternal life. And our officers are, equally with them, ministers in the church of God...[13]

The dilemma of clericalisation

So, the Army had attempted to maintain a sectarian equality of believers, resisting the idea that its officers were clergy. At same time, it adopted a military, hierarchical structure which expedited the process of clericalisation. Conditions of officers' service would constitute their professional milieu in way not true of other Salvationists. The mystique of the Call to officership, the intensive nature of officer-formation and sessional group bonding, the extent of personal commitment involved in the Covenant and Undertakings, the ranking and appointment systems, the expectations of the rank and file, the distinctive and all-absorbing work of officers, the sense of corporate identity and *esprit de corps*, together with the organisational advantages of claiming status as celebrants and chaplains, gave officership a character which was clerical compared with that of soldiers. External aspirations, such as the appointment of officers as military chaplains, reinforced this development.[14]

The end result: the Army became another denomination, its officers were regarded, and regarded themselves, as clergy, and its soldiers thought of themselves as laity. Despite a strong tradition of soldier-participation, officers became a professional religious class. The Army inherited and carried forward the ecclesiological contradictions of Methodism (and of most other sects). It has recapitulated, in its brief life, the history of the church as a whole. This denominationalising tendency consolidated throughout the 20th century, even though the Army's official rhetoric long remained sectarian.

The usual "routinisation of charisma" profile is that a period of consolidation and reflection ensues in a Movement's second century as it adjusts to operating in different world from that of its origins. In the Army's case, this was manifest from the 1960s in a debate over whether officership was simply a functional role or enjoyed a higher status. The same ambiguity or

---

[12] Roland Robertson, "The Salvation Army", in Bryan Wilson, *Patterns of Sectarianism* (London: Heinemann, 1967) 80.

[13] W. Bramwell Booth, *Echoes and Memories* (London: Hodder and Stoughton, [1925] 2nd edn. 1977) 82.

[14] The Judge Advocate General's decision (USA War Department) in 1917 is acknowledged here, although officer chaplains had been appointed earlier in other jurisdictions, beginning in New Zealand in 1911.

polarisation became apparent in this debate as we have seen in the writings of the Founders – it remained part of the Army's DNA. Commissioner Hubert Scotney, for example, resisted the drift to clericalisation:

> The distinction made today between clergy and laity does not exist in the New Testament... The terms layman and laity (in the current usage of those words) are completely out of character in a Salvation Army context... It is foreign to the entire concept of Salvationism to imagine two levels of involvement. Any distinction between officers and soldiers is one of function rather than status.[15]

Conversely, Colonel William Clark welcomed it:

> [By] a direct call from God into the ranks of Salvation Army officership, we have been given particular spiritual authority... Whatever our role ...happens to be for the time being... we are primarily spiritual leaders...Our spiritual authority lies not only or chiefly in what we do, but in what we are... Our calling is to be a certain kind of person and not ... to do a certain kind of job... The "ordained" ministry of the Church – to which body we belong by virtue of our calling, response, training and commissioning – is a distinctive ministry within the body of the whole people of God, different from that "general" ministry of the Church which is defined in the New Testament as "the priesthood of all believers".[16]

Ordained or Commissioned?

Inevitably the debate amongst Salvationists eventually found expression in official pronouncements, the first of which was General Arnold Brown's introduction of "ordination" in commissioning. The Chief of Staff's 1978 letter to Territorial Commanders stated:

> It is the General's wish that a slight modification should be made to the wording of the Dedication Service during the Commissioning of cadets, in order to emphasise the fact that Salvation Army officers are ordained ministers of Christ and of His Gospel.
> After the cadets have made their Affirmation of Faith, the officer conducting the Commissioning should then say: "In accepting these pledges which you each have made, I commission you as officers of The Salvation Army and ordain you as ministers of His Gospel."[17]

General Brown's introduction of "ordination" provoked a new round of discussion. Captain Chick Yuill opposed this change:

---

[15] *Officer* (July 1969) 452.
[16] *Officer* (July 1976) 289-90.
[17] Letters in IHQ Archives.

May I suggest that we need to re-emphasise the truth that there is no real distinction between officers and soldiers, that the difference is simply of function... If that little word 'ordain' has crept in because of a subconscious desire that other Christians should realise that we are as 'important' as the clergy of other denominations, ... in the end it matters not a jot where we stand in the estimation of any who would compile a league table of ecclesiastical importance.[18]

Brigadier Bramwell Darbyshire supported it:

In spite of all the stuff about the priesthood of all believers, ordained and commissioned officers are different from non-officer Salvationists. They are not cleverer, wiser, more loved of God than their fellows, but they are special, set apart for Jesus ... No one is more grateful for the Army's dedicated lay staff than this old warrior; but let's get it right. They may be as much involved as officers, but there is for an officer a sacramental dimension and if we lose sight of this the Army is finished.[19]

A pragmatic voice was that of Major Cecil Waters:

We will go on looking for a definition of officership unless and until we recognise that officership exists firstly as a convenience by which we organise the Army and secondly as one function, among many, to which we feel "called of God. [It is] impossible to define a concept of officership which is plainly and clearly distinct from that of soldiership. [He concluded] (a) That it would seem that the Army needs full time workers... Most, but by no means all, these workers are officers. (b) That we believe we may be called to be such workers – and this call may refer to officership (rather than employee or envoy status). (c) That to be so called and so engaged is sufficient to sustain our work, our spirit and our identity... we need look for nothing more special than this." [20]

Brown's decision did not command universal support even among the hierarchy. It was reviewed in 1988 and 1992, and in 2002 the rubric was amended by General John Gowans to read:

The commissioning officer will say to each cadet in turn: "Cadet (name): Accepting your promises and recognising that God has called, ordained and empowered you to be a minister of Christ and of his gospel, I commission you an officer of The Salvation Army." [21]

---

[18] *Officer* (October 1985) 438-40.
[19] *Salvationist* (18 April 1998) 6.
[20] *Officer* (July 1992) 317.
[21] IHQ Archives.

Significantly, "ordination" was now seen as something already done by God rather than in this ceremony by a representative of organisation. Commissioner Shaw Clifton was amongst those who disagreed with this change, and reversed it when he became General himself (2006-2011), although both rubrics may now be variously encountered in practice.

Meanwhile there had been other occasions for discussion. The 1982 World Council of Churches *Faith and Order Paper 111 on Baptism, Eucharist and Ministry* (The "Lima" document) was circulated amongst churches for comment. In its response, on the question of how Salvation Army ministry was perceived in relation to traditional Church belief about ordination, the Army missed significant areas of difference. It was vague about meaning of language of ordination and confused the concept of indelible character of orders with Army's own expectation that officers had life-long ministry. It identified with the theology of "radical reformation" but also sought to be included in the fold of "mainstream" ecclesiology by claiming to be just like everyone else but with different terminology. Or in the use of "ordination", the *same* terminology.[22] At time of writing, The Salvation Army had yet to respond publicly to similar issues raised in *Faith and Order Paper 214, The Church: Towards a Common Vision* (2013).

Prepared at General Eva Burrows' request as a further response to "Lima", Major Philip Needham's *Community in Mission, A Salvationist Ecclesiology* was published 1987. Needham's basic premise was that "a Salvationist ecclesiology stands as a reminder to the Church that its mission in the world is primary, and that the life of the Church ought largely to be shaped by a basic commitment to mission."[23] His ecclesiology deals with ministry of the Army as a whole, and only incidentally with that of the officer corps in particular.

Needham "raised serious questions about interpretations of ordination that stress the conferring of a unique spiritual status". He claimed its significance was best expressed in the word "commissioning", used of both officers and soldiers taking up specific tasks, while "ordination" was commonly used in connection with "ministries that require theological training, specialised skills, pastoral leadership and a full-time vocation... the ordained ministry can only be understood as functional..."[24]

The Doctrine Council's 1998 edition of the *Handbook of Doctrine*, *Salvation Story*, described the evolution of the Movement from an agency for evangelism to a denominational church. On Ministry, it noted that all Christians are "ministers or servants of the gospel... share in the priestly ministry... In that sense there is no separated ministry." However:

---

[22] The Army's response was included in *Faith and Order Paper 137* (Geneva: World Council of Churches, 1987) and also published as *One Faith, One Church* (London: Salvation Army, 1990).

[23] Philip Needham, *Community in Mission* (London: Salvation Army, 1987) 4, 5.

[24] Needham, *Community*, 65.

Within that common calling, some are called by Christ to be full-time office-holders within the Church. Their calling is affirmed by the gift of the Holy Spirit, the recognition of the Christian community and their commissioning – ordination – for service. Their function is to focus the mission and ministry of the whole Church so that its members are held faithful to their calling.[25]

Leadership in a missional community

Like *Community in Mission, Salvation Story* made clear the principle that ministry of particular persons arises out of ministry of whole Christian community, and attempted to explain and justify how this happened in practice.

The Doctrine Council's later work *Servants Together* was prepared because the 1995 International Conference of Leaders' recommended that:

> The roles of officers and soldiers be defined and a theology of "the priesthood of all believers" be developed to encourage greater involvement in ministry (for example, spiritual leadership, leadership in general), worship, service and evangelism.[26]

Servants Together clearly stated that there was no distinction in status between soldiers and officers, although it then struggled to establish what was unique about the officer role, admitting that a variety of opinion was held on the subject. As an official response to the debate of the previous forty years, *Servants Together* entrenched the Army's traditional ambiguity about its "separated ministry" – although the 2008 edition, with its inclusion of the new *Minute* on Commissioning amongst other things, took the Army back in a clericalising direction.

Nevertheless, we may still sum up the progression after the introduction of ordination in 1978 at least to *Servants Together* in 2002, by saying that in the 1970s the pendulum had swung far in direction of status for officers, while the Army's subsequent official publications tried to correct the imbalance and restore a functional view – while retaining Movement's traditional ambiguity about the question.

As a kind of counterpoint to this debate on officership, discussion continued on the place of Salvationists who perform officer functions without officer status. These include non-commissioned and warranted ranks – Envoys, Auxiliary Captains, (and Lieutenants between 2001 and 2008, when that rank was not treated as an officer one) – and also soldiers. The ambiguity about the status of officers – whether they are clerical or lay – has implications for them too. To have people doing identical work, under similar conditions, but accorded differing status and privileges is unjust and illogical, running counter to the principle that officership is simply functional. If people are treated

---

[25] *Salvation Story* (London: Salvation Army, 1998) 108.
[26] *Servants Together* (London: Salvation Army, 2002) 127.

differently because of what they *are* rather than what they *do*, that implies an essentially different priesthood.

The late twentieth century saw more soldiers in ministry roles – as youth workers, pastoral workers, corps leaders, social workers and administrators – particularly in western countries with declining officer strength. Debate about the respective roles and status of officers and soldiers has paralleled similar controversy in the Roman Catholic Church.[27] The difference between Church and Salvation Army lies in fact that the Army does not in theory reserve spiritual ministry and leadership roles for a sacerdotal class. The similarity is that, because of its hierarchical structure, the Army behaves in the same way as the Catholic Church, so change in this area occasions similar tensions.

Against the tendency for officers to become clergy and soldiers to think of themselves as laity, there has always been counter-movement, a consistent tradition of soldier initiative and participation in Army's work. There is always some tension between the belief that soldiers are the front line of evangelism, in *real* "full-time service", to be resourced by officers; and the assumption that soldiers are "cannon-fodder", whose lives are co-extensive with Army programmes. The second approach happens in a clericalising context.

In the "Western world" Army, the second half of twentieth century saw attempts to introduce consultative machinery on both the local level, with Corps Councils, and the territorial level, with a variety of "laymen's advisory" groups. Three weaknesses may be discerned in such attempts to spread the ownership of the Army:

Firstly, as Peter Price has observed of Catholic Church: "The consultative structures of the Church are still only 'recommended' and 'advisory'. They do not necessarily facilitate Lay participation in real decision-making. Such participation as well as its authority are dependent on the individual Bishop or Parish Priest, and may be dismantled at will."[28]

Secondly, the default, officer-centred position attributes omnicompetence to commissioned rank, so that too often business decisions are made by commercial amateurs, with commensurate loss of credibility in eyes of soldiers.

Thirdly, conversely, there is a danger that people see the professional business of the church as the "real" work of Christians, instead of their being light and salt in the world. This also "clericalises" the "laity".

In an attempt to resolve such questions, an International Commission on Officership was set up by General Paul Rader on the recommendation of the 1998 International Conference of Leaders "to review all aspects of the concept

---

[27] Mary Ann Glendon, "The Hour of the Laity", *First Things*, 127 (November 2002) 23-9.

[28] Peter Price, "Vatican II: End of a Clerical Church", *Australian Ejournal of Theology*, February 2004.

of officership in the light of the contemporary situation and its challenges, with a view to introducing a greater measure of flexibility" into officer service.[29]

Concerning the status of officership, the Commission was asked to do two incompatible things: to strengthen the ideal of life-time service and to explore possibilities of short-term service. The first would shore up the "clerical" assumptions behind officership; the second would permit a greater degree of flexibility based on an "all-lay" ethos. The Commission offered both alternatives. General Gowans tried to have it both ways but ended up perpetuating the two-tier model, with two groups performing the same ministry roles but only one having the status of officership. Lieutenants in 2002-2008 were not officers. Under General Clifton the Army reverted to the pre-2002 status quo.

Options for clerical status

In my view the Salvation Army had three options regarding clerical status:

1. There *are* priests/clerics/people in orders in Church, with status distinct from laity, but we *do not* have them in Salvation Army. That would mean the Army's acceptance of an "all lay" status for soldiers and officers, implying a second class clergy status for officers. The Army would be something like an "order" rather than a stand-alone entity like a "denomination". Booth rejected that option in 1882 in negotiations with the Anglican Church.

2. There *are* priests/clerics/people in orders in Church, and we *do* have them as officers in Salvation Army. This is what General Brown claimed by adopting "ordination", and assuming that the Army's commissioning was always equivalent to ordination. It endorsed officially what Salvationists already assumed, partly in consequence of the ambiguity about church order inherited from Methodism, and partly the desire to be accepted by other Christian denominations as one of them. *But* that is a position difficult to hold without sliding into clericalism.

3. There are *no* priests/clerics/orders in Church, and Salvation Army does *not* aspire to any. All Christians are "lay", all belong to the people of God, without distinction of status. This was Booth's theoretical position. However, the Army's ecclesiology was shaped instead by his autocratic temperament, the need for organisation, the twin demons of militarism and bureaucracy, the susceptibility of human nature to pride and ambition, and historically conditioned expectations. So the Salvation Army became "clericalised". The difficulty lies in the tension between the hierarchical institutional structure and the more egalitarian "Priesthood of all Believers" ethos inherited from our radical Protestant antecedents.

Clericalisation has had two related adverse effects on the Church – and on the Salvation Army. Firstly, clericalism fosters a spirit incompatible with the

---

[29] Norman Howe, "The International Commission on Officership: A Report", *Officer* (August 1999) 19.

"servanthood" Jesus modelled and undermines the kind of community Jesus calls together. Secondly, by concentrating power and influence in the hands of minority, clericalisation disempowers majority of members of Church, thus diminishing the Church's effectiveness in mission.

Of the first adverse effect, Bramwell Booth was aware. In 1894 he was complaining that "the D.O.'s [Divisional Officers] are often much more separate from their F.O.'s [Field Officers] than they ought to be. Class and caste grows with the growth of the military idea."[30] Thirty years later he was still anxious about Divisional and Territorial leaders in that "they are open to special dangers in that they rise and grow powerful and sink into a kind of opulence…"[31] (Unfortunately Captains are as susceptible as Colonels to the tendency.) Dr Laura Petri of Sweden, in her thesis "Catherine Booth and Salvationism", regretted that "military persons easily become arrogant, unrestrained and tyrannical" – though in quoting her, Commissioner Tor Wahlström also noted that "Salvationist lack of humility is apt today to be more frequently seen in the anxiety of many a Jack to prove himself at least as good as his master!"[32]

General Albert Orsborn acknowledged to the 1949 Commissioners' Conference that

> …dissatisfaction and decline… is blamed on our system of ranks, promotions, positions and differing salaries and retirements… that it has created envy and kindred evils and developed sycophancy, ingratiation, "wire-pulling", favouritism, etc… It is a sad reflection that we are in character, in spirituality, unable to meet the strain of our own system.[33]

All of which is to say that it is in the nature of systems to undermine the reason they exist. Human nature will take its course, and a system which actually encourages it to do so requires extra vigilance.

And the second adverse effect, the disempowerment of the many by the exaltation of the few? The American Nazarene Kenneth E. Crow sums up: "Loyalty declines when ability to influence decision and policies declines. When institutionalization results in top-down management, one of the consequences is member apathy and withdrawal."[34]

---

[30] W. Bramwell Booth, letter of October 1894, in Catherine Bramwell Booth, *Bramwell Booth* (London: Rich and Cowan, 1932) 218.
[31] W. Bramwell Booth, letter of 17 April 1924, in Catherine Bramwell Booth, *Bramwell Booth*, 437.
[32] "Aristion" (Tor Wahlström) in *The Officer*, November-December 1967, 413.
[33] Quoted by Eric Wickberg, in "Movements for Reform". Address at the 1971 International Conference of Leaders, Minutes, 9.
[34] Kenneth E. Crow, "The Church of the Nazarene and O'Dea's Dilemma of Mixed Motivation", www.nazarene.org/ansr/articles/crow_93.html) downloaded 30 March 2005.

Proposals for leadership ministry

It would be difficult to say whether clericalisation had led to a loss of zeal, or loss of zeal had been compensated for by a growing preoccupation with status, or whether each process fed the other. There is a paradox here: the military system, quite apart from the fact that it fitted Booth's autocratic temperament, was designed for rapid response, and is still officially justified in those terms. The Army's first period of rapid growth followed its introduction. However, the burgeoning of hierarchical and bureaucratic attitudes came to exert a counter-influence. The reason for success contained the seeds of failure. The longer-term effect of autocracy was to alienate many hitherto enthusiastic, and to deter subsequent generations, more habituated to free thought and democracy, from joining. Unfortunately clericalism is to clergy as water to fish. It is pervasive and taken for granted. We may find it encapsulated by the question of an incoming Territorial Commander, meeting for the first time with a group of Youth Officers and Youth Workers in a conference; "Which of you are the *Officers*? *You're* the ones I'm interested in!"

Clearly this argument refers to what we may loosely call the "Western" Army. In much of the "Third World" the Army is both expanding rapidly *and* also extremely rank-conscious! The cultures are different, but the long term results are yet to be seen.

If clericalisation *is* a bad thing, how may its ill-effects be moderated? Leadership is indispensable to the effectiveness of any movement. Structure is necessary, and needs continuity, accountability and legitimacy to mitigate the effects of unrestrained personal power. But if institutionalisation is inevitable, the prophetic critique, the Reformation's *ecclesia semper reformanda*, is essential.

There are two ways the problem can be approached: one is structural, the other attitudinal.

Had General Gowans been able to seize the opportunity offered by the Commission on Officership and abolish the two-tier vocational system, this would have mitigated an injustice and encouraged the variety of options of vocational service available. If all leaders in full-time paid employment were called officers, the soldiers' covenant would suffice for all. Appointments could be by application and held under employment contract rather than the anomalous "employed by God" fiction we cling to – a relic from a Christendom we no longer inhabit.

However, the 2002 edition of *Servants Together* did make the following suggestions for structural change "in order to facilitate servant leadership":

- Develop non-career-oriented leadership models.
- Dismantle as many forms of officer elitism as possible.
- Continue to find ways to expand participatory decision-making.[35]

---

[35] Servants Together (2002), 121.

Unfortunately the whole paragraph quoted was deleted from the 2008 edition of *Servants Together* (in which "participatory" was everywhere replaced by "consultative"). That leaves *attitudes*. The 2002 text of *Servants Together* made one other subversive suggestion, also deleted from the 2008 edition:

- Teach leaders to be servants by modelling it.[36]

This is the only suggestion most of us can aspire to implement, but it is also the most important: to model servanthood. And where opportunity affords, to name and challenge its shadow, which is the abuse of power. Nevertheless, an intentional reversal of the clericalising tendency might yet enhance the Salvation Army's vocational – and non-vocational – ministry.

---

[36] Servants Together (2002), 121.

8. '… and the church in her house'[1]

Women in Ministry in the Salvation Army

JoAnn Shade

In the beginning…

From its inception, the Salvation Army has affirmed that women, equally with men, should share in the government as well as the work of the Mission. The initial theological underpinnings for that position were heavily influenced by Catherine Booth, a formidable force in the fledgling Christian Mission (to be re-named The Salvation Army in 1878), especially in the area of the role of women within its organization and pulpits. In practice, single women have held significant leadership positions, and the Booth's daughter, Evangeline, was the National Commander in the United States from 1904 until she was elected the General of the international Salvation Army in 1934. In 1986, another single woman, Eva Burrows, became the second woman leader of the worldwide Salvation Army, and a third (Linda Bond) followed in their footsteps in 2012

How did this come to be? As has often been the case in the history of the church, the most significant opportunities for women in ministry in the 18th and 19th centuries came through new movements, perhaps because 'manpower' is badly needed in the initial stages of religious movements. Malcolm suggests that 'the greatest breakthrough in opportunities for women to proclaim the gospel came with the Wesleyan revival in England in the eighteenth century',[2] as the women of early Methodism were given ecclesiastical opportunities not known to women in other denominations[3] So while Catherine Booth was influenced by her own study, she was always positioned within a Wesleyan heritage, and the experience of women within the holiness movement, planting the seed of preaching women once again.

One such woman was Phoebe Palmer, who travelled and preached throughout the East Coast of America, Canada, and Great Britain as a part of the burgeoning Holiness movement. She spoke to the needs of women and the church: The church in many ways is a sort of potter's field where the gifts of

---

[1] Col 4:15

[2] Kari Torjensen Malcolm. *Women at the Crossroads: A Path Between Feminism and Traditionalism,* (Downer's Grove, IL: InterVarsity Press, 1982), 111

[3] Diane Leclerd, *Singleness of Heart: Gender, Sin and Holiness in Historical Perspective,* (Lanham, Md.: The Scarecrow Press, 2001), 69

women, as so many strangers, are buried. How long, O Lord, how long before man shall roll away the stone that we may see a resurrection? [4]

In her writings, Catherine Booth was committed to the principles of equality. Writing to her fiancé William in 1855, Catherine's words foreshadowed her later determination that men and women should have equal opportunity within the fledgling Army.

> May the Lord, even the just and impartial One, over-rule all for the true emancipation of woman from the swaddling bands of prejudice, ignorance and custom which, almost the world over, have so long debased and wronged her . . . If indeed there is in Christ Jesus 'neither male nor female,' but in all touching His Kingdom 'they are one,' who shall dare thrust woman out of the church's operations or presume to put any candle which God has lighted under a bushel? I have not written so much to thee as for thee. I want thee to feel as I do, if thou canst. [5]

It was Palmer who led Catherine Booth to a public defence of female ministry as early as 1859. At that time, Palmer had begun a four-year speaking tour in England, and was attacked by Reverend Arthur Augustus Rees in a pamphlet, 'Reasons for Not Co-Operating in the Alleged Sunderland Revivals', where Palmer was scheduled to preach. Catherine Booth's response to Rees was titled, 'Female Teaching: or "The Rev. A. A. Rees versus Mrs. Palmer, Being a Reply to a Pamphlet by the Above Named Gentleman on the Sunderland Revival'. Green indicates that while William Booth did the copying of the pamphlet, the argument was Catherine's alone. [6] It was this pamphlet that became the theological basis for the role of women within the Christian Mission and subsequently the Salvation Army.

William and Catherine lived within an ever-changing climate for women in ministry. While Wesley had allowed for preaching women, by the early 1850's, sectarian Methodism had largely closed its doors to women in the pulpit. However, a new wave of revivalism, beginning in 1859, again opened doors for a few exceptional women to preach, and this number included Catherine Booth, first in the Methodist New Connexion, and then in the Salvation Army. [7]

---

[4] Phoebe Palmer. *The Promise of the Father*, (Boston, Henry V. Degen Palmer, 1859), 341

[5] John Waldron, *Women in the Salvation Army*. (Toronto, Canada: The Salvation Army 1983), 40.

[6] Roger Green, *Catherine Booth* (Grand Rapids, MI: Baker Books, 1996), 125.

[7] Andrew Mark Eason, *Women in God's Army: Gender and Equality in the Early Salvation Army* (Waterloo, ON: Wilfrid Laurier University Press, 2003), 25

Theological Understanding

If the Salvation Army's practice has claimed to embrace full opportunity for women in ministry practice, what then is the theological position of the Salvation Army that supports that practice in regards to women in ministry? The Salvation Army has historically outlined its theological positions in its *Handbook of Doctrine*, which is revised every 15-20 years, and it outlines its practices in volumes entitled *Orders and Regulations for Officers*.

In *The Handbook of Doctrine*, printed in 2010 there is no mention of gender in the doctrinal component of the portion of the publication, and it is only in an appendix, on one of the last pages, that we find *The Salvation Army in the Body of Christ, An Ecclesiological Statement*, a statement issued by the International Headquarters of The Salvation Army in 2008 by authority of the General, in consultation with the International Doctrine Council and the International Management Council. The only statement that mentions gender is found on p.315, and reads, 'its recognition of the equal place within the Body of Christ of men and women in all aspects of Christian service, ministry and leadership including the holding of ecclesiological authority'.[8]

Based upon this scanty text, we are thus left with Catherine Booth's *Female Ministry*, first published in 1859, with its 3rd (and final) revision in 1870, still Christian Mission days. Based upon its origin, it is clear that the pages are formed as an apologetic, as described by Catherine: 'In this paper we shall endeavour to meet the most common objections to female ministry, and to present, as far as our space will permit, a thorough examination of the texts generally produced in support of these objections'.

In the pamphlet, Booth takes on the major arguments of the day against female preachers; she begins by addressing those who say that public speaking is unnatural and unfeminine. Booth answered that custom does not equal nature, and women have the necessary abilities, persuasive speech, graceful form and attitude, winning manners and finely-toned emotional nature.[9]

A second argument was that public speaking or preaching is an indulgence of ambition. Booth answered bluntly: why should that matter more in a woman than a man? A woman's commitment to the Gospel shields her from coarse and unrefined influences, and she gave examples of the successful ministry of Madame Guyon and Susannah Wesley.[10]

A third point of contention that is of more importance from a twenty-first century perspective, is that speaking in church by a woman is forbidden in Scripture. In addressing this, Booth first writes of the public ministry of women

---

[8] *The Salvation Army Handbook of Doctrine* (London: The Salvation Army International Headquarters, 2010), 315

[9] *Terms of Empowerment: Salvation Army Women in Ministry*, (West Nyack, NY: The Salvation Army, 2001), 1

[10] *Terms of Empowerment*, 2-3

as recognized and described by Paul in I Cor. 11:4,5, and suggests that the question of women's public participation was settled at Pentecost. She then addresses what we would refer to as the problem texts, first in I Cor. 14:34, 35, 'Let women keep silence'. Booth describes that as a different kind of speaking (inconvenient asking of questions, ignorant talking), and speaks to the verb usage – *lalein,* 'to speak', used in variety of settings, meanings, and is modified by the context. She suggests that the improper speaking is that of chatter, babble, the loquaciousness of a child, or speaking imprudently.[11] She also discusses 1 Tim. 2:12, 13, teaching that the injunction in that passage is regarding personal behaviour at home, as in teaching that usurps authority, and suggests that an ignorant or unruly woman is not to force her opinions on the man whether he will or no. She believes it has no reference whatever to women sent out to preach the Gospel by the call of the Holy Spirit.[12]

Fourth, she addresses the contention that speaking/preaching is to be confined only to men by recognizing that it is not confined only to men in the Scripture. She points the reader to Joel as quoted in Acts 2:16-18, as the Spirit is poured out on all flesh, and the daughters are to prophesy. She also presents the Biblical examples of Phoebe (Rom. 16), Junia, and the historical witness of Justin Martyr, Irenaeus, and Eusebius.

An additional point made against women preachers was that it was unnecessary for women to preach, because after all, a woman can visit the sick and poor and work in the church instead. Booth responds by noting that Jesus did not show horror at public proclamation by females, and that individual decisions must be dictated by the teachings of the Holy Spirit and the gifts with which God has endowed each woman. Again, she notes the scriptural precedent in Deborah (Judges 2), Huldah (II Kings 12), Anna (Luke 2), 'Great was the company of women evangelists', Psalm 68:11, Miriam classified with Moses and Aaron, and Mary Magdalene who made the first and public announcement of the resurrection She noted as well that in Acts 1:14, 2:1,4, women were present and assembled on the day of Pentecost, filled with the Holy Ghost, given the gift of tongues, and notes as well the four daughters of Phillip the Evangelist (Acts 11:9), Priscilla (Rom. 16:3,4) and Tryphena, Tryphoa, and Persis (Rom. 16:12).[13]

With a few final points, she concludes her presentation by quoting Galatians 3:28, that there is 'neither male nor female, for ye are all one in Christ Jesus'.[14] As Booth wrote, 'This is a subject of vast importance to the interests of Christ's kingdom and the glory of God, we would most earnestly commend its consideration to those who have influence in the Churches. We think it a matter worthy of their consideration whether God intended woman to bury her talents and influence as she now does? And whether the circumscribed

---

[11] *Terms of Empowerment,* 3-7

[12] *Terms of Empowerment,* 12-15

[13] *Terms of Empowerment,* 19-20

[14] *Terms of Empowerment,* 26

sphere of woman's religious labours may not have something to do with the comparative non-success of the Gospel in these latter days'.[15]

In Practice

Despite her early championing of women's involvement in the church, Catherine Booth may not have been fully convinced of the role women should take in leadership of this new mission. Writing of his mother, Bramwell indicated that, 'the Army Mother had never quite contemplated placing women in positions which would involve their authority over men'. [16] Yet the Constitution of the Christian Mission (soon to become the Salvation Army) indicated that 'Godly women . . .shall be eligible for any office, and to speak and vote at all official meetings'. Even after Catherine Booth's death, William said 'I insist on the equality of women with men. Every officer and soldier should insist upon the truth that woman is as important, as valuable, as capable and as necessary to the progress and happiness of the world as man. Unfortunately a large number of people of every tribe, class and nationality think otherwise. They still believe woman is inferior to man'. (William Booth, 1908). [17] [18]

How well did the Salvation Army do in following Catherine's lead and its public statements of egalitarian opportunity? Linda McKinnish Bridges has studied many religious movements, and she commonly finds the 'Lydia phase', in which women begin in positions of leadership in the early days of the institution, but then are relegated to secondary roles in order for the movement to gain cultural legitimacy and to diminish the feminizing effect of women's leadership.[19] Did this pattern hold true within the Army?

This fledgling army was a product of its Victorian England roots, and it appears that The Salvation Army's public declaration of equality did not always extend to its practices, especially when its young women officers began to marry. Writing on the period between 1865-1930, Andrew Eason undertook a critical, historical examination of female experience and opportunity within the Salvation Army in Britain. While its pulpits remained open to women, were the public pronouncements factual when they claimed the Salvation Army 'refuses to make any difference between men and women as to rank, authority

---

[15] *Terms of Empowerment*, 27-28
[16] Bramwell Booth, *Echoes and Memories* (London: Hodder and Stoughton, 1925), 168-169.
[17] William Booth. *Messages to Soldiers* (London; The Salvation Army, 1908), referenced on the Salvation Army international website, www.salvationarmy.org
[18] Allen Satterlee, *Turning Points: How the Salvation Army Found a Different Path.* (Alexandria, VA: Crest Books, 2004), 5
[19] Linda McKinnish Bridges "Women in Church Leadership." *Review and Expositor* 95, no. 3 (1998), 333

and duties, but opens the highest positions to women as well as men'?[20] Eason's research exposed the gap between its declared position and the actual place of women within the organization. As one example, a review of the leadership of the Salvation Army in Great Britain in 1930 found that, with the exception of the Booth women, the percentage of female leaders was negligible.[21]

Eason's conclusion is revealing:

> If the history of the early Salvation Army teaches us anything, it is the fact that recommendations and principles, however well-intentioned, are not enough to ensure equality between the sexes. Although Salvationists made numerous pronouncements on the subject of sexual equality between 1870 and 1930, they failed to address the deep-seated assumptions and the discriminatory practices that worked against the possibility of an egalitarian environment.[22]

In her historical review of the urban religion of the Salvation Army in the United States, Diane Winston suggested that, 'as the first Christian group in modern times to treat women as men's equals, the Army offered a compelling, if sometimes contradictory, vision of gender'.[23] It appears that the evolving role of women within the Army was strongly influenced by its American leaders, first Ballington and Maud Booth, followed by Frederick and Emma Booth-Tucker, and then Evangeline Booth (Emma, Ballington and Evangeline were all children of the elder Booths).

Early Army leader Maud Booth (married to the Booths' son, Ballington) offered two main roles to women. The first was that of the slum sister, whose 'dress indicates extreme poverty; her face denotes perfect peace'.[24] Self-abnegation was the spirit desired in these women, mostly single women of simplicity and deep faith (and also likely limited ability). Maud also proposed a second image for the Salvationist woman, that of a woman warrior. The woman warrior combined 'tender, gentle, loving attributes' with 'courage, strength, action, sacrifice, and loyalty'.[25]

Her female successors, sisters-in-law Emma Booth-Tucker (1896) and Evangeline Booth (1904), proved more conventional in their approach. While experiencing their own leadership opportunities, more likely to be because of their lineage than their gender, they accepted both the Army's stated goal of equality for women and the limitations imposed on it by contemporary

---

[20] Eason, *Women in God's Army*, 160
[21] Eason, *Women in God's Army*, 151
[22] Eason, *Women in God's Army*, 157
[23] Diane Winston, *Red Hot and Righteous: The Urban Religion of the Salvation Army.* (Cambridge, MA: Harvard University Press, 1999). 95
[24] Winston, *Red Hot and Righteous*, 73
[25] Winston, *Red Hot and Righteous*, 78

society.[26] Emma, a mother of six, represented the 'womanly woman', one with a 'mother's heart, a nurturing image resonant with the cult of domesticity', [27] whose work reflected a form of 'enlarged moral housekeeping'.[28]

Evangeline Booth, United States leader from 1904 to 1934, encouraged the image of the doughnut girls who served at the front in World War I. She was less than sympathetic to more flamboyant approaches to womanhood (although she herself was known for her eccentricity and dramatic flair). History tells of Captain Rheba Crawford, the 'Angel of Broadway', whose independence, popularity, and sexual charisma disturbed Army leaders to the extent that she was ultimately placed on rest furlough because of her unorthodox theology and dress. Winston suggests that it was Crawford's 'success at transforming the doughboy's goddess into a real live girl that caused her undoing'.[29] Summing up the changes in the position of women during Evangeline's reign, Winston concludes, 'Confronted by societal changes in women's roles, Salvationists portrayed their female followers as exemplars of freedom and equality who eschewed the excesses associated with the New Woman or the flapper'. [30] It is interesting to note that Evangeline Booth was forbidden to marry by her father, because of his fear that her marital status would severely limit her leadership opportunities.[31]

Evangeline Booth went on to become the first woman international leader of the Salvation Army, serving in that position from 1934-1939. Little appears in the history books of the role of women until the next female General, who shared both her name and marital status (single), was elected in 1986. The selection of Eva Burrows brought a hope that she would address issues in relation to women officers, especially married women, but it was not to be. Writes Henry Gariepy, her biographer: 'Many married and single women officers had high hopes that the disproportion (lack of women in top leadership positions) would be corrected when a woman was elected General, but have not seen the results for which they had hopes'. [32] She did, however, establish a commission to consider the matter.

In 1994, Paul Rader was elected as general, and, joined by his wife, Commissioner Kay Fuller Rader, became known for their commitment to broadening the role of women in ministry. Said Kay, 'I desired to help women realize their potential for ministry . . . to be someone to stand in the gap for them in any way I could, to keep Catherine Booth's dream alive'. Commissioner Doris Noland spoke of Kay's leadership: 'Kay helped raise

---

[26] Winston, *Red Hot and Righteous,* 95

[27] Winston, *Red Hot and Righteous,* 111

[28] Winston, *Red Hot and Righteous,* 141

[29] Winston, *Red Hot and Righteous,* 206

[30] Winston, *Red Hot and Righteous,* 207

[31] Margaret Trout. *The General was a Lady.* (NY: The Salvation Army, 1980)

[32] Henry Gariepy, *General of God's Army: The Authorized Biography of General Eva Burrows* (Wheaton, IL: Victor Books, 1993), 240

awareness of the long drift away from Catherine Booth's ideas on women's ministry'. [33]

As Kay Rader discovered, her encouragement of expanded roles for women was not always welcomed. One leader, Commissioner Don Ødegaard, described her work: 'She has done more for married Salvation Army women than anyone . . . not through feminism, but by producing excitement. She role modelled . . . she stepped on toes unafraid . . . irritated some people, but the days of wasting women are gone', [34] a conclusion not shared by all Army women (or men).

Rader's biographer, Carroll Hunt, speaks to the status of Army women:

> The Salvation Army legacy as told in literature and history reveals a divided heart when it comes to its women officers, trained and commissioned equally with the men, and at times handed what the Christian world considers "a man's job" but at other times ordered to stand back and stir the soup, preferably quietly. But the world contains an Army of women warriors called by God to service, and they are not about to disappear by drowning or discrimination. [35]

Recently retired international leader General Shaw Clifton added his voice to the conversation: 'I do not believe the Army has gone far enough in using its women, and I refer here not only to its officers, but also to its women soldiers, and its women local officers'. [36] However, despite his hopes in this area, few strides were made in this critical area under his leadership, perhaps because of resistance in the levels of governance within the Salvation Army.

To put the situation in a historical perspective, The Salvation Army wasn't alone in its struggles on this front. MaryAnn Hawkins, writing from a Church of God (Anderson, IN) position raises a similar question: 'So what happened that the Holiness movement, that gave an unprecedented opportunity for women to join equally in every aspect of ministry, began to marginalize women who were called to ministry?' [37] She quotes Marie Strong and Juanita Evans Leonard:

> Vision [gave] way to routine. Organizational maintenance was substituted for evangelization and the healing of the ills of people and society. More effort was spent on maintaining the organization and less on ministry to the world. Flexibility gave way to inflexibility. Those in

---

[33] Carroll Ferguson Hunt, *If Two Shall Agree*. (Kansas City, MS.: Beacon Hill Press, 2001), 167

[34] Hunt, *If Two Shall Agree*, 184

[35] Hunt, *If Two Shall Agree*, 150

[36] Warner, Sue Schumann. "A Passionate Look Towards the Future: A Conversation with General Shaw Clifton" *New Frontier* 24, no. 10 (2006)

[37] MaryAnn Hawkins, Wesleyan Holiness Women Clergy e-mail, 2-26-12

power whose identities were entwined with position and status had a vested interest in maintaining the status quo of the institution . . . a passion for people [gave] way to a focus on programs. Success was measured in programs and buildings. As the institutional machinery continued to grow, white women and ethnic minorities were increasingly detached and alienated from the Church. . . . Impersonalization was rampant and the majority clergy controlled the institution; the Church was no longer sensitive to women's needs and goals for service. The egalitarian informality of the Church's beginnings had hardened to become an entrenched hierarchy. The sense of camaraderie as "the whole people of God" had all but died. There remained an intellectual assent to women in ministry, but the realized vision needed once more to be fanned into flame by the Holy Spirit's power and those empowered by the Word.[38]

The Current Day Situation

While the Salvation Army does not have any recent statement internationally that reflects its theology regarding women in its ministry, Colonel Janet Munn succinctly summarizes her understanding of The Salvation Army's theological position:

- We believe that women are created in the image of God as sure as are men and are of equal value before God and before each other.
- We believe that in Christ there is no male or female (Galatians 3:28).
- We believe that females have the same capacity as males to learn, to develop, to lead, to teach, to preach and to decide.
- We believe that these assertions are biblically and theologically sound, and they are Salvationist essentials.
- We believe that the Holy Spirit gives gifts as the Spirit desires, for the building up of the body of Christ.
- We believe that any person, male or female, could potentially have any gift, talent, ability given by the Spirit and developed by diligence.
- We believe that the Salvation Army has historically desired to be a progressive and prophetic example of female leadership and empowerment to the world and the church, and that there is still a need in the world for Salvationist witness in this regard.

While Munn does not make mention of marriage in her list, she would be sure to note that we also believe in the egalitarian marriage model that expresses mutuality and shared responsibility.[39]

---

[38] Marie Strong, Juanita Evans Leonard *Called to Minister, Empowered to Serve:, 2nd edition. (*Warner Press 2013*).
[39] Janet Munn, Personal Correspondence, March, 2013.See also: Janet Munn, *Theory and Practice of Gender Equality in The Salvation Army*, (Ashland: Gracednotes Ministries, 2015)

Women make up more than half of the officers in the Army internationally, a statistic that is partly determined by the requirement that both spouses serve as officers in most territories of the world, yet few are in top leadership roles. An International Commission on Officership in 2000 articulated the concerns: 'A number of women officers experience frustration and lack of fulfilment, perceiving that they are not considered for certain appointments due to gender or marital status'.[40] In speaking of present realities regarding women in Salvation Army ministry, Allen Satterlee muses: 'The Army proved that women could handle leadership and ministry in all phases of its work. Now it may find itself passed by, viewed as being mired in tradition instead of as a tradition-breaker'.[41]

Gender and ministry issues in Salvation Army circles continue to be debated on personal blogs, on-line journals,[42] and in regional discussions such as the Gender Issues Commission held in the United Kingdom territory, which affirmed that 'our policy and practice must reflect our theology [there is no theological conflict in the ministry of women in all spheres of service]'.[43] While front-line opportunities continue to be available to women, both single and married, the stained-glass ceiling remains an obstacle for leadership positions, particularly for married women. As William Booth acknowledged in 1888, 'the male officers are joined [in marriage] with the female officers, and then, by some strange mistake in our organization, the woman doesn't count'.[44] It appears that William understood at that early date the tension between the dual clergy requirement and the Army's commitment to women in ministry.

While women are theoretically given equal opportunity by policy, practice proves a contradiction, as Eason points out historically. Women were considerably less likely to be in leadership, and women often took a lesser role upon marriage (Eason, 2003). Upon appointment of their husbands to leadership roles, women officers were called 'to a less conspicuous part of His great vineyard', and urged to 'not judge as to the relative importance of the work we do for Him, whether this or that'.[45]

As the Army acquired respectability, the role of women declined.[46] While it appeared to the uncritical observer that the Army was an 'egalitarian

[40] The Salvation Army International Headquarters, "Commission on Officership Report," 2000.
[41] Satterlee, *Turning Points*, 10
[42] see www.armybarmy.com's *Journal of Aggressive Christianity*, beginning with the Feb/Mar 2006 edition
[43] The Salvation Army United Kingdom Territory, Gender Issues Commission, 2005.
[44] Roger Green. *The Life and Ministry of William Booth*, (Nashville, Tenn.: Abingdon Press, 2005), 201
[45] Catherine Higgins, (Mrs. General) 'Opportunities and responsibilities of wives of headquarters officers', *The Officer* 52 (1931), 265-268
[46] Flora Larsson, *My best men are women*. (London: Hodder and Stoughton, 1974), 170

religious body that gave its female officers unparalleled opportunities to work in every area of its institutional life', the reality was that 'it largely failed to implement sexual equality beyond the pulpit' and did not 'promote an egalitarian sharing of roles by women and men'.[47] As Satterlee points out, there remain many challenges to women in leadership in the Army, in that leadership of the Salvation Army remains dominated by men, restrictions are placed on a woman's development because of stereotyping, and women have not always been given the opportunity to explore their leadership skills. He also comments that, "this leadership (of women) is actually more restricted in Western countries than in non-western countries",[48] as evidenced in part by the fact that women officers in the United States who are married receive no financial compensation in their own name either in their active years of ministry or in retirement, unless widowed.

, while in local, pastoral leadership the ministry is shared between a married couple, in the major leadership roles around the world (Territorial Commander, Chief Secretary, Training Principal and Divisional Commander) only 9.07% of those position are held by women, with only 1.73% of the total held by married women.[49]

Given this scenario, some women are leaving officership for other opportunities, but given the spiritual sense of calling, financial implications, and the marital necessity of both spouses being active officers in most territories, the attrition rate is not yet high. Other women are 'defecting in place', remaining in the church but identifying patriarchy and its impact, while taking responsibility for their own spiritual lives.[50]

Looking to the Future

The Salvation Army is at a critical point in regards to the issue of women in ministry. There is a cognitive dissonance between its historical and theological position of full acceptance of women in ministry roles of all kinds, and the actual practices that create a stained glass ceiling for married women. While this is not a new phenomenon, cultural factors, at least in the western Salvation Army, and perhaps throughout the world, are making this a vital issue to the future of the Salvation Army.

The following was a press statement issued from Washington, D.C. in 2013:

---

[47] Eason, *Women in God's Army*, 154-155
[48] Satterlee, Turning Points, 8-10
[49] Sue Swanson, Jolene Hodder (International Conference of Leaders July 2012, International Management Council March 2012).
[50] Miriam Winter, Adair Lummis, and Alison Stokes. *Defecting in Place: Women Claiming Responsibility for their own Special Lives.* (New York: Crossroads, 1995), 5-7

The Obama Administration has made it clear that advancing the rights of women and girls is critical to the foreign policy of the United States. This is a matter of national security as much as it is an issue of morality or fairness. President Obama's National Security Strategy explicitly recognizes that "countries are more peaceful and prosperous when women are accorded full and equal rights and opportunity. When those rights and opportunities are denied, countries lag behind. [51]

It would be expected that the Salvation Army, with its emphasis on social justice, would be in agreement with Clinton's statement for the women of the world. Many of its officer women would say that it needs to begin within its own camp (see Joshua 7:1-13). What could make a difference?

1. A contemporary theology of women, of gender.
2. Preaching, teaching, ministering, leading female role models (single and married) at all levels of the organization.
3. An acknowledgement of the level of frustration experienced by its women officers due to the inequities that are in place.
4. A recognition of the role of expectations and exhaustion, especially in the lives of young officer mothers.
5. An understanding of the potentially negative influence of conservative evangelical Christian writings and teachings upon Salvation Army women.

Having just retired after 34 years of active service as a Salvation Army officer, I have watched my sisters wrestle with this issue. I've watched as an officer was assigned to be the laundress at camp for the summer. I've watched the corps officer's wife (as she was then known) wash and iron twenty junior soldier uniforms each week. I've been blessed under the pulpit ministry of many women officers. I've attended celebratory events such as commissionings and congresses and wondered why women tended to be the pray-ers instead of the preachers. I have written, I have wept, I have strategized and I have been called 'that radical woman' because of my passion to see myself and my sisters in full and complete ministry and leadership.

The week before she died (1890), Catherine Booth called for her husband at 4 a.m. to give him a solemn message: 'she feared the women of The Salvation Army were not going to rise up to take the place she wished for them'. [52] It would appear that her fears were well-founded, and it is still to be determined as to whether a new wave of women (and men) will rise up to challenge both the systemic and practical barriers to her dream.

---

[51] Hillary Rodham Clinton, Secretary of State Press Statement, (Washington, DC, 31 January, 2013)
[52] Green, *Catherine Booth*, p. 298

9. 'My life must be Christ's broken bread'[1]

Non-practice of the Sacraments in The Salvation Army: Re-considering the Decision 130 Years Later

Philip D. Needham

Introduction

Having been asked to write this paper on the non-practice of the sacraments in The Salvation Army, I decided to approach it with a mind open to reconsideration of the decision. With a few exceptions writings by Salvationists on the subject, myself included, have defended the 1883 decision and argued for its continuing legitimacy and usefulness. I have never opposed the reintroduction of the sacraments *per se*. I usually find spiritual blessing, benefit, and challenge when I participate in the Lord's Supper while visiting another church. I have been able to live with the 1883 decision because: first, most of the reasons for the original decision to discontinue were valid in light of The Salvation Army's focus on inclusive mission; and second, the challenge of re-introduction after intentional non-practice for 130 years in this very diverse international Salvation Army seemed to be overwhelming and unrealistic; and third, I intend to be a Salvationist till the day I die, whether or not the sacraments are re-introduced in The Salvation Army. (Note: I use the word 'sacraments' in this paper to designate baptism and the Lord's Supper and not to imply, by use of the word itself, any particular sacramental theology.)

I have gradually come to the conclusion, however, that the first reason for discontinuance has lost almost all of its validity and force. In other words, I have concluded that almost all, if not all, of the original practical, theological, and missional arguments for discontinuance are either no longer valid or require views of sacramental practice that are too narrow and limiting. Furthermore, I have come to the conviction that there would be great benefit to The Salvation Army to restore sacramental practice as a medium of grace, blessing, and missional challenge, and as a visual expression of our unity and participation in the Body of Christ. If this is shown to be true, then the huge challenge of re-introduction seems to be the big task. Whether The Salvation Army finds the way to do it will, I think, depend on the will to do it.

The Salvation Army's position with respect to the two sacraments practiced by practically all Protestant denominations evolved early

---

[1] Albert Orsborn, *The Song Book of the Salvation Army*, 512

in the movement's history. For a few brief years, however, they were practiced. There may have been a generally agreed prescribed order, presumably borrowing primarily from the Wesleyan provenance of the Founders, William and Catherine Booth. Records of those early days sometimes associate the practice with great blessing and spiritual outpouring.

Why, then, did the early leaders, and William and Catherine Booth in particular, come to the decision to discontinue practice of the sacraments? What was gained by it? And whatever the gains at the time, do they still stand as such? Can the sacraments now give no benefit with regard to The Salvation Army's spiritual life and the advancement of its mission? To push the question even further, does continuation of this position, in fact, now work against the mission? And finally, given the establishment of non-observance these 130 years to the present, would the decision to re-instate the practice of the sacraments of water baptism and the Lord's Supper be too divisive for this international movement that spans the globe and has been held together by common ecclesial practice? And is this especially so in light of the strong possibility that certain national, regional, and ethnic constituencies might well be adamantly against re-introduction? These are the matters this paper will first seek to address.

Do the supports for the decision to discontinue still stand?

What were the original *practical advantages*? In the Victorian era the idea of women preachers was radical. The use of women preachers, however, was not negotiable for The Salvation Army; Army leaders firmly decided on principle to withstand the criticism. The idea of a woman presiding at the administration of a sacrament, it seems, was an even more radical idea, and eliminating the sacraments allowed the Army to avoid that particular opprobrium. In our day, however, the offence of women administering sacraments is largely gone in most Protestant denominations, and those denominations that still find it offensive would also be offended by women preaching.

Another advantage for this young missional movement was that its needed mobility was not hampered by obtaining and transporting the furniture, accoutrements, and elements needed for the sacraments. Furthermore, it was extremely difficult in those days before refrigeration to obtain unfermented grape juice. Now, most Salvation Army church (corps) facilities are stationary, and unfermented grape juice is available, and where it is not, other non-alcoholic juices would be available.

I am convinced that the primary reason for the decision to discontinue was *missional*. A large number of early Salvationist leaders came to the conclusion, probably justified, that the debate and argument between denominations over sacramental practice in Victorian England was divisive. Also at issue were the small number of trained clergypersons in the movement – most officers were lay leaders – complicating the issue further. As many other major changes and innovations were made to facilitate the mission to the poorer classes (renting unchurch-like places, replacing traditional hymns with more popular tunes wedded to new words, brass bands, etc.), the decision to simplify further by foregoing the 'complication' of sacramental practice also made sense. At first, Salvationists who still wanted to take the sacraments were encouraged to do so at an existing church or chapel. To be sure, The Salvation Army was becoming the spiritual home and family to a growing number of Salvationists, but it was to be many decades later before it was even willing to refer to itself as a 'church.' Furthermore, it worked across denominational lines and probably did not want something like the establishment of a particular sacramental view and practice to create a barrier to working alongside any Christian group or denomination.   It had enough opposition from churches early on over its radical methods without fueling theological fire over the sacraments, as well! The Salvation Army could move forward in its mission without the baggage and divisiveness of sacramental debate.

The question now at hand is *whether non-observance still carries any real missional advantage.* In other words, what arguments could be made for claiming that sacramental practice would measurably limit either service outreach or evangelism and member recruitment? The fastest-growing part of the Church today is charismatic-pentecostal. Their practice of the sacraments certainly does not hinder recruitment – and probably enhances it. Speaking from personal experience, I know of people who decided not become Salvationists because of the absence of sacramental observance. I also know of Salvationists who left The Salvation Army because they wanted to become members of a church where the sacraments were practiced. Conversely, I have never met anyone who said they were drawn to membership in The Salvation Army because the sacraments were *not* practiced.

One wonders if some leaders of The Salvation Army in the Western world hold the view, or suspect, that re-institution of the sacraments would be crossing a line that would have serious implications for the public and private funds the organization heavily relies upon in order to carry out the community services for which it is so well known. If The Salvation Army began practicing the sacraments (so the view goes), it would let the cat out of the bag, so to speak, exposing the organization as a Protestant church, and thereby sowing seeds of doubt in the minds of many current financial supporters who would then begin wondering why they should or want to give money to support another *church*. This is an understandable concern, but in light of the fact that almost all mainline denominations have community service arms for which funds are elicited from the public, the concern is undoubtedly greater than what the actual funding loss might be. (Many contributors to The Salvation Army understand it is a church and that its community service is an explicit expression of Christian compassion.)

One should not, however, underestimate the difficulty of making such a major change as resuming the celebration of the sacraments in The Salvation Army. It would have been far easier if William Booth had reintroduced the sacraments once it had become clear that The Salvation Army had actually become a church (a worshipping, serving body of believers) -- if a missional, evangelistic, social-action oriented church at that. After all these 130 years, however, changing things that have become part of an organization's 'sacred tradition' is far more difficult, especially in an international organization. Later in this paper we will discuss possible ways to approach this major change. At this point I simply want to note a new reality (certainly in the Western world) in regard to 'denominational loyalty': it is on the wane, especially in Protestantism. I saw strong denominational loyalty when I was young. When Salvationists moved from one city to another, they typically looked for a SA corps at which to 'soldier.' Also, when a Salvationist family moved out to the suburbs, or across town, they continued to drive further to retain their soldiership at the same corps if no corps were located near where they now lived. This still happens, but mostly with older Salvationists who have a longer history in The Salvation Army. I am now observing that fewer and fewer young adult and sometimes middle-aged Salvationists do so. As with other denominations, loyalty to The Salvation Army as a denominational affiliation is definitely on the wane, certainly in the West. This trend teaches us that we can rely on such 'loyalty' less and less, certainly with the younger generations. There are too many other options, plus there are the growing number of 'Nones,' people who profess belief or faith in God, perhaps even Christian faith, but do not care to affiliate with any particular congregation.

This marked decline in denominational loyalty is a fairly recent emergence which it would be foolish not to take into consideration in our present discussion. Whatever the institutional observances or non-observances that are the distinctives of a particular denomination, they are less and less likely to be significant factors in keeping a more mobile populace committed to the denomination, especially among younger adults. And it seems to me highly unlikely that non-observance of the sacraments will be a significant factor in keeping emerging generations in The Salvation Army committed to the organization.

This is not at all to say that re-introducing the sacraments alone would bring in new members of younger generations. There must be other factors present (e.g., solid biblical teaching; inspiring, helpful worship; a caring community; effective outreach). It *is* to say that the practice of the sacraments is no longer the contentious issue it once was. There is far greater recognition and acceptance in church circles of different sacramental views from denomination to denomination. People will be drawn to a corps by seeing the grace of God, the compassion of Christ, and the power of the Holy Spirit in action; and if sacramental practice can be beneficial to this end, The Salvation Army should take another serious look at the question.

It is my view that not only would there be no detrimental effects on The Salvation Army's mission, but more importantly, there would be positive results for the mission by observing the sacraments in a way that is consistent with Salvationist theology and the Army's calling. Clearly, where non-observance has been a barrier to some prospective members, that barrier would be removed. Equally, if not more importantly, the sacraments could be practiced in such a way as to culminate in Christ's missional command: in baptism, the newly baptized could be commissioned for discipleship and mission; and in the nurture and sustenance of the Lord's Supper, commissioned to be willing, like Jesus, to give their love and their lives for the world. Participants could be challenged to take the grace and nurture received as not only a personal blessing but also as an enablement to share the blessing with the world. The Salvation Army's early critique of much sacramental practice of that day as too self-centered can be transformed from critique to a different Salvationist baptism and Lord's Supper, sacraments now pointing to mission, practiced by a missional Army.

What about the *theological rationale* for non-observance? It is worth noting that some of this rationale was developed once the decision to discontinue had already been made. This is an important point, as theological justification *after* the point is often forced or even contrived. We must therefore look very closely at the real theological strength, or lack thereof, of these rationales.

The foremost theological rationale began with the obvious fact – at least for those Christians who do not believe that failure to observe some specific ecclesiastical ritual consigns them to outer darkness – that water baptism and/or the Lord's Supper are not necessary to salvation. This premise, correct in and of itself, was then used – and still is – to argue for the acceptability or even desirability of non-observance. To say that something is not necessary, however, is not to say that it is not desirable, helpful, or nurturing. It was not necessary that I marry my wife Keitha, but my life would have been far poorer had I not. To say that the sacraments are not necessary to salvation does not at all mean that they could not nevertheless be a medium of *grace* and enormously helpful for one's *journey* with Jesus, one's development as a *disciple* of Jesus, and one's participation in *the Body of Christ*, his Church. The question for today is whether the sacraments, practiced in a way consistent with The Salvation Army's theology and encouraging for its mission, are now desirable for their potential in providing nurture, strengthening faith, building community, and stimulating the compassion of Christ among Salvationists.

This leads us to look more closely at what the sacraments would mean or signify practiced in the context of, and consistent with, Salvationist theology, and ecclesiology in particular. One of the abuses of some of the churches which The Salvation Army critiqued was empty ritualism. It appeared to many early Army leaders that the sacraments were frequently seen by participants as rituals which in and of themselves bequeathed needed grace (*ex opera operato*), apart from the personal faith of the recipient and without a sincere desire and intention to follow the way of Christ. The convenience of the sacraments was embraced, the inconvenience for what they intended for the life of the recipient was easily ignored and unaccounted. For many, the sacraments of Christ's grace were transposed into sacraments of easy Christianity. Baptism and occasional participation in the Lord's Supper was quite enough.

There can be no question that this was the case for many Christians who received the sacraments at the time of The Salvation Army's beginnings, and it may still be.   On the other hand, there can also be no question that for many Christians the sacraments are transforming means of grace because they approach them with open minds and believing hearts, allowing the palpability of water or a meal, combined with the power of words evocative of Jesus, to signify and invite the transforming and enabling grace of their Lord to continue to perfect them in Christian love. In receiving the sacrament, they look back at who they have been to the present, they turn their eyes on Jesus, and they look forward to who they are becoming and the next step toward it. This is similar to how Salvationists see the mercy seat (kneeling rail) used, usually during an 'appeal' following preaching in a worship service. The question that must be asked, therefore, is whether the mercy seat is equally subject to abuse of its intention.   Can it also become a place of cheap grace – easy forgiveness, emotional catharsis, self-indulgent spirituality, attention-getting, serial confession, and other abuses – instead of costly grace – forgiveness leading intentionally to spiritual and moral change, empowerment leading to progress in discipleship, sanctification leading to love's ongoing perfecting? The answer is a strong Yes! and the experience of any honest observer within The Salvation Army supports that conclusion. The mercy seat itself carries no more innate prophylactic against the worst abuses than do the sacraments. In both cases, the spiritual benefit has to do with a readiness to risk receiving grace and living in it.

In the case of the mercy seat in The Salvation Army, what precedes and leads into the invitation to come forward and kneel is typically the sermon. Its purpose is to provide the context and content for new grace that can be received by responding either through coming forward publicly or through praying privately. To be sure, the appeal may extend beyond the sermon's subject matter, or the worshipper, on his own, may respond with respect to a matter having little or nothing to do with the sermon or appeal but which he himself or the Lord has brought to the moment. Again, anyone who has observed these appeals in Army worship has seen instances of extreme disconnection between the sermon and the appeal, with the appeal being an extremely broad and ever-developing invitation to respond to a range of spiritual needs. Further, it has been observed that some sermons are very weak, and the appeal itself almost a desperate begging or clever manipulation appealing to guilt feelings and low self-esteem. All this to say that the coming forward to kneel and pray at the mercy seat is no less subject to abuse than are the sacraments. It can further be pointed out that this practice of coming forward without receiving the Lord's Supper is a fairly recent development over the course of the Church's 2,000-year history, and The Salvation Army's initiation into membership in Christ's covenant community *without* water baptism is a practice extremely exceptional in the wide spectrum of Christian denominations.   One has to ask: Did God give to this small band of Salvationists, and earlier the Society of Friends, an insight He has withheld from the overwhelming majority of Christians for almost 2,000 years?

One wonders if there is potential theological weakness, or even heresy, imbedded in another oft-referenced theological rationale for discontinuance. I refer specifically to the idea of 'the immediacy of grace.' Here, 'immediacy' goes back to the Latin *immediatus*, comprised of *im* (meaning 'not') and *mediatus* (meaning 'intervening'). It means 'without intervention.' The idea is that in Jesus Christ and through the Holy Spirit, the Christian can access grace without the need of a mediating element or medium and can do so immediately. (I once attended a service in The Salvation Army where the preacher invited the congregation to come forward for 'the Lord's Supper,' which he 'administered' without any physical elements. It was a kind of disembodied spiritual meal.) Such a position represents a dualistic separation or even contradiction between spiritual and physical, which suggests a greatly weakened doctrine of Creation and leans toward a form of gnosticism. As The Salvation Army began as a redemptive mission, it is understandable why its articles of doctrine, though naming God as Creator, do not include a stated doctrine of Creation. (Only in very recent years has The Salvation Army shown interest in the ecology of the planet, and then only in exceptional instances.) In reality, Salvationists *do* believe in the importance of physical media to communicate spiritual reality. The mercy seat itself is a physical thing at which most Salvationists believe it is important to kneel. There are even Salvationists hymns about it. Speaking of hymns, it is worth noting that music is actually physical things vibrating, and most Salvationists have little difficulty in speaking of 'the sacrament of music,' both vocal and instrumental. The Bible and other helpful spiritual books are physical things, even on an iPad! The enrollment of a new soldier and the commissioning of an officer are almost always accompanied by physical things (flag, Bible, uniform, etc.). Most experiences of grace, even by Salvationists, are accompanied and often stimulated by such things as the presence of another person, reflection on Scripture, a poignant event, a group meeting, the witnessing of a spectacular manifestation of God in His Creation, or some other physical stimulation. Those who have meaningful times of personal devotions are usually greatly helped by a familiar physical setting. Very few, if any, are the experiences of grace that are totally divorced from the world around us.

The immediacy of grace, carried to its logical conclusion, requires no Creation, only a disembodied spirituality. It disparages countless means of grace and can encourage a spiritual haughtiness toward those who find great benefit in using certain physical media of grace. I would argue that both logically and experientially there is probably no mediation of grace without a physical medium of some kind. Even the great mystics who are given a profound experience of union with God begin that journey in a specific setting and with tangible means of spiritual discipline. God created the physical world and declared it to be good. He then created humans as *embodied* souls. His intention for humankind at the very beginning is that they embrace the *unity* of their spirituality and their physicality. It is no accident that the Christian vision of life after death is not an unqualified immortality of the soul, but a resurrection of the *body*. As our destiny is not disembodied, so our present life is to be lived by both spirit helping flesh and the physical world becoming conduits of heavenly grace.

We can only conclude, therefore, that all believers, as embodied souls, experience the grace of God in mediated ways. We can do no other because our physicality is inseparable from who we *are*.

From this understanding of biblical anthropology, we can then move on to consider the two sacraments as media or means of grace. We are asking if there would be value in reintroducing them into Salvationist practice. We have discussed the absence today of certain conditions which encouraged discontinuance early on. We have also questioned the legitimacy or applicability of theological rationale used to support the decision. We now consider the value of again opening the door to this sacramental practice.

Interpreting the Sacraments

In order to do so, we must ask what exactly we mean by 'sacrament.' According to the general definition from *The Book of Common Prayer*, a sacrament is 'an outward and visible sign of an inward and spiritual grace given unto us, ordained by Christ himself as a means whereby we receive the same, and a pledge to us thereof.' There is nothing here that is inconsistent with Salvationist theology, which allows of any number of physical things – whether persons, objects, events, music and art, words – that may serve as signs of grace or become mediums through which grace is at work. As we well know, over time the Church developed further interpretations of what the two sacraments actually signified, theological descriptions of what actually happened whenever the sacraments were administered, and exactly how they were to be administered properly in order to be effective. While The Salvation Army would be wrong or presumptuous to deny its debt to church history – or what Wesley referred to as 'tradition' – its own approach to the sacraments issue would be first to explore heuristically the relevant New Testament material, asking the question, 'What is really going on here, what are the persons experiencing?' rather than 'What is the theology that rigidly defines – and therefore confines -- it?' When this investigation has been completed, the next step would be to review the development of sacramental interpretation and practice, in all its permutations, and weigh the merits based on the life, work, and teaching of Jesus.

There is one more issue relative to the biblical material that must be addressed. Some Christian traditions refer to baptism and the Lord's Supper not as sacraments but as 'ordinances' (an authoritative order), and base this preference on Jesus' command to make disciples and baptize them (See, e.g., Matthew 28:19.) and with respect to the Lord's Supper, to 'do this in remembrance of me' (Luke 22:19c; I Corinthians 11:24c). These traditions tend to be uncomfortable with the high-church, mystical theology that has become associated with the sacraments in other traditions. They are convinced that Jesus did not intend to initiate 'sacraments' in that sense. What they see in the biblical accounts is Jesus' command for his disciples 1. to follow as initiation into Christian faith the ceremony used by John the Baptist and submitted to by himself and 2. to remember his sacrifice on the cross for them when they come together as a community of his followers around a meal.

There are two specific questions that must be addressed as The Salvation Army considers these two commands, to baptize and to remember Christ's redemptive sacrifice in connection with a meal. The first is: When Jesus spoke of his disciples baptizing, was he necessarily using the word in the literal sense, thereby requiring a ceremony with water, or in the metaphorical sense (as in 'the baptism of the Holy Spirit' over against literal water baptism), or in both senses? If the latter, is there some defect in not using water where it is readily available? The second question is: When Jesus commanded his disciples to 'do this in remembrance of me,' was he referring to the context of an actual meal (as in this translation: 'as often as you do this [i.e., share a meal together with fellow Christians] remember me.'), to a symbolic meal in the context of a worship service, or to both? If the latter, is there some defect in choosing either the first or the second option alone? These questions must be kept in mind as we now consider contemporary options for The Salvation Army.

Baptismal Practice

What we can say with respect to *baptism* is that Jesus voluntarily identified himself with the human race by submitting to the baptism of John and that this act elicited the heavenly Father's expression of pleasure. We can further say that Matthew records the resurrected Jesus commissioning his disciples to a mission which included baptizing and teaching those who would become disciples through that mission. (Mt. 28:18-20) Whether or not fulfilling that command of Jesus *requires* water baptism is admittedly open to question.

What *is* clear is that the Church from very early on has practiced water baptism as its initiation rite, signaling the 'death' of the old man or woman and the 'birth' of the new through the saving act of Jesus. (Col. 2:12) To be sure, there have been a number of different understandings of the exact meaning of the act itself and the conditions of its efficacy, but practically all Christian traditions and denominations have practiced the rite of water baptism as the sign of conversion and adoption by Christ. The Salvation Army is part of a very tiny minority who do not. Is there good reason theologically for the Army to continue to set itself apart from practically all other Christians on the matter, especially in light of the apostle Paul's appeal to 'preserve the unity of the Spirit' by confessing 'one Lord, one faith, one baptism....'? (See Eph. 4:2b-6, CEB.)

The literal meaning of 'baptize' is 'to dip under water.' Obviously then, Christian water baptism (by immersion) is a powerful metaphor of the old person dying and the new person emerging. Further, it is also a vivid metaphor of the cleansing from sin through God's forgiveness in Christ. Further still, when baptism is communal (a group of converts baptized on one occasion), as it almost always was in the early Church and usually is in most churches today, the power of entering or receiving the water as a community speaks of our unity with one another and with all humanity, as it did with Jesus in his baptism in the Jordan.   When the resurrected Jesus in Mt. 28:19-20 commanded his disciples to 'go and make disciples of all nations' by 'baptizing them in the name of the Father and of the Son and of the Holy Spirit' and also 'teaching them to obey everything that I've commanded you,' there can be little doubt that the baptism he was speaking of was a baptism of the Holy Spirit *expressed through water baptism.* If he had any other expression or sign in mind, there is nothing in the Gospels that suggests it. And if he intended to leave it entirely open to future disciples as to how they would signify or sign or express in ritual this baptism of the Holy Spirit, he gave no indication to that effect.

There is a clear difference between the baptism of John and the baptism 'in the name of the Lord Jesus' which the early Church followed. In the New Testament the baptism of John is described as a baptism of repentance, to be followed by certain life changes. (See Mk. 1:4; Lk. 3:3-14; Mt. 3:1-12; Acts 13:24; 19:4.) It was carried out in the context of John's mission to prepare the way for the Messiah whom he identified as the man Jesus. (See Mt. 3:11; Mk. 1:7-8; Lk. 3:15-16; John 1:6-8, 29-34.)   Later, as the Church was beginning to be established in Ephesus, the apostle Paul explained to the believers there, who only knew 'the baptism of John,' that John's baptism also proclaimed 'the one who was coming after [John], namely Jesus, 'the one in whom they were to believe.' After hearing Paul explain this, the people 'were baptized in the name of the Lord Jesus,' and 'when Paul placed his hands on them, the Holy Spirit came on them....' (See Acts 19:1-6a, CEB)

Using the distinction between John's baptism and the subsequent Christian baptism in the name of the Lord Jesus to seem to support a distinction between baptism by water and a seemingly superior Christian baptism bearing no particular relationship to water is begging the question, given that water continued to be used by Christians from the beginning of the Church. As we have said, the fact that water baptism is not necessary for salvation does not mean there is no great meaning, value, and help in practicing it. The meaning is the cleansing of the soul, the death of the old person, and the birth of the new, starkly visualized. The value is Salvationists standing alongside almost all other Christians on an equal footing with no one needing to defend or rationalize the practice or the non-practice. The helpfulness is in remembering and re-enacting the joyful stories in the New Testament of a water baptism that signed a spiritual revolution, and in receiving the courage to claim and live out the revolution in the same way Jesus did.

There appears to be no theological reason, then, not to rejoin the historic Church of Jesus on this matter, so long as baptism is clearly understood and practiced as a sign of what has happened or is happening in the life of a person through the saving, sanctifying, and transforming grace of Jesus. Furthermore, following the example of Jesus who, though perfect, identified fully with us by being baptized, Salvationists may do well also to humble themselves and place themselves alongside their Savior, with other brothers and sisters in Christ, in the waters of a redeemed humanity.

Significance of The Lord's Supper

With respect to *the Lord's Supper*, whether or not Jesus actually commanded the ritual observance of a Supper, he certainly did not command a 'sacrament' as such. (A Greek equivalent of the word does not appear in the New Testament accounts of the last Supper.) There can be no question, however, that 1. he used the bread and the wine of the last Supper with his disciples as signs or metaphors of his broken body and shed blood for the salvation of the human race, 2. he saw meals as powerful settings for spiritual intimacy and growth, and 3. he wanted his disciples to mark and remember that last Supper. Certain meals are sacred in almost all religions, Judaism had its sacred meals, and Jesus spoke of the Kingdom of God as an all-inclusive banquet. It is not surprising that the early Church celebrated the presence of Christ at their meals together and that as Christianity became accepted by the Roman Empire and worship moved from homes and secret meeting places to public places, the last Supper was incorporated into worship as a poignant and powerful evocation of saving, inclusive grace. It remains so to this day. Various traditions have different views of how the meal can be a means of grace or helpful to participants, but all of them affirm and testify to their value in the life of the Church and the Christian. Salvationists do not have to agree with every interpretation of what 'happens' in the observance of the Supper to find it to be a helpful means of grace and blessing, personally and corporately.

The Salvation Army's decision to discontinue practice of the Lord's Supper was made at a time when the movement saw itself primarily as an evangelistic and evolving social service agency and not as a 'church' as such. Today we would use the term parachurch to describe that understanding. Denominational debates over how the Lord's Supper should be observed and what its efficacy was were seen as theological distractions to the evangelical movement's purpose. Converts were at first referred to churches and chapels for membership and affiliation. When the welcome mat was usually not put out for them, many returned to The Salvation Army. By this circumstance The Salvation Army (reluctantly) became their church home, a church home without the sacraments. As we have noted, early on Salvationists were allowed or even encouraged to visit the churches to take the sacrament if they desired, but over time as non-observance became established policy within the movement, the encouragement ceased, with increasing numbers of Salvationists coming to believe participation was a 'betrayal' of The Salvation Army's position. Over the years The Salvation Army has resisted outright calling itself 'a church' though claiming always to be part of the universal Body of Christ. It has seen itself as a missional arm or expression of the one Christian fellowship on earth, maintaining its 'distinctives,' including non-practice of the traditional sacraments. In recent years, however, there has been a strong movement toward self-identification as a Christian church expressed in official Salvationist publications. (This writer, upon official assignment from The Salvation Army's International Headquarters, wrote an interpretation of The Salvation Army's ecclesiology titled *Community in Mission*, 1986.)

This evolution in self-understanding also raises the question whether re-introduction of the Lord's Supper should be considered. Of the two sacraments the Lord's Supper speaks most powerfully of the Body of Christ and the unity of the diverse expressions of the one Church under one Lord. It also speaks of the eloquent power of grace to sweep away our pathetic, failed works righteousness and offer us the bread and wine of Jesus' finished work, always a more than adequate renewing. Like the nourishment of a good meal the grace received becomes an empowerment to grown as Christ's disciples and serve his compassionate mission. The Supper is made all the more poignant by evoking the memory of that last meal of Jesus with his disciples; and those who participate in the celebration of the Lord's Supper place themselves around that same table and face the same consequences of discipleship.

Holiness as the sacramental life

Finally, it is worth discussing an important theological conviction of The Salvation Army (grounded in Wesleyan interpretations) that has helped to frame a re-interpretation of the idea of sacrament. I refer to the doctrine of sanctification and the call to holy living (or holiness of life). Once the decision was made to discontinue practice of the sacraments, the call to holiness and the experience of sanctification continued to gain increasing prominence. The weekly Holiness Meeting was designated specifically to invite Salvationists to seek 'the second blessing.' Attention was strongly focused on this 'deeper experience' of sanctifying grace, and one could well argue that this seeking of the blessing at the 'holiness table' took the place of coming forward to receive the Lord's Supper. (The holiness table in a SA sanctuary is located at the same place as the communion table in most Protestant churches.)

Over time, some Salvationist writers occasionally referred to holiness as 'the sacramental life,' the idea being that all of life is a sacrament of grace, a celebration of grace in the everyday, and that the Christian is to live his holiness in the world, avoid the dualism of sacred and secular, and seek the presence and grace of God everywhere. The sacramental life means that holiness is grounded in the world. In a sense, the Lord's table was moved from the sanctuary to the streets.

This is not only a commendable view, it is also a profound insight into the Christian life as an undivided journey and discipleship as focused primarily on the Christian's life in the world rather than in church. The question we now ask, however, is whether in The Salvation Army renewed practice of the Lord's Supper would now strengthen, or weaken, this understanding. Could bringing the Lord's table back into the sanctuary weaken its presence in the streets where Salvationists live and serve? Conversely, could it strengthen that presence in the world? It can well be argued that the Lord's Supper could be celebrated in The Salvation Army in such a way as to 1. give Salvationists the opportunity to experience the unity and mutual love of a holy people made possible by Christ's broken body and poured out life, 2. strengthen Salvationists' historic awareness of Christ's redemptive sacrifice for the whole world, and 3. dramatize Christ's calling of his people to sanctification and to the giving over of their lives for a world needing his redeeming love. If the Lord's Supper were observed in this way, it would encourage Salvationists to see their calling to holiness as that call into the world which the early SA took so seriously, and not narrowly as an invitation to a private spirituality. And it would bring Salvationists together as one body united in the outpoured love of Christ, the call to holiness, and mission in the world.

Sacraments in the context of Salvation Army theology

Let us now consider the two sacraments as a whole and ask if their re-adoption would in any way contradict Salvationist theology and if they could actually be practiced in a way that supported and dramatized Salvationist theology.

First, there are the deep Wesleyan convictions of its Founders and the lack of any intent to 'improve' on them. They were not forming some purist sect with new, perfectionist doctrines and practices. They believed they were called to a mission, not a theological improvement project. Their doctrines were Wesleyan throughout and neither mention non-observance of the sacraments nor articulate any specific theological rationale for non-observance. In short, the Eleven Articles of SA doctrine say nothing that would call observance of the two sacraments into question. As we have suggested, the 'theological support' tended to appear as add-ons. There is no inconsistency between sacramental observance per se and Salvationist theology.

Furthermore, Salvationist belief that The Salvation Army is a part of the universal Church and the near-unanimous conviction by Salvationists that The Salvation Army is, in fact, 'church,' 'a church,' 'a Protestant denomination,' continues to raise the question of why The Salvation Army continues to except itself from the almost universal practice of observing these two sacraments which have their roots in the New Testament. The Salvation Army frequently participates in ecumenical events as a Protestant denomination, and SA officers, at least in the USA, are classified as ministers of religion for tax purposes. What is now gained by continuing non-practice of the sacraments? And what is lost, especially if the sacraments can be understood and practiced in ways that enhance Salvationist theology, spirituality, and mission, while avoiding implications that are not helpful or even acceptable?

General John Gowan's description of the three purposes for which The Salvation Army exists has resonated with Salvationists around the globe. It seems to capture the whole of the Army's mission. The Salvation Army exists, said Gowans, to

- save souls,
- grow saints, and
- serve suffering humanity.

Could the practice of baptism and the Lord's Supper inspire, strengthen, and reinforce that mission? Could the visibility of a washing, the symbol of death and resurrection powerfully evoked by immersion, the participation and identification with Jesus' own baptism in the Jordan, and submission to this testimony to conversion by millions of Christians since Jesus' time, reinforce the convert's awareness of the power of his salvation through the grace of God? Could the ingestion of bread and 'wine' as a powerful metaphor of spiritual sustenance and needed grace for the journey, and the encouragement of the community gathered around the table, a family united by the Holy Spirit as one Body in Christ, strengthen the nurture and growth of saints in The Salvation Army? Could the radical change symbolized by baptism point to a life now devoted to serving suffering humanity? Could the welcoming hospitality of an inclusive Lord's Supper encourage the least and the lost to find their way home to the family where they belong? I firmly believe the answer to all these questions is 'Yes'.

Let us then project how this could take place in a way to help to undergird The Salvation Army's mission, enrich Salvationist theology, and fan the flames of mission.

Possible steps for implementing the re-introduction of baptism and the Lord's Supper in The Salvation Army

For the foregoing reasons, it is worthwhile for The Salvation Army to engage in open-minded conversations about the desirability and benefit of practicing the two Protestant sacraments. Making such a change in ecclesial practice after 130 years of non-observance is no small matter, and the decision should not be taken without realistic consideration of how best to take advantage of the opportunities and address the obstacles. Furthermore, the consternation and grief of Salvationists who oppose such a step and see it as a violation of an important part of their heritage as Salvationists – and for some, even as an outright betrayal of that heritage – must be taken seriously and treated with utmost respect and sensitivity. Fortunately, in this proposal nothing is put forward that takes away anything essential; rather, something is added that is voluntary.

How the issue is discussed, debated, and prayed over, and a final decision reached at the international level is crucial. One possibility is for the General (advisedly at the beginning of his or her term) to appoint a study group comprised of Salvationists who are effective officers and lay leaders, competent thinkers, and persons with strong biblical knowledge and conversant in ecclesial and Salvationist history. The study group gives its report and recommendations to the General within a year, before a meeting of the International Leaders Conference where the report then comprises the lion's share of the agenda.

Following the Conference, the General further considers the study group's report and recommendations, and the recommendations of the ILC, further consults and engages him- or herself in prayer over this important matter, and then reaches a decision. If the decision is to open the door to voluntary practice of the sacraments, the General appoints a group to assist him or her in developing rationale and guidelines for practice of the sacraments in SA corps, as well as guidance for territorial and divisional leaders. These are then presented to another International Leaders Conference.

The matter of implementing the change at the local level is crucial. To begin with, not only must participation be voluntary, but great care taken to eliminate attitudes of spiritual superiority on the part of both participants and non-participants. One way to do this is to make sure all words spoken by the officer administering the sacrament are applicable to non-participants as well as participants. None of the words spoken can be construed to exclude non-participants from receiving the grace referenced in the baptism or the Lord's Supper. There are other ways, as well, to enable non-participants to be full participants. The inclusive SA must never practice the sacraments in ways that exclude anyone, and very clear guidelines about inclusion will be given to every officer and lay leader.

Let us now consider the matter of *how* to implement practice of the sacraments. Attempts to implement in a peremptory fashion would be insensitive and would ignite unnecessary conflict. There should be no great hurry to implement across the board. The sacraments should be observed only where there is readiness.

The first important step is to *educate the entire SA world* about The Salvation Army's openness to the practice of the sacraments in ways that are consistent with Salvationist theology and mission. Assurance would be given that Salvationists have *a choice* about their own participation and that any Salvationist can participate in a sacrament in The Salvation Army even if he or she does not take the physical elements at the Lord's Supper or is not immersed in or sprinkled with actual water at baptism.

The next consideration would be *regional differences*. My own conversations with officers from around the globe reveal that in some regions the majority of Salvationists are strongly in favor of the sacraments, in others Salvationists are more divided, and in others there seems to be either little interest in the matter or definite resistance to sacramental practice. As participation would always be voluntary for Salvationists, once the decision and the rationale behind it are announced and thoroughly disseminated, sacramental practice would be left to individual regions for implementation in ways sensitive to the prevailing attitudes of Salvationists in that region and in individual corps. Orientation and training of officers takes place at every level:

divisional commanders at TEC and corps officers and other field officers at either territorial or divisional officers councils.

The biggest challenge is implementation in individual corps, especially where views are divided over the matter. In every corps, of course, there is a period of orientation and study, so that every Salvationist has the opportunity to learn and have questions answered with respect to both the rationale and the benefit of the decision to make the sacraments available to Salvationists who wish to avail themselves of this opportunity. At the conclusion of this time of study, the corps holds an extended prayer meeting, inviting Salvationists to search their own hearts, seek God's will, and come to some clarity about where they now stand with respect to their personal participation in the sacraments. The meeting concludes with united prayer for the unity of the corps around the call of Christ.

In corps where the majority wish to participate physically in the sacraments, implementation can take place following the above process, with care taken to assure those who choose not to receive physically that they are full recipients in the grace shared by all present. The ceremony addresses *everyone gathered*, and of course the invitation to be present for the sacrament is extended to everyone.

In corps where only a minority choose to participate physically in the sacraments, implementation is more complicated. As the decision has been made internationally to allow the sacraments to be practiced in corps, those who wish to participate, even though a minority, have the right to the sacraments. In most of these situations, however, it is unwise to include the sacraments in regular public worship services (holiness meetings, e.g.). It might well be seen by the majority as an insensitive disregard of their own convictions, even making them feel like outsiders. A better strategy is to conduct a separate worship and prayer service centered on the sacrament. There could be a Service of Rebirth centered on baptism and a Service of Christ's Table centered on the Lord's Supper. Again, no one is excluded, everyone is invited. If, over time, receptivity to the sacraments evolves into a strong majority in that corps, then the sacrament can be included as part of some regular public worship service.

In corps where there is no support whatsoever for including the sacraments in the life of the corps, even after the international policy allowing voluntary participation has been explained, rationale reviewed, and benefits outlined, the corps officer will not allow sacraments to be practiced in the corps, so long as non-practice is the wish of every member. The convictions and wishes of the whole congregation will be respected.

Possible general guidelines for practice of the sacraments in The Salvation Army

These or similar guidelines could be taught as part of the training program for cadets and continuing education for officers, and clarified whenever a sacrament is administered:

Guidelines for practicing the sacraments
- Sacraments will be administered for reasons of need, desires, and appropriateness, not as part of a required liturgical calendar, thereby preserving the freedom so characteristic of Salvationist worship as affirmed by the International Spiritual Life Commission (1989). When the sacraments become institutionalized as part of a liturgical calendar, they can easily lose their radical nature and purpose.
- It must be said whenever the sacraments are celebrated in The Salvation Army that the sacrament itself has no spiritual efficacy or power apart from the openness and risk of the person receiving it. The grace of God (by whatever means conveyed) may come quite unexpectedly as a surprise or even a shock. At the same time it does not force itself upon an unwilling recipient. The invitation to come to the sacrament is an invitation to those who, while they may be hesitant or uncertain about the outcome, trust what God may do.
- There is no prescribed formula or sequence or order for the celebration of the sacrament. Certain essential words will be spoken, referencing the sacrament to particular New Testament texts, but there will be no set liturgy. It may be that a resource book of different approaches and wordings will be provided.

Guidelines for practicing baptism:
- It must be stated that water baptism is a sign and seal of a covenant the initiate (or recruit) has or is making with God through redemption in Christ, forgiveness of sins, and regeneration and sanctification by the Holy Spirit. The water baptism is a visual, vocal, physical enactment of the person's death to sin and rebirth with Christ, celebrated by followers of Jesus from the very beginning of the Church to the present.
- Salvationist theology and no clear evidence in the New Testament of a command to baptize infants would, of course, require that baptism signify a choice consciously made by the person. In The Salvation Army infants would continue to be dedicated in a special ceremony where the child's parents, family, and the faith community commit themselves to nurture the child in love and discipleship training.
- It must be said clearly that this baptism is an event that testifies to a changed life and way of living. It signifies the launching of a new journey in a different direction. The old man/woman has died, and the new man/woman is alive and well in Christ. Baptism does not stand alone! It points to a radical change of life that *must* prove itself in the days and years following. In this sense, baptism must include a *commissioning for discipleship and mission*. There are

different ways this can be indicated as a part of the baptismal event. And in response to the commissioning, each person can be asked to testify to a particular voluntary life change he or she is commencing. And/or a spiritual guide and accountability partner can be identified during the event. The baptism must testify to both a benefit received and a sacrifice made, a costly grace, or it will be a mere ceremony, a custom.

- The matter of how water baptism is administered to the initiates (total immersion or sprinkling) can and probably must be left to individual corps or locales. (Sprinkling may be the only alternative where a large enough body of water or a sufficiently large immersion container is not available.) Of course, totally immersion is the more powerful visually in terms of death and resurrection.

Guidelines for practicing the Lord's Supper:

- It must be stated that as baptism is the sign and seal of a covenant a person has made with God, the Lord's Supper is an invitation to *remembrance*. It is first and foremost a remembrance of *Jesus*. Specifically, it is a remembrance of his sacrifice for our salvation, which he himself symbolized at his last meal with his intimate company of disciples. Importantly, it is a remembrance not only that we are saved and sanctified but also sustained and nurtured by this grace, experienced palpably in a holy meal presided over by the grace-giving Jesus and open to all. As Jesus symbolically shared his broken body and shed blood with his twelve disciples, so he shares himself with his entire Church, binding all Christians together in this wide circle of grace. When a corps experiences the Lord's Supper, they experience their unity with one another and the whole Church in the grace of Jesus. (The love feast of the early days of The Salvation Army was designed as a reconciliation meal. It never was practiced that often or universally. Could it be the reason it never really 'took' was that it had no strong, explicit tie to the reconciling work of Christ as in the Lord's Supper, and it was usually conducted when there was an obvious 'problem' of broken relationships in a corps that needed addressing. Perhaps the Lord's Supper would help far better in resolving unity issues in SA corps by nurturing an *ongoing* atmosphere of grace and a reliance on the presiding presence of Jesus.)
- The elements of the Lord's Supper, bread and the juice of the grape, are specifically used because they replicate the bread and wine used by Jesus at that last Supper, and the remembrance is thereby made palpable. The words of Jesus are repeated (Mk. 14:22-25; Mt. 26:26-29; Lk. 22:19-20) to associate the actions of the Lord's Supper (eating the bread and drinking the wine) with the supreme sacrifice of Jesus for the world and with the saving, sanctifying, enabling grace received through it. Also, Jesus' command to use meals together as a way to remember this and to testify to the whole world can be recalled. (I Cor. 11:23-26) The elements are helps to remembering and as such can be vehicles of grace if the participant is open to receive. They carry no efficacy in and of themselves.

- The Lord's Supper is inclusive and open to all, those who take the elements and those who do not. It is also a way of using all the senses in proclaiming the gospel. Roger Green points out that Wesley opened the communion rail to the sinner as well as the saint. The Lord's Supper practiced in The Salvation Army can actually be a means of leading persons to faith.

10. 'They devoted themselves to the apostles' teaching…'[1]

Discipleship and Learning in a Salvation Army context

Alan Harley

The Salvation Army – A Discipleship Movement

'The ministry of the New Testament is silent about education. Learning is scarcely mentioned…'[2] So said Bramwell Booth in 1899. Eleven years earlier Samuel Logan Brengle had been rebuffed by the Founder on the grounds that he was of 'the dangerous classes.'

On the face of it these comments suggest an opposition to learning on the part of early Salvationist leaders. Closer examination, however, reveals something different.

Bramwell Booth's words appear in a chapter written by him on the training of officers. His concern was that the first task of a training programme was to make disciples. In that same chapter he described a typical day at the Clapton Training Homes. The 6.45 a.m. bugle call was followed by a packed day of in-class lectures and practical training, including a 6 p.m. oral examination of the day's lectures, and at 8 p.m. a one-hour lesson in 'Arithmetic or similar subject'. This intensive regimen lasted for five months and was basic training which could hold its own with that of other non-conformist and evangelistic bodies of the time. Bramwell's philosophy of training was simple: everything was with the view to producing disciplined, godly disciples of Christ. He wrote:

> I am far from depreciating the value of the book-teaching which goes on (at Clapton). It is all good, and so also are the drills, the regular habits which are formed, the instruction in the great facts and doctrines of the Bible, the singing, and speaking, and public-house visiting, the dealing with the sick, the fighting in the streets, the praying with people in the dark, dark slums and homes of filth and vice – it is all good, it is all proper to equip the men and women of God for their great work in the future, and without it they would often be of very little use, but it is not what I am thinking of just now as being the *great* work done in the Training of our Officers, the results of which I have been observing at every point of the compass for a quarter of a century. That work is rather

---

[1] Acts 2:42
[2] Bramwell Booth, *Servants of All,* (London: The Salvation Army, 1899), 52

the work done in the very warp and woof of their nature, in the essential qualities which make what we understand by character – *in the training of the heart.* [3]

Mind and Soul

Brengle's initial encounter with the Army needs to be put into context. What the Founder said to him was 'You belong to the dangerous classes. You have been your own boss so long that I don't think you will want to submit to The Salvation Army. We are an Army, and we demand discipline.'[4] While there may have been some disquiet regarding candidates with university training, Booth's stated concern was to assure that those whom he recruited embraced the disciplined life of a Salvationist soldier.

That Booth was anything but anti-intellectual is evidenced by his grand vision in 1903, when he prepared a *Proposal for a World University for the Cultivation of the Science of Humanity in Connection with the Salvation Army.* Roger Green describes what the Founder had in mind:

> Booth simply did not find the training of officers or soldiers sufficient to meet the needs of the world and his expanding Army. Therefore, he envisioned the establishment of a university 'having its main Wings in England and the United States, with affiliated Colleges throughout the world, and to provide it with Officers of every rank capable of supplying the training needed for the discharge of every variety of work at present engaged in by The Army, or in which it may feel called upon to engage in the future.' He envisioned that training would be given in four areas: evangelistic work, missionary and medical work, social work, and departmental work including instruction in medicine, engineering, architecture, accounting and auditing, finance, and editorial and literary work. To Booth, this would include a broad educational training in what he called 'the science of humanity.' [5]

Such was Booth's vision: a Christian university unlike anything in the world – particularly within evangelicalism. At the same time the early Salvationists were evangelical pragmatists. Education for its own sake held little appeal to them. What was needed was 'boot camp' training to equip young men and women – in as short a time as possible - for the war against sin. But in so saying it needs to be noted that while university training was the norm for Church of England clergy, such was not generally the case within the nonconformist community. The Methodist New Connexion which prepared William Booth for ministry is a case in point. In 1861 the Connexion's annual Conference resolved to develop 'a training institution for the preparation of

---

[3] Booth, *Servants of All*, 52, 53
[4] Eric Court, *The Brick and the Book,* (London SP&S, 1960)
[5] Roger Green, *The Life and Ministry of William Booth,* (Nashville, TN Abingdon, 2005), 209

young men for the ministry.'[6] It became a reality in 1864 and in 1880 it had nine students and one tutor.[7] Booth had by that time founded The Salvation Army and thus missed out on this provision. He nevertheless received a good introduction to theology under the New Connexion's earlier 'apprenticeship' programme. In 1854 he was enrolled as a student of Dr William Clarke, who taught the principles of sermon preparation, grammar, logic, writing, Elementary Greek, Latin and moral philosophy.[8] He found academic work hard-going but there is no evidence that he adopted an anti-intellectual attitude as a result. Indeed, Booth's high regard for John Wesley would make such a stance unlikely. Wesley himself once received a letter from a devout correspondent who told him, 'The Lord has directed me to write to you that while you know Greek and Hebrew, he can do without your learning.' To this Wesley replied,

> Your letter received, and I may say in reply that your letter was superfluous as I already know that the Lord could do without my learning. I wish to say that while the Lord does not direct me to tell you, yet I feel impelled to tell you on my own responsibility that the Lord does not need your ignorance either. [9]

His Brother Charles endorsed this principle in a hymn written for the opening of the school at Kingswood:

> Unite the pair so long disjoined,
> Knowledge and vital piety;
> Learning and holiness combined
> And truth and love, let all men see. [10]

Another has written

> Christianity and scholarship comprise two sides of the same coin of God's truth. A Christian commitment reminds the scholar that all truth ultimately comes from God, while scholarship cautions the believer not to descent to superstition or fanaticism. These commitments do not preclude, but rather supplement, each other. [11]

---

[6] George John Stevenson, *Methodist Worthies,* (London Thomas Jack, 1884), 62

[7] It is noteworthy that during this same period The Salvation Army had some three hundred cadets and a regular training staff of twenty five officers in residence at Clapton (Bramwell Booth, 51)

[8] Green, *The Life and Ministry of William Booth,* 68

[9] A. Leonard Griffith, *God and His People, (*Methodist Church of Australasia, 1960)

[10] *A Collection of Hymns for Use of the People Called Methodists*, Hymn 461, in *The Works of John Wesley, (*Oxford: Clarendon, Press, 1983), Vol. 7, 644

[11] Smith, Robert, *Christ and the Modern Mind,* (Downers Grove, IL: IVP, 1973), vi

Booth agreed. The Lord did not need ignorant disciples. The call was for sanctified officers and soldiers – possessors of vital piety - who knew what they believed. Hebrew and Greek may not be required, but a pure heart and knowledge of sound doctrine were. In an address to officers at a Council of War in 1876, Booth instructed his hearers,

> Teach your people. Teach them sound doctrine; if you do not give them the *truth*, somebody else will give them *falsehood*. The best method of keeping the weeds out of your garden is to stock it well with good, useful plants, and I know no better plan to prevent the devil and ignorant, mistaken teachers sowing the seeds of error in the minds of your people than to anticipate them with sound scriptural doctrine. There are three old-fashioned practical truths which you must frequently and emphatically insist upon. They may be regarded as three pillars which mainly carry the entire building of experimental godliness; and if your people are thoroughly grounded in these, they will not be easily moved. They are REPENTANCE, FAITH and HOLINESS. [12]

Knowledge and Piety

In truth the Army was established on the principle of discipleship. Few denominations have made the same demands upon their constituency. Booth's co-workers were termed 'soldiers'. Discipline and devotion were set forth as the marks of soldiership – the type of discipline and devotion spoken of by Jesus whenever he talked of discipleship. This gave a sharp focus to the type of training implemented by the early Salvationists. Booth established his training programme at a time when Bible institutes were springing up around the English-speaking world. Many were created to counter the teachings of Darwinism, Higher Criticism and 'Modernism'. Others existed to promote or repudiate the nascent Pentecostal movement or to disseminate Dispensationalism. None of these matters were of much concern to the Salvationist educators. Their task was to equip people for the holy war by firmly establishing them in the core evangelical and Wesleyan truths of repentance toward God, the life of faith, and holiness of heart – each of which represents a key component of New Testament-style discipleship. Discipleship language was not prominent in the writings or the preaching of early Salvationist leaders – a fact probably true of other evangelical preachers and teachers of the same period – but the essence of discipleship was set forth in a profound and clear manner in the writings, teaching and sermons on holiness and the 'holiness' songs produced by Salvationist authors. Directory classes were implemented to catechize the children. Company meetings, Junior and Senior Soldiers' Preparation Classes and Corps Cadets all had as their objective the making of disciples Jesus and soldiers of the Army. All had well-prepared teachings tools written and produced by the Army. A succession of editions of

---

[12] *Salvationist Soldiery,* (London: John Snow, 1889), 68

the *Handbook of Doctrine* has appeared, in each instance providing Salvationists with solid, biblical expositions of their beliefs. Instead of 'morning worship' the Holiness Meeting was created, with a view to instructing believers in godly living. The disciplined life demanded of Booth's soldiers reflected that demanded by Christ of his disciples (e.g. Luke 9:23). This was the life into which the cadets at Clapton were introduced with the view to such a life being the outstanding quality of their future lives and ministries. Indeed what emerged was something remarkably akin to that of the discipleship found in the Book of Acts. E. E. Kellett wrote of 19th century Nonconformity:

> Those who dwell on its narrowness and darkness can never have seen, as I have seen, humble privates of the Salvation Army, after being beaten, stoned, or otherwise maltreated, then punished by magistrates for their sufferings. The faces of these martyrs, as I can personally bear witness might be scarred with wounds, but they shone with joy. [13]

It is worth noting that Booth's approach to training produced a movement passionately evangelistic and Bible-based while at the same time not embracing an excessively conservative doctrinal stance. It steered clear of the debates which birthed Fundamentalism in the early 20th century and did not get caught up in subsequent internecine evangelical battles such as the more recent and ongoing inerrancy of Scriptures debate. Indeed, its position regarding women in ministry and the sacraments marked it out as a movement quite different from Fundamentalism both in theological outlook and biblical understanding. It is unlikely that the Archbishop of Canterbury would have suggested to William Booth that the Army become part of the Church of England[14] had he seen the young movement as heretical or extremist.

The doctrinal standards compiled in the fledgling years of the Army, and to which Salvationists still subscribe, embrace a Nicene position on God and the Trinity ('three Person in the Godhead'), a Chalcedonian doctrine of Christ ('truly and properly God and truly and properly man'), a Reformation view of the Scriptures ('they only constitute the divine rule of Christian faith and practice'), an evangelical Arminian view of grace[15] ('an atonement for the whole world'), and a Wesleyan understanding of the Christian life ('the witness in himself', 'wholly sanctified'). To this the movement added a Quaker understanding of the sacraments. In other words it was committed to a theology which was nuanced, ecumenical, orthodox and evangelical and which would

---

[13] Quoted by Kenneth Young in *Chapel*, (London: Eyre Methuen, 1972),224
[14] Green, *The Life and Ministry of William Booth*, 140 - 145
[15] I use the adjective 'evangelical' to distinguish Wesleyan/Salvationist Arminianism from that of 17th century Laudian 'Arminianism' and that understanding of Arminianism, widespread amongst its detractors, which is in essence Pelagianism. Some Wesleyans and Salvationists may have lapsed into Pelagianism, but their respective movements acknowledge God as the prime mover in a person's salvation. For them, as with Calvinism, salvation is 'all of grace.'

provide material to challenge the sharpest theological minds both then and on into the future.

Patterns of Discipleship

Booth's vision of a company of Christians whose lives were marked by discipline and holiness and committed to the saving of souls reflected the heart of the New Testament. He wanted to do more than make converts; he sought to make men and women into soldiers of Christ. For him true Christianity was synonymous with discipleship. In this he undoubtedly was correct. Jesus did not command his apostles to 'go and make converts' but to 'make disciples' (Matt. 28:19). It is to this principle that we now turn.

Joachim Jeremias suggests that Jesus sets forth his pattern of discipleship in terms of (1) a new motive – love, (2) the sanctification of everyday life and, (3) a loving understanding of the poor which is marked by renunciation of possessions.[16] These were the very qualities which made Booth's Army distinctive. They were expected of every officer, and were the foundation for all that was taught to the cadets. God's soldiers were to live a life marked by love to God and to all. They were to experience God's sanctifying grace in every part of their lives. They were to live a life of self-denial and service to others.

Further, these qualities constitute an accurate description of the character and life of Jesus. When Jesus called men to follow him with a view to their becoming his disciples, it involved their following his teaching, his leadership and his example (Matt.4:19; 8:22; 9:9; Mk. 2;14; 8:34; 10:21; Lk. 9:59; Jn.12:26). As George Eldon Ladd says, 'Discipleship to Jesus involved far more than following in his retinue; it meant nothing less than complete personal commitment to him and his message.'[17]

Donald Bloesch says, in distinguishing an evangelical understanding of discipleship from that of the monastic, '… discipleship is interpreted not in terms of withdrawal from the world into a cloister but of wounded servanthood, bearing the cross in the midst of the agony of the world'. [18]

Such an understanding reflects the nature of Christ's call to discipleship. But it represents a development of the original meaning of 'disciple'. The basic meaning of 'disciple' (*mathētēs*) is 'a learner' (from *manthanō*, to learn). In the papyri it was used of an apprentice, e.g. of a physician, a weaver or a flute player.[19] One papyrus refers to a young man who 'is regular in attendance at his studies (*mathēma*), for he is eager in acquiring

---

[16] Joachim Jeremias, *New Testament Theology*, (London SCM Press, 1972), 211- 213
[17] George Eldon Ladd, *A Theology of The New Testament,*, (Grand Rapids, MI: Eerdmans, 1994), 106
[18] Donald G. Bloesch, *The Essentials of Evangelical Theology*, (San Francisco, CA: Harper Collins, 2006), Vol. 2, 53
[19] *Theological Dictionary of the New Testament*, (Grand Rapids, MI: Eerdmans, 1967: Vol. IV, 416.

knowledge (*mathēsin*)[20]. In the New Testament it is used of those who follow a teacher (*didaskalos*). Once it speaks of the disciples of Moses (John 9:28).

Prior to the calling of Christ's disciples, John the Baptist gathered disciples around him. (Matt.22:16). John was a *didaskalos*. Among other things he taught his disciples how to pray (Luke 11:1). Jesus was recognised by the authorities as a *didaskalos* (Jn. 3:2). Indeed he is seen as 'a teacher sent by God'.

The term gained a heightened meaning when used by Christ in reference to his followers. He said, 'This is to my Father's glory, that you bear much fruit, showing yourselves to be my disciple' (Jn. 15:8, NIV).

Mathētēs is widely employed of those who followed Jesus (Jn.6:66; Lk.6:17), including those who followed in secret (Jn.19:38). Jesus invited people, 'come to me ... take my yoke upon you and learn (*mathete*) of me' (Matt.11:29).The Twelve Apostles were styled 'disciples' (Matt.10:1; Lk.22:11; John 20). The term is employed in speaking of those who would continue to follow Christ's teachings (Jn.8:31). In Acts it designated those who placed their faith in Christ and bore testimony to him (6:1,2,7; 14:20, 22, 28; 15:10: 19:1, etc.) In other words, there appears to be a development it the meaning of 'disciple'.

In Judaism 'disciple' (Hebrew: *limmud*) was used only of men. It was held that 'religiously women are on a lower level and cannot give themselves to the work of learning and teaching.'[21] In the New Testament, however, we read in Acts 9:26 of Tabitha, a female disciple (mathētra). In Acts 19:26 we are told that Priscilla and Aquila teaching the things of God to Apollos, with Priscilla being mentioned first.

By the time of the Acts there was little place for 'secret disciples'. Such a term would by that time be deemed an oxymoron. But this development in meaning actually took place in the ministry of Jesus. He said to those who believed him 'if you hold to my teaching, you really are my disciples' (John 8:31, NIV). His disciples, he taught, were those who not only aligned with his mission but who followed his example (Jn.8:31; 15:8). He taught them by what he said, by how he ministered to people, and by how he lived. Discipleship and learning thus are inextricably linked. And the result of this is a transformed life - a life which 'bears much fruit' (Jn. 15:8).

John Wesley and William Booth understood this. For them to be a Christian was to follow a path of devotion, discipline, cross-bearing and holiness. The rules which they wrote for their people, some of which today sound quaint[22], were their way of reminding their people that they were not called merely to a new form of religious commitment but to a total 'life-style' – something which affected every part of their being. The movements which

---

[20] J.H. Moulton and G. Milligan *The Vocabulary of the Greek Testament,* (Grand Rapids, MI: Eerdmans,1930), 385
[21] *The Vocabulary of the Greek Testament,* 433
[22] These include such counsel as the type of undergarments to be worn, the number of inches for keeping the bedroom window open, etc.

developed under their leadership demanded more of their people that sound doctrine, church attendance and good behaviour. They were to be disciples, in the full New Testament sense of the word. Thus Christ's commission was to 'make disciples of all nations .... teaching them to obey everything I have commanded you" (Matt.28:20, NIV). It was not enough that Christ's disciples *believe* everything he had taught; they were to *obey* every command he had given. To bring this about, the apostles were instructed to teach those whom they discipled. That this instruction was not confined to the apostles is made clear by the fact that a similar command is later given to Timothy (2 Tim.2:2).

Further, it is clear that New Testament discipleship is more than teaching and learning; it is all about vital relationship with the Teacher. Dietrich Bonhoeffer wrote,

> Discipleship means adherence to Christ, and, because Christ is the object of that adherence, it must take the form of discipleship. An abstract Christology, a doctrinal system, a general religious knowledge on the subject of grace or on the forgiveness of sins, render discipleship superfluous, or in fact they positively exclude any idea of discipleship whatever, and are essentially inimical to the whole conception of following Christ. With an abstract idea it is possible to enter into a relation of formal knowledge, to become enthusiastic about it, and perhaps even to put it into practice; but it can never be followed in personal obedience. Christianity without the living Christ is inevitably Christianity without discipleship, and Christianity without discipleship is always Christianity without Christ. [23]

Further, New Testament discipleship, as Bonhoeffer implies, has to do with all Christians. At times the impression is created that the true disciple, the truly dedicated person is the one who becomes a Salvation Army officer. A young person in the corps who shows exceptional commitment to the Lord and the Movement is so often encouraged to apply for officership. But surely the Lord wants Spirit-filled and totally dedicated men and women who are accountants, school teachers, bankers, mechanics and politicians. In the same way he wants that every member of a local corps be just as dedicated as the spiritual leader of that corps. The Reformation doctrine of the Priesthood of all Believers does away with Grade 'A' and Grade 'B' Christians and says all are called to full-time service, regardless of their occupation. This is not to denigrate officership but to elevate discipleship in the whole of life and in the entire Body of Christ.

Teaching and Discipleship

In this regard, teaching and discipleship have not always gone together. Some teaching has actually pointed away from the discipleship yoke to which Jesus

---

[23] Dietrich Bonhoeffer, *The Call to Discipleship,* (New York, NY: Macmillan 1965), 63,64

called his followers. In second century work, *The Teaching of the Twelve Apostles (*the *Didache)* it is stated that 'if you can bear the whole yoke of the Lord, you will be perfect; but if you cannot, bear what you can.'[24] That such truly reflects the teaching of Christ's apostles is to be questioned. Jesus taught that to qualify as a disciple a person must be willing to turn his or her back on family and home, carry a cross, and give up everything (Luke 14:25 – 33). Through the course of Church history there runs a narrow stream of men and women who sought to bear 'the whole yoke.' Franciscans, Puritans, Pietists, Methodists and Salvationists stand in that 'apostolic succession.' Their terminology may have differed according to their history and tradition, but their aim was the same – to produce disciples of Christ. They sought to pursue the path of holy living and obedience to their Master, and their respective movements produced teaching materials designed to assist others to do the same.

In order to be a disciple-making movement, one which is committed to making every one of its members a disciple of Jesus, it must have in place the kind of training which equips future spiritual leaders for that task. Before creating a training programme its objectives and end-product must be determined and made clear. This implies that some, but not all of the methods of earlier times will now be appropriate or effective. It further suggests that different movements have different needs and thus develop their own distinctive training programmes. This was clearly the case when the Clapton Training Homes programme was created. It was focussed sharply on producing disciplined and godly soldiers of Christ who would be able to carry out the onerous tasks of an officer of The Salvation Army. Since that time training methods have changed – as has the role of an officer[25] - and the initial vision modified to suit the changing nature of the Movement.

Theological and ministerial training institutions have tended to fit into one of four categories, with some overlapping, with the following objectives: (1) Some institutions, particularly within the Bible college tradition, have majored on the cultivation of Christian character. For such the spiritual life of the student is paramount. Men and women attend such a college in order to deepen their knowledge of God, cultivate their Christian character, increase their knowledge of the Scriptures, and all with a view to becoming a true disciple of Christ. (2) Others exist to the teach their denomination's confessional standards, This is the model favoured by churches which give priority to their doctrinal position as set forth in a statement such as the Westminster Confession of Faith. Those enrolled in colleges within this model

---

[24] Edgar J. Goodspeed, *The Apostolic Fathers, (*London Independent Press, 1950), 14

[25] This is evidenced by Bramwell Booth's description of a typical week in an officer's life (*Servants of All*, 88-90). Each day began at 7 a.m. with non-stop activities until late in the evening. There was no provision for free time, family time, or days or evenings off. Nor, it must be noted, was there significant provision for prayer, Bible study, and sermon preparation, even though meetings were held each night of the week. Happily, this was gradually modified.

have as their objective the mastery of their church's beliefs with the view to instructing others and of defending their doctrinal standards. (3) For others, the development of a professional ministry is paramount. Colleges in this stream see the ordained minister as a professional person, and are thus committed to equipping future clergy as such. The Doctor of Ministry degree emerged largely within this context. Those who offer and those who attend these university-style training programmes have in mind a ministry governed by high professional standards and competence. (4) The *raison d'etre* of others is the training of missional workers. Their prime commitment is to mission and service. In these, men and women train for practical ministry which is based on biblical foundations. The focus here is less on reflection and research than on training for a 'hands-on' ministry.

Each of these is a worthy model for theological education. It would seem that a well-rounded training programme will reflect all four. Indeed, that is probably the case in most instances, at least within the context of accredited theological and ministry training. Few, if any, exist to offer only one area of speciality.

Future officers need to be shaped by each in order to be grounded in the Christian life, their Movement's doctrines, requisite skills for their ministry, and a firm commitment to and understanding of the Movement's mission. The first and the fourth of these seem to fit clearly into the early Army's training philosophy. It could seem that, while not standing within the confessional tradition of the Reformed and Lutheran churches, a clear need exists for officers to be well trained in their Movement's distinctive theology, with its Nicene, Chalcedonian, Arminian, Wesleyan and Quaker components. Above all, officer training should be with a view to developing a discipleship lifestyle and discipling skills in those who are to be commissioned to make disciples.

The churches of the western world have, over the past half century or so, undergone major changes. Membership has diminished, as has church attendance. Ways of worship are in some instances unrecognizable when compared to the largely unchanging style of earlier generations. The community's respect for the churches and the clergy has waned dramatically. Most denominations face a shortage of clergy and dwindling applicants for theological training. And what is true generally is true specifically for The Salvation Army. In the 1950's and earlier, the Movement boasted many more soldiers and officers than now – probably twice as many in western countries. It arguably was the most colourful of denominations, with some of the world's finest brass bands, well trained songster brigades, huge Congresses, Divisional Holiness Meetings, Open Air meetings, street marches, and uniformity not only of dress but of worship style. With its own insurance company, musical instrument manufacturing plant and publishing house, immigration schemes, hospitals and children's homes and the like, it was a formidable force in society. Little remains of these activities. For some, this means great loss. All that made the Movement what it was a half-century ago spoke of a style of Christianity in many respects now a distant memory. Bishop Gerald Kennedy once said of American Methodism, of which he was a leader, that his denomination was so well organized that the Holy Spirit could depart completely from its midst and no would notice. It is not just the cynic who says something similar regarding the Army in the heady days of the mid-century. Not that it lost its way. People were still being converted and many Salvationists were leading godly lives. But some of us who grew up in that era were conscious that something was missing. Perhaps it was the busy life of the corps officer – a life which made it difficult to develop strong biblical teaching and preaching; perhaps it was, as some have said, that many of us were 'band-saved'. Perhaps it was that the Movement itself was so colourful, so rich and satisfying in so any ways that the very features which made the Army great became for some a substitute for true discipleship.

But that is not the whole picture. It would have been easy for the Army to drift into something far removed from its original moorings and to have become a company of nominal Christians with a liberal leadership or a philanthropic organization with no significant Christian commitment. But these things didn't happen. And they didn't happen because even in those much-criticised days there were in every Territory officers and soldiers firmly committed to saving souls and to holy living. The type of discipleship spoken of by Joachim Jeremias: discipleship marked by love-motivated service, the sanctification of the whole life, self-denial – were much in evidence. Through the entire history of the Movement there has been a succession of godly and wise leaders at the highest levels. There has been an unwavering loyalty on their part to the Movement's doctrines. Today there is a strong, renewed commitment to the preaching and teaching of holiness of life and the publication of books and materials promoting such a life. Seminars and conferences are convened for the purpose of equipping people to be disciples.[26] Around the world there are multitudes of young people who are not overly interested in playing in the band but who are passionately committed to being disciples of Jesus. These things may not constitute revival, but they are encouraging signs of renewal in the ranks. The need is for well-equipped teachers who can assure that the zeal of these young disciples is matched by their knowledge. At the same time, as more and more officers pursue higher academic studies, it needs to be said that in their case knowledge must be matched by zeal if their studies are to have value in terms of their calling. It seems reasonable to suggest that where possible, officers should be encouraged to study with institutions within the same general theological tradition as their own, take courses which will deepen their grasp on their denomination's doctrinal position, and encouraged to write theses which are of direct value in terms of their faith and their ministry. There is little point is spending a great deal of time and money in obtaining a degree which either has no bearing on one's ministry, calls into question the doctrines of one's denomination, or in the

---

[26] An example of this is *Roots,* teaching and worship conferences in the United Kingdom.

long run prepares for service in another church. Nor is there much point in having officers who can explain to their people the fine points of the Documentary Hypotheses, the number of people it took to write Isaiah, or the views of *avant garde* theologians, but who cannot teach from Scripture the basic principles of discipleship and godly living.

For both teacher and student the knowledge required for disciple-making is that set forth in Scripture, and to this end the great need is for officers and others who know the Bible and are able to communicate its teachings. Disciples in the mould of those in the Acts of the Apostles are made by the Word of God and prayer. Methods are subordinate to these. Without this Bible-based approach, even the most zealous disciple is vulnerable to alien teaching. As stated previously, the Eleven Doctrines represent a mainstream, evangelical understanding of the Christian faith, whereas a great deal of the popular material available in Christian bookstores stands outside this tradition or reflects a position other than that of the Doctrines.

Surely, those called to be officers are of that number whom the Lord has placed in the church as 'pastors and teachers.' These are to care for and to teach their people with the view to 'equipping God's people for the work of ministry.'(Eph.4:11,12).

These pastors/teachers will need solid training in their movement's theology and in the principles of biblical exegesis. Cadetship itself will be seen as an experience of serious learning and discipleship training. The making of saints and scholars (i.e. professional scholars) will not be its primary objective (although some surely will eventually become such) but the developing of saints and students – disciples of Jesus with a commitment to a life-long study of Scripture and doctrine will be. The result of such training will be men and women who live as disciples and servants of the Word in their respective appointments. Their task will be to make biblically and doctrinally literate disciples in those appointments. In the times of reformation and revival when the Church has been called back to its apostolic roots and rediscovered a new vitality in the Holy Spirit, this type of learning, and this type of discipleship, have been at the heart. This can be true once more. It can be true of 21st century Salvationism. It will keep the Army from becoming a quasi-religious charitable organisation or a religious body which has lost its theological moorings. Our calling, to re-phrase Wesley, is to 'unite the two so long divided, learning and vital discipleship,'

11. 'Let us come before him with... music and song'[1]

Communicating the Gospel Message through Music in 'Traditional' Salvationist Worship

Ronald W. Holz

Introduction

Music has always been a strong component of the Salvationist mission to spread the Gospel of Christ to the 'whosoever.' Music ranks in many ways as the most recognizable aspect of The Salvation Army's unique form of Christian worship. In this essay I purposefully limit the discussion to the role of music and musicians in Salvationist public worship services. In doing so, I do not mean to lessen the importance and role of worship, and music, in other aspects of a Salvationist's life. All that we do may be considered, in essence, worship. However, here we will examine 'traditional' Salvation Army music past and present in three broad categories: 1) congregational song; 2) choral music; 3) brass band repertoire. These will be briefly studied in the context of their purpose within the following forms of public worship side by side with a very short survey of the development of this sacred repertoire in the context of Salvation Army 'meetings': Sunday services or meetings, including the older demarcation between the morning Holiness Meeting, the evening Salvation Meeting. It is not my intent to provide an apologetic for the existence of traditional music sections and their music literature in this short essay, as I have written extensively on that subject in other projects.[2]

Salvation Army music sections also offer concerts, or festivals, and some continue in many locations to hold outdoor evangelistic services, what used to be called the Open Air. The size and scope of this article does not allow for more than tangential treatment of these aspects of Salvation Army evangelism and worship. Likewise, in terms of specific musical repertoire that has developed for Army music sections, in this chapter I focus on music written for Army brass bands and choirs (Songster Brigades).

---

[1] *Psalm 95:2*

[2] For a comprehensive discussion of SA music past and present, see Ronald W. Holz, *Brass Bands of The Salvation Army: Their Mission and Music, Volumes 1 and 2*, (United Kingdom: Streets Publishers, 2006, 2007). Volume II contains a detailed bibliography dealing with most aspects of SA music and music history.

Congregational song, and the close connection between the development of the *Song Book of The Salvation Army* and music for Salvation Army sections, will also be given a central position.[3]

Since its earliest days, Salvation Army worship services have been loosely structured. Starting in the early Christian Mission, they have mostly taken their lead from the form of the Wesleyan Song Service: Song - Testimony/Scripture Reading – Prayer – Song - Testimony/Scripture - Song/Collection - Vocal Solo - Bible Address - Invitation/Invitational Song – Dismissal/Benediction. The number of songs sung, witnesses given, and other components, including the worship order, were left to the ingenuity of the leader. In many ways that is still the case, though as the Salvation Army became more sectarian and its' music sections emerged, and a supportive repertoire grew, the new components added to the worship did not essentially change this *potpourri*, or string of pearls format.

General Frederick Coutts (General 1963—1969) explained this unstructured approach to worship in an essay on Salvation Army meetings. 'No-one is more free to be led of the Spirit than he who is responsible for conducting a Salvation Army meeting. There is no liturgy which he must follow'.[4] Officers are cautioned, however, to pursue careful coordination of any music and song with the general tenor or theme of the service. For years, however, the only basic requirements for an Army meeting, aspects that should, or must be present, were a prayer, a bible reading, personal testimony, congregational singing, and a Bible address.[5]

William Booth began his Christian movement in an effort to reach the unconverted and the socially outcast within Victorian England. Booth's message stressed Redemption for all through Jesus Christ. He consciously avoided liturgical 'form' in his meetings. Those traditional church sacraments that were part of early Army meetings were eventually discontinued. We are intentionally non-sacramental, non-liturgical, but we have added our own 'rites' and certainly our own yearly calendar that only occasionally aligns with the traditional church calendar. Certainly the Salvation Army follows no lectionary! The Open Air meeting served to attract outsiders to the two main indoor services on Sunday, and, in early eras, on multiple weeknights. Neither the Open Air, the freest of Salvation Army services in which the band essentially makes loud, entertaining sounds in order to attract attention and maintain interest, nor the indoor services followed any consistent organizational plan. This is somewhat the case even in present-day meetings, except that certain practices have now, after six generations, become fixed in the generally non-liturgical 'liturgy' or format of Army meetings.

---

[3] The best overview of SA song and choral music is still Brindley Boon, *Sing the Happy Song: A History of Salvation Army Vocal Music*, (London: SP&S, 1978).

[4] Frederick Coutts, *In Good Company*, (London: SP&S, 1980), 133

[5] *Orders and Regulations for SA Officers*, Part 2, Chapter 3 (London: SP&S, n.d.), 45

William Booth, Song and Music

William Booth in a preface to a song collection called *Salvation Music Volume 2*, published December 1883, just two months after establishment of the Salvation Army's first music department, stated the following: 'The Salvation Army must always be singing new songs whilst it continues to win new victories. Old songs will not do where there is plenty of new life'. He and the Army embraced the boastful imperative of the psalmist to 'sing unto the Lord a new song'. From its' earliest days the Salvation Army has been basically obsessed with encouraging and acquiring new songs. For Booth, singing by a 'congregation' was a major element in his evangelism. In choosing any song, a good melody was also key for him. In 1877, as 'General Superintendent' of the Christian Mission, Booth delivered a remarkable address on 'Good Singing' published that year in the *Christian Mission Magazine* that contained the essence of his practical approach to music.

> [I have] ever found choirs to be possessed of three devils, awkward, ugly and impossible to cast out. They are the quarrelling devil, the dressing devil, and the courting devil, and the last is the worst of the three. . . . Merely professional music is always a curse and should you ever find a choir in connection with any hall in this mission, I give you my authority to take a besom [broom] and sweep it out. Promising that you do so as lovingly as possible. You must sing good tunes. Let it be a good tune to begin with. I don't care much whether you call it secular or sacred. I rather enjoy robbing the devil of his choicest tunes, and, after his subjects themselves, music is about the best commodity he possesses. It is like taking the enemy's guns and turning them against him. However, come whence it may, let us have a real tune, that is, a melody with some distinct air in it, that one can take hold of, which people can learn, nay, which makes them learn it, which takes hold of them and goes humming in the mind until they have mastered it. That is the sort of tune to help you; it will preach to you, and bring you believers and converts.

Notice that in this same address he attacked organized musical groups, especially choirs, essentially telling his leaders to avoid using anything that resembled traditional, sacred music making. While by 1878 he began to allow a role for brass bands in outdoor evangelism only, gradually permitting them indoors for the Sunday evening service, it took him till 1898 to sanction the formation of choirs, or songster brigades.

 Throughout his years of leadership Booth greatly encouraged congregational singing and the composition of new songs. He contributed several notable ones himself, such as 'O Boundless Salvation,' and 'O Christ of burning, cleansing, flame'. He would feature soloists and small singing brigades or 'parties', but these should not be confused with established choirs. Congregational song gained priority place in Booth's practical use of music. It took decades for him to allow the fuller participation of what we now consider 'traditional' sections in Salvation Army worship. Richard Slater, the 'father' of

Salvation Army music, once wrote the following that sheds light on the gradual 'evolution' of the movement's formal music:

> As to our Brass Bands, The Founder was keen and wise enough to perceive their value as revealed by facts. Although he did not personally gain much pleasure or help from them in his meetings. He never used a Brass Band in his meetings but to accompany singing, although in the latter part of his life he permitted them to play while audiences assembled, but then only from a list of pieces made out by the Music Dept. at his request, of Salvation music such as would be in place in a Sunday night's meeting.[6]

It is for this reason that this discussion will first focus on the growth of Salvation Army song, and then continue with an examination of the growth of Salvation Army music for bands and choirs in the context of the use of such materials in Salvation Army worship.

The Song Book of the Salvation Army

As this chapter is being completed the Salvation Army intends to release a new edition of its' *Song Book*, in conjunction with the summer 2015 'Boundless' International Congress. Booth's Christian Mission, as it was called by September, 1869, grew large enough by the early 1870s for Booth and his wife, Catherine, to compile several hymnbooks: *The Christian Mission Hymnbook, Hymns for Special Services, The Penny Revival Hymn Book*, and *The Children's Mission Hymn Book*. By 1876 *The Christian Mission Hymn Book* contained 531 standard hymns, spirituals, and songs set to popular and national tunes, a combination that would be main sources for decades to come. Early song choices naturally first came from other denominations' hymn and songbooks, and gradually we have added to it so that with each succeeding edition of our *Song Book*, the percentage of songs by Salvationists has increased significantly.

The current English language *Song Book of The Salvation Army* (1987; Revised edition) contains 962 songs and 251 choruses, words only, the exception being in the American—Canadian edition that contains a *Supplement* with 30 songs with music, 2 with text only. The keyboard edition, *The Salvation Army Tune Book* contains the music for 871 tunes plus music for the 251 choruses. Our congregations usually see only words, and songs may be sung to a variety of tunes. That we are still going to print a words-only *Song Book* is a highly significant matter—despite Booth wanting good melodies, words count most.

---

[6] Richard Slater, *The History of Salvation Army Music, Part II: Instrumental Music*, unpublished manuscript housed in SA Heritage Centre (UK, London), 22

The Salvation Army *Song Book* has had and continues to have a vibrant history of growth and change. The first official, full-size congregational songbook, entitled *Salvation Army Songs*, was printed in 1899 along with the release of a companion instrumental tune book entitled *Band Music No. 1*. Three further editions of these primary sources were issued in the 20th century. The first appeared in 1928-31, the second, in 1953 (with supplementary song collections and *Tune Books* released in 1963 and 1978), and the third in 1987.

In between editions of our *Song Book*, new congregational songs and choruses have been released on a steady, consistent basis in such periodicals as *The War Cry*, the choral journal *Sing to the Lord* (formerly titled *The Musical Salvationist*), or especially in recent decades, gleaned from a host of other outside Christian publishers. The fast-changing nature of Salvationist worship is shown in the significant number of so-called contemporary "praise-and-worship" songs and choruses that will appear in the new edition. I point out that the greatest surge in such songs into Army worship came just as the 1987 edition entered wide use. As a result, music departments were swift resource Salvation Army musicians and congregations with accompaniments of contemporary songs. Two notable examples are the USA Central Territory's *Hallelujah Choruses* and the British Territory's *Scripture-Based Songs* series.

While still a majority of songs and tunes in our *Song* and *Tune Books* are derived from standard Western church hymn and Gospel song traditions, with each successive edition, a larger number of them are the original work of composers and poets who are or have been members of the Salvation Army. In the only published study of this facet of our *Song Book* that I know of, William Metcalf, author of the *Concordance to the Songbook*, found that the change went from as little as 5% of the songs in 1899 written by Salvationists, to 15% by 1930, then doubling, or approximately 30% by the 1953 edition.[7] My rough estimate for the 1987 edition is about 38% of Salvationist origin. In our earliest days, say before 1880, we only had 5 new, truly 'Salvation Army' songs, but soon the floodgates opened, so that in the various song compilations—not the congregational *Song Book*--of the 1880-90s, a great, explosive period in Salvation Army song, the range was as high as 90% in the 1880s and just under that in the 1890s. Almost all of that would have been 'solo song' items, not congregational, nor choral.

Songbooks almost by definition must be compilations 'after-the-fact.' They will contain songs that have gradually entered into Salvationist worship within the time period since the last edition. The 1987 edition, for example, contained a good number of songs from Gowans—Larsson musicals that became congregational in the period 1965--1985, at first unofficially or adapted from choral settings in *The Musical Salvationist*. Similarly, 'pop' songs by Major Joy Webb, for example, gradually received official blessing via various

[7] William Metcalf, "The Pattern of Song in Our Development," *The Officer* (XVI, 7, July 1965), 483-487

types of settings. Interestingly enough, despite the gradual inclusion of Salvationist songs, by far the largest single hymn writer in the 1987 edition is the 18th-century lyricist Charles Wesley, with some 60 songs. However, a strong connection has developed between songs and choral pieces written by Salvationists that have gradually been accepted as congregational, suitable for all to sing.

As one of the primary responsibilities of Salvation Army bands is to accompany congregational singing, it is not surprising, therefore, to find that the Army's hymn and song literature is the basis of all its instrumental music. All Salvation Army brass music makes reference in the course of its development to a hymn or song text through complete or partial quote of a melody associated with that text. Only classical transcriptions and certain rarities in the *Festival Series* are exceptions from this policy. The first twenty years of published band music in the Army, 1883—1902, consisted solely of hymn tunes, Gospel songs, and transcriptions of vocal works from the organization's principal vocal publications, primarily *The Musical Salvationist*. This was a direct order of the General William Booth. It was intended to limit musical performance to items with a clear message, or textual basis. All Salvation Army music is, therefore, referential music, music that refers the listener beyond the notes to spiritual ideas and concepts. For the Salvationist, soldiers or officer, the *Song Book* becomes a central tool for both private devotion, and corporate worship.

One of the key roles of the Songster Brigade after 1898 was to introduce new songs, especially those written by and for Salvationists, to the soldiery or congregation. In this way many fine songs first appeared in mixed voice settings within the *Musical Salvationist*, then eventually became part of the *Song Book*. This process could take a considerable number of years, the transformation of a choral song to congregational song sometimes taking many decades. What I stress here is that there arose a tight relationship between the music sections of the Salvation Army and the growth and use of new songs with a particular Salvationist stamp. This blossomed side by side with not only the development of a sophisticated choral and instrumental repertoire but also with the more specifically sectarian appearance and practice in Salvation Army 'forms' of Sunday worship.

A Division in Salvationist Worship Services

Salvation Army modes of worship continue to undergo significant, even radical change. The traditional bifurcation between Holiness and Salvation Meetings that developed in the first three decades of the 20th century has been blurred, or changed, with many corps having to adjust their times for and styles of worship in ways that can still attract people to the Army hall. In order to understand, however, the broad development of Salvation Army music suitable for use on indoor worship services a more detailed look at the traditional types of services in which music sections gradually were called upon to participate in is essential.

If early Army worship sometimes resembled a musical hall entertainment, or was marked by 'spectacle,' by the turn of the 20th century Salvation Army worship began to take on a certain shape for which the immerging music written for Salvation Army sections would play a larger and more important role. Salvation Army worship became more 'refined' if not highly structured, and a division was made between services aimed inwardly at the already converted and services designed as overt evangelism. In this way the Salvation Army unconsciously embraced an old division that dates back to the earliest days of the Christian church where within the developing Mass a split was made midway between part 1, *Synaxis*, in which the non-baptized could participate and be instructed in the Word, and part 2, *Eucharist*, the celebration of the Lord's Supper for baptized believers only.

Fred Brown once gave a clear, official clarification of the difference between the two principal Sunday worship services that gradually took shape in the first few decades of the 20th century.

> The morning gathering [Holiness Meeting], primarily for Salvationists and adherents (though it is still a public meeting), could be called a holy community service. Not that the people who attend preen themselves with a "holier than thou" look upon their faces, but their motive is the worship of God and the sincere wish to learn more of scriptural holiness. They assemble, not because they imagine themselves righteous, but because they want to offer to Almighty God the sacrifice of their love and thanksgiving.
>
> The night meeting [Salvation Meeting] is for the proclamation of salvation to the unconverted, nothing more and certainly nothing less. Self-evidently the two meetings should be completely different in character: broadly speaking, one is for saints, the other for sinners; one devotional (even sacramental), the other evangelical; one deepens faith, the other seeks to communicate it; one is for the offering of worship to God; the other for the offering by the same worshippers of Christ to the people. [8]

Up until World War II, in most Salvation Army territories, the brass band and songster brigade participated in any outdoor Open Airs, evening Salvation Meetings, and intermittent Praise Meetings held on a Sunday, not only by accompanying or encourage the singing but also by providing separate instrumental or choral musical items of a direct, familiar nature to aid in the

---

[8] Fred Brown, *The Salvationist at Worship* (London: SP&S, 1950), 69-70. See also Richard E. Holz, "Music and the Arts Among the Churches: The Salvation Army." *The Complete Library of Christian Worship, Volume 4, Music and the Arts in Christian Worship*, (Nashville: Star Song Communications, 1994), 245—247. Additionally, Richard E. Holz, "A Salvation Army Model of Worship." *The Complete Library of Christian Worship, Volume 2, Twenty Centuries of Christian Worship.* (Nashville: Star Song Communications, 1994), 70—73

corporate worship. In the morning Holiness Meeting of the not too distant past, if the band or choir was permitted to participate other than in a short prelude and, for the band, by accompanying the opening song, the music chosen was usually of a more devotional, meditative, and thought-provoking nature. More recently, many territories have provided broader guidelines in their *Orders & Regulations* allowing for fuller participation. However, in many corps, if any prelude item was given, the group or groups were then seated in the audience, with keyboards only used to accompany further singing. In America, it must be noted that bands and songster brigades began to offer on a regular basis specific musical items during the Holiness service in the period directly following World War II, while this did not take place elsewhere until considerably later, especially in the UK.

The Origins of Brass Band Music Suitable for Use in Worship

The Salvation Army commenced publishing its regular *Brass Band Journal* in 1884, a scant six years after the first Salvation Army 'band' – the Fry family quartet – heralded salvation on the streets of Salisbury. By this date there were over 500 corps in the UK alone, with at least 400 of them having some kind of 'brass band.' For six years they had been using music from a range of British publishers. This included hymn tunes, street marches that featured a hymn, and even some of the more extended selections with a sacred theme that were available at the time. Many of the bands also relied on local arrangers, who scored out tunes, tailor-made for each unique combination. Within a year, 1885, the Army felt comfortable enough to demand that their bands play only music printed by the organization. Autocratic control soon replaced the improvisation that had fueled the rapid growth of bands within the emerging movement. That control was needed for a variety of reasons, several of which related to the inappropriate use of music by bands at various Salvation Army gatherings.

From 1884 through 1901 Salvation Army band music had to be based on a vocal model, whether an existing hymn tune, gospel song, or a transcription of SA vocal music appearing in *The Musical Salvationist* or *War Cry*. Starting in 1901 William Booth agreed to permit the use of band music for which no words had been composed or intended. Richard Slater, head of Music Editorial, and 'father of Salvation Army music' was then given further latitude, subject to conditions, for decisions regarding instrumentation, arrangement, and compositional style. Three basic forms emerged, from which others developed: the meditation, the selection, and the march.

The first 'Selection' for Salvation Army band, *Old Song Memories*, made its debut in the January 1902. In a selection the arranger combines two or more songs around a given subject. These can be devotional or praiseful in mood and style. In the meditation, the more serious, demanding musical form akin to the Baroque chorale prelude, the composer illustrates successive verses of one song or hymn to project a highly personal, spiritual message. The march functioned both outdoors and indoors for the obvious purposes of attracting attention and rallying the troops. Out of these three basic forms came a diverse series of musical forms especially for use in concert settings: tone poems, suites, festival arrangements, instrumental solos, variations, and more.

A prototype hymn meditation, *Jesus, Hope of Souls Repentant*, was released in February 1902. The first Salvation Army March, *The Morning Hymn March*, appeared in April. From these early efforts an impressive sacred literature gradually emerged for Salvation Army brass bands unmatched by any other Protestant denomination. Behind it all, however, was General Booth's caveat about avoiding 'idolatry' in the use of music with the Salvation Army's mission. He once expressed it this way just one year (1900) before he opened the floodgates to new musical practice:

> . . . you must be careful not to over-estimate its importance [Salvation Army band music] or come into bondage to it. Music, in itself, has neither a moral nor a religious character. This can only be imparted to it by the thoughts or feelings of the soul when under its power. That is to say, if music is to have any holy, any Divine influence on the hearts of those who listen, it must be associated with holy feelings and with Divine thoughts. It is this that makes good singing more important to us than the grandest music the Band can play, unless accompanied by the singing of words calculated to carry home its appeal to our hearts. [9]

Primary Functions for Bands and Songster Brigades

Since at least the remarkable 1916-17 Commission of Inquiry during which the Salvation Army took a very detailed look at its musical practices, the Salvation Army has formally stated three primary functions for each of its key musical ensembles.[10] For the brass band, these may be summarized as follows, as drawn from the 1998 *Sing and Make Music: Orders and Regulations for Music Organizations in the USA* [duplicated in other countries and territories]:

    1. "Attracting people to the meetings" [both indoors and outdoors]
    2. "Accompanying the singing thereby helping and enriching it"
    3. "Conveying, by association of ideas, salvation messages direct to the heart of hearers."

The Songster Brigade exists primarily for the following three functions:
    1. "Singing to the people. Soul-stirring words articulately and

---

[9] William Booth, "All About the Local Officer—Singing," *The Local Officer* (III, #8 March, 1900), 181-182

[10] For further discussion of this important event in SA music history, see Ronald Holz, *History of the Hymn Tune Meditation and Related Forms in Salvation Army Instrumental Music in Great Britain and North America, 1880—1980*, (Ph.D. Dissertation, University of Connecticut, 1981), 32—35. A facsimile of the final report, and a summary of recommendations, actions, and achievements emerging from the Commission of Enquiry appear in the appendices of this dissertation, 212—235

musically presented, provide an effective means of worship."
2. "Singing with the people. By doing so, the vocal groups stimulate congregational efforts of the best kind..."
3. Introducing new Army songs and choruses...vocal groups should launch new congregational songs and choruses." [11]

Of course, corps music sections take on many other tasks in addition to these fundamental functions. Bearing in mind these essentials, however, is helpful when reviewing how Salvation Army musicians mainly 'communicate the Gospel message.'

Taking Stock—One Recent American Example of a Salvation Army Worship Service

It seems appropriate to now provide an example of a recent Salvation Army worship service in which traditional music sections played a major role, and embraced their 'functions.' The corps, Atlanta Temple, Georgia, USA, has a brass band of about 31 and a songster brigade of approximately 30 members. The bandmaster (Robert Snelson) and songster leader (Daniel Meeks) are members of the corps Worship Committee that meets with the corps officer each week in shaping the service order. These music leaders are in close communication with their officers, Captains Kenneth and Amy Argot, regarding the focus of each service, choosing music appropriate to the topic or theme of the service, or in some instances, series of services.

Atlanta Temple now holds but one service on a Sunday, so that this service must become, in essence, a blend of the old Holiness and Salvation Meetings. To put it simply, the service must feed the saints while reaching out to the sinner. The corps is following the Salvation Army's international call to read and study the New Testament during 2015, *The International Bible Reading Challenge*. Captain Argot has been shaping his sermons and the themes of each service along this trajectory provided by the Salvation Army, but one he is not required to follow. On February 22, 2015, the focus was on the nature of a true spiritual cleansing, and the scripture chosen for particular attention was Mark 7: 1—23:[12]

---

[11] *Orders and Regulations for Music Organizations in the USA* (Alexandria, VA: The Salvation Army, 1999), 2. Functions for both bands and songsters detailed here and in successive portions.
[12] Phil Layton, Rachel Castle, and Tracey Davies, *Boundless—The Whole World Reading The International Bible Reading Challenge*. Pamphlet produced in 2014 by SP&S, Ltd, for use throughout 2015.

Service Outline 22 February 2015

Prelude by Band (Two short hymn tunes)
Words of Welcome by the Corps Sergeant Major
Circle of 10—Short time of Informal Greeting for all gathered
Call to Worship: *Power in the Blood* (arr. Nicholas King) by Songsters
Congregational Song: *All Creatures of Our God and King*
        (using Festival Fanfare *St Francis* by William Himes) SB 2
Short Video on Lent
Prayer Song: *Holy Ground* (Piano and Praise Band accompaniment)
Pastoral Prayer
Service of Giving, with Offertory by Band, Meditation--*Gift for His Altar* (Leslie Condon)
Congregational Song: *Whiter than the Snow*, SB 459; organ and piano
Message: "Wash Your Hands" – Mark 7: 1—23 Captain Ken Argot
Altar Call Solo Song: *Nothing But Thy Blood* (Richard Slater—Donna Peterson) Heather Goodier, soloist
Closing Song: *In Christ Alone* (*Hallelujah Chorus* brass band accompaniment by Williams Himes)
Benediction
Short Postlude by Band—final section of *In Christ Alone*

Music <u>almost</u> dominates this service, though the sermon is indeed the focal point. There are four congregational songs, two accompanied by the band in more extended settings. The corps Praise Band (singers, keyboard, bass guitar, drums) handles one song, while 'traditional' keyboards another. Two songs have been drawn from the *Song Book*, one an older, 'outside' worship chorus ('Holy Ground'), and one is a reasonably contemporary, non-Army hymn-anthem, *In Christ Alone*. This is typical of the Salvation Army blending its own song repertoire with other appropriate sources (old and new), as well as a blend of musical styles, in this instance, from symphonically shaped hymn accompaniments to rock-style backings. PowerPoint projection of texts makes for good singing and for careful 'referencing' when songs are not taken from the *Song Book.* PowerPoint projection also allows associated texts of band items, like Leslie Condon's meditation on successive verses of Slater's song 'I have not much to give Thee, Lord' to be 'streamed' during the offertory. Bands realize very few in the audience know such an old song! The songster item revives in a modern setting an older American Gospel song, as does the solo sung during the 'appeal' or Altar Call, Donna Peterson's update of Slater's 'Nothing But Thy Blood'.

On any other given Sunday, the Praise Band might take on more of the song accompaniments, and all the music sections. 'traditional' or otherwise, covering various, changing spots as detailed by the Worship Committee. Granted, this is a larger corps with many resources, but the model shown here is one that has been developed and followed in traditional English-speaking

Salvation Army for decades. The congregation is highly involved in the worship, and music sections enhancing, <u>not</u> dominating, the scene. The congregation is diverse in age, socio-economic status, and ethnic background— quite the challenge for the Worship Committee.

Such a brief review could be duplicated across the globe. The degree to which Salvation Army musicians succeed in enhancing mission through what they offer in worship is directly tied to their choice of music <u>and</u> the word/idea associations connected with any particular piece of music. For the songster brigade, the task is an easier one, a matter of selecting quality music in a variety of styles, for they sing the words. For the brass group, the task is more daunting, for the bandmaster can no longer assume any cultural consensus among any given 'congregation' or audience, no previous knowledge of hymn and song texts.

A Brief Reflection on Brass Band Repertoire Suitable for Salvation Army Worship

By the second decade of the 21st century the Salvation Army had provided its brass bands nearly 10,000 individual pieces of music, from the humblest hymn tune to the most sophisticated symphonic variations or tone poem. The choral repertoire is even larger. Speaking to the hearts and minds of listeners becomes, however, a great challenge. So much of our best quality band music is deeply meditative, thought provoking, requiring a fully engaged listener. A classic like Dean Goffin's *The Light of the World*, a beloved musical portrayal of not only a hymn text ('O Jesus, Thou art standing outside the fast closed door'), and also illustrative of the famous 19th-century painting by William Holman Hunt, would now only connect with most audiences by the addition of PowerPoint projection of the painting itself, with hymn texts interspersed. One can't or shouldn't give a 10-minute spoken explanatory introduction to a 6-minute meditation. Similarly, Erik Leidzén's great sermon in sound, *The Call*, once a quintessential example of evangelical appeal through music, needs texts provided. It may move an audience member on just an emotive level, but can they follow the sequence of the songs that leads to a *stretto* of pleadings from the first song, "Come With Thy Sin," ending with the great question that must be answered as the music fades, "what will your answer be?"? Only the middle tune might still have some slight connection to the average audience member— "Softly and Tenderly Jesus is Calling." This five-minute musical 'appeal' can still effectively prepare a congregation for the Gospel message. However, the bandmaster should carefully weigh the *why-how-when* issues in consultation with the speaker and those that shape the service.

While attracting attention with up-tempo music of whatever style (brass bands perform many styles as well as just about any musical medium) will be easier to supply (both indoors and out), it is the music with a direct evangelical appeal that is not only wherein Salvation Army composers have created an amazing achievement and repertoire, but also presented the bandmaster with the greatest dilemma. Salvation Army band music tends to be strongest in highly personal, reflective music, especially in the meditation and the more serious selection. Salvation Army song encourages this, for so many effective Army songs are highly personal, 'I' focused, rather than the corporate 'we.' In this, the Salvation Army joins the long line in Christian hymnody that balanced what the Lutherans in the Baroque era called the *Ich Lied*—the subjective 'I song' -- with the corporate voice of praise and supplication ('Now thank we all our God').

So our best music stands polarized, excellent in the extremes: upbeat, sophisticated festival--concert features and marches versus quiet, contemplative offerings. I have always thought that in the latter category, the well prepared Salvation Army band meditation or selection can become a 'sacramental' moment within Salvation Army worship. Some consider this experience almost, but not quite, akin to 'Communion.' Numbers of pieces leap to mind for this, starting with Arthur Gullidge's selection *Divine Communion* or Wilfred Heaton's masterful meditation, *Just As I Am*. However, lest idolatry loom, better that the best Salvation Army music for serious worship be more akin to what J.S. Bach might have offered on any given Sunday within one of his cantatas that served as the introduction to, the musical meditation upon what would be more elaborately discussed in the lengthy sermon to follow that same morning!

A Brief Reflection on Choral and Solo Song Music Suitable for Salvation Army Worship

If the choir's role and task in choosing appropriate music for proclaiming the Gospel message are much more straightforward, we should consider that what the songsters sing can have a profound influence on not only the immediate tenor of a given service, but have a lasting impact on congregational practice. One brief example may suffice, Oliver Cooke's 'I know a fount where sins are washed away' (SB 257). The song dates from 1922, appearing as a choral setting in the April 1923 *Musical Salvationist*. It did not become part of the *Song Book* until the 1987 edition, though sung congregationally, especially the chorus, for decades before. Cooke tells of being frustrated one day at work when sorting on his accounts, not being able to correct some mistake. To clear his mind, he took a short bus ride, during which the text for the famous chorus came to him. By the end of the trip he had added words for the first two verses. Later at home he added the music, plus two more verses.[13]

Cooke provided a quintessential Salvation Army song, one filled with evangelical fervor and appeal—'Say are you weary...'. The message is unequivocal, and the imagery, the fervent appeal to the lost, right down our alley, so to speak. It would also provide the source for a profound piece of

---

[13] Gordon Taylor, *Companion to The Song Book of The Salvation Army* (London: SP&S, 1989), 161

Salvation Army brass music, Dr. Thomas Rive's *Variations on 'I Know a Fount,'* itself very much more than a 'concert' work for musical and technical display. So many other examples of Salvation Army songs that are doctrinally sound and enrich Salvation Army worship could be cited. Many continue to be updated stylistically, as in Marty Mikles' and Phil Laeger's resets a few years ago for the Salvation Army rock group Transmission of both 'I Know a Fount' and Stanley Ditmer's 'I'm In His Hands'. The best songs are inspired (Holy Spirit-filled) and transcend their age and the initial circumstances in which they emerged.

Still Proclaiming the Gospel to the Whosoever? [14]

I recall a category on the evaluation sheet used for many years when the USA Eastern Territory's Music Council rated brass band music for its *Band Music for Evangelism* band journal: What is the potential and strength of this music to reach the proverbial 'the man on the street?'[15] Even as our music became more and more sophisticated, our musical groups in some locations almost of professional level, perhaps we were becoming less and less effective in proclaiming a clear spiritual message to the general public. We played more and more to ourselves, our own narrow conclave, though no doubt doing much good in encouraging those still fighting the Great Salvation War in the trenches. Stirring up the troops while maintaining evangelical thrust is always the challenge, plus we have been prone since our earliest days to confuse entertainment and worship—an old problem!

Our music sections must face a multi-cultural congregation and public with sensitivity and spiritual insight. We no longer debate the intrinsic merits of traditional brass bands and choirs versus electronically driven Praise Bands versus 'ethnic' instruments in our diverse congregations. All can be positively and effectively used for the extension of the Kingdom. Paramount will be how best to communicate the character and message of Jesus Christ in any given social and cultural setting.

A new openness is needed in Army worship and evangelism so that cultural baggage can be removed to allow true ministry to take place. This could and should prove helpful as more reflection takes place concerning the mission of Salvation Army music sections and the music and musical styles chosen for those tasks. The Salvation Army faces many other, graver concerns besides the state of their music program. The Salvation Army needs its brass bands and songster brigades, but in recent years the focus, the priorities have been placed on spiritual, educational, and theological renewal first. If anything, the success of the Salvation Army music program in whatever dimension it is

---

[14] The issue of the relevance of musical ministry by SA bands in particular is addressed in more detail in Ronald Holz, *Brass Bands*, Volume I, Chapter 10, "Function, Mission, and Music in the Future of SA Bands."
[15] A facsimile of this form, a recently revised version, can be found in Ronald Holz, *Brass Bands*, Vol. II.62

examined is one of the great achievements of the Salvation Army and one of its great gifts to Christendom. It is not surprising that bands, or traditional SA music in general, are not at the top of the list of priorities to be addressed in reviving and expanding the Army.

What else is of concern that starts as a sociological problem and becomes a musical and theological one? 1) The lack of quality in some recent Praise and Worship texts and music that gets blended into our public worship, resulting in the loss in the use of theologically sound song and hymn repertoire; 2) the widening gap and possible lack of cooperation between the ever expanding Gospel Arts sections beyond the traditional formations, a category under which all groups are now being grouped.

On a positive note, within another front Salvation Army bands are interacting with the outside music community in ways they have never done in the past. The old regulations restricting individual participation in other musical organizations have been lifted or modified; Salvation Army bands join with all kinds of other organizations for joint concerts and worship. As a result, Salvation Army brass bands and choirs and their members have wider influence. This can be musical and, if you allow, at least 'moral,' if not directly or overtly spiritual in some contexts. I am convinced that such 'outside' involvement is a powerful way for the Salvation Army musician to be - using an evangelical buzzword - a witness. We are not an isolated movement.

Conclusion: The Future Is Bright

Salvation Army music still has a vital role to play in the movement's mission and, especially, Salvationist worship. Our published music and our organized music sections are among the brightest 'jewels in the crown' of our movement.[16] Our composers, band members and songsters continue, with God's grace, to tell the Good News via musical means both within their own encouraging fellowship and to the general public to the degree that they are open to direction of the Holy Spirit that has so far richly guided our movement's role in the Church's great task. All that comes to fruition when Salvation Army musicians and their music meet up with mission and submit to the priority that must be placed on communicating the Gospel in various worship settings, while placing less emphasis on, but not ignoring, the artistic quality of the music, the shared aesthetic experience, and each musician's

---

[16] This year marks my 50th as a commissioned SA bandmaster (first commissioned at age 16). It has been my privilege as a musicologist to not only chronicle the history and music of SA bands, but to be actively and intimately involved in SA musical mission on so many levels, plus be engaged in many educational efforts to renew our music and musicians. This has included hosting the biennial North American Composers' Forums since 2002, and most recently contributing to the forward-looking North American Song Writers' Forum that met in January, 2015, Atlanta, GA, with a primary goal to reinvigorating SA song in 'contemporary' styles. It is in that context and experience— the Lord leading us—that I write the future is bright.

personal achievement and satisfaction. Richard Slater put it well, as quoted by his younger colleague, Frederick Hawkes:

> The music of the Army is created to meet certain well-defined and specific needs. The Army does not exist as an entertaining society, to provide a series of concerts. It exists for the direct purpose of winning souls and of helping men and women to be good. It is, or ought to be, secondary and subservient to this great purpose—a means to an end....The Army does not necessarily need the best music, but that which best assists it in the accomplishment of its supreme purpose.[17]

That supreme purpose continues to undergird all that SA musicians undertake within Salvation Army worship:

> Salvation Army music organizations exist to proclaim the Army's message: salvation from sin through Jesus Christ, and to accomplish the Army's purposes: The glorification of God and the salvation of souls.[18]

---

[17] Richard Slater, quoted by Frederick Hawkes in "Fifty Years of Army Music, Part 2," *The Officer* (Jan-Feb, 1951), p. 113.
[18] *Sing and Make Music*, p. 1.

Part Three: Serving Suffering Humanity

12. 'Go into all the world...'[1]

An Overview of Salvationist Missiology

Andrew M. Eason

Andrew Walls has defined missiology as 'the systematic study of all aspects of mission.'[2] Such a description is broad by intention, reflecting the fact that this academic field is approached from a number of diverse angles: biblical, theological, historical and cultural. Each of these emphases can be detected to varying degrees in this chapter, which aims to provide a brief overview of Salvationist missiology. In the process, it answers a number of important questions about the purpose, character and assumptions of Salvation Army missions. What principles have guided Salvationist missionary work over the decades? To what extent have these notions been implemented effectively? How have they changed over time? Given the daunting nature of this task, which encompasses roughly 150 years of global ministry, the narrative that follows is divided into three chronological periods. While this arrangement may reflect the historical bias of the author—who is a religious historian by training—there is perhaps no better way to appreciate the depth and complexity surrounding the Army's ongoing efforts to fulfill the Great Commission.

If the multifaceted features of Salvationist missiology could be reduced to one overriding imperative, it would lie in Christ's command to make disciples of all nations. Such a biblical conviction was stressed repeatedly during the earliest days of the Salvation Army, so much so that the title of its international journal, *All the World*, was inspired by the parting words of Jesus to his followers in Mark 16:15: 'Go ye into all the world and preach the Gospel to every creature.'[3] While some critics may have dismissed the missionary enterprise as nothing more than a religious fad, countless Salvationists of yesteryear exhibited a missionary spirit that was deemed to be 'nothing less than the often unconscious effort to obey Christ's command' to spread the Good News to the ends of the earth.[4] Judging from the movement's current international mission statement, the same impulse—a divine call to preach the gospel of Jesus Christ—is meant to frame the activities of Salvationists today.[5] What remains in the pages ahead is to demonstrate exactly how this Great

---

[1] Mark 16:15
[2] Andrew F. Walls, 'Missiology', in Nicholas Lossky, José Míguez Bonino et al. (eds.), *Dictionary of the Ecumenical Movement* 2nd ed. (Geneva: WCC Publications, 2002), p. 781. For an equally inclusive approach see Stanley H. Skreslet, *Comprehending Mission: The Questions, Methods, Themes, Problems, and Prospects of Missiology* (Maryknoll, NY: Orbis Books, 2012), 9-15
[3] See *All the World* 1, 1 (November 1884), 1
[4] *The Cry of a Thousand Millions* (London: The Salvation Army, 1921), 1
[5] *The Salvation Army Handbook of Doctrine* (London: Salvation Books, 2010), 266

Commission has been manifested in the three distinct periods of Salvationist missionary history.

Salvationist Missions between 1865 and 1889

Four principles of mission quickly came to define the earliest work of the Salvation Army at home and abroad. There can be no doubt that the chief of these was direct evangelism. Preaching the gospel to the unsaved not only motivated William and Catherine Booth to establish a mission among the poor of East London in 1865 but also convinced them of the need to transform their Christian Mission into an army of salvation in 1878. The Good News was not something that the Booths and their followers could keep to themselves. As William explained at the time: '[W]e publish what we have heard and seen and handled and experienced of the word of life and the power of God . . . soul saving is the great purpose and business of our lives.'[6] A privatized gospel was no gospel at all, for the Great Commission commanded all true Christians to share the liberating message of salvation with the world. To ignore this biblical directive was to leave people in sin and in danger of eternal damnation. Complacency about such grave matters could not be tolerated in a movement that increasingly became known for pursuing an aggressive and public expression of Christianity.[7] Evangelism was meant to be the prime occupation of the Salvationist, soldier and officer alike.

This theological conviction was expressed with particular force once the Salvation Army began to send missionaries to non-Christian lands in the 1880s. The task at hand was simply the evangelization of the so-called heathen, not the establishment of institutions to educate and civilize them. Therefore, when plans were put in place to begin work among the Zulus of Natal in the late 1880s, the Army's weekly *War Cry* candidly remarked: 'We need hardly tell our soldiers and friends that we are not going to attempt anything whatever in the educational or industrial way. . . . It is for their souls, and their souls only that we shall attempt to provide.'[8] Such a strategy was commonplace during the early days of the organization, most notably because it reflected the will and mindset of the founders. As Catherine crisply expressed the matter in June 1888, in what was destined to be her final sermon: 'Christ did not come to civilise the world, but to save it, and bring it back to God.'[9] Roughly a year later, in mid spring 1889, her husband echoed this viewpoint in an important speech delivered at London's Exeter Hall. Referring to recent controversies

---

[6] William Booth, 'Our New Name', *The Salvationist* 1, 1 (January 1879), 3
[7] Catherine Booth, *Papers on Aggressive Christianity* (London: S.W. Partridge and Co., 1880), 3-16; William Booth, 'Satisfaction', *The War Cry* 31 December 1884, 1-2. Unless otherwise specified, all references to *The War Cry* in this chapter come from the edition published in London, England.
[8] 'Our Campaign in Africa', *The War Cry* 5 November 1887, 9
[9] 'Mrs. Booth's Last Public Address [Part 1]', *The War Cry* 18 October 1890, 2. See also Catherine Booth, 'What is Your Purpose?' *The War Cry* 9 August 1884, 1

about the validity of conventional missionary methods, Booth condemned the Victorian civilizing mission in the strongest of terms; charging it with being costly, inefficient, destructive and unbiblical, he argued that it was up to converts to 'clothe, house and educate themselves.'[10] At this stage in his life and ministry, he held stubbornly to the belief that the salvation of the soul was the only legitimate goal of mission work overseas. The genuine missionary laboured after the fashion of the apostles, seeking only to lead sinners to Christ.

Efforts to replicate this apostolic model ultimately led Salvationists to embrace a second missionary principle, cultural adaptation. There was, of course, nothing new about this precept, which had been implemented first among the impoverished inhabitants of East London. As *The Nonconformist*, a leading religious newspaper, reported on the Booths' organization in 1868: 'The great bulk of its advocates are working people, the language used is that of the working people [and] its habits are made to harmonise with those of the working people.'[11] Religious services, for example, invariably mirrored the format of the Victorian music hall: missioners not only attached sacred words to popular secular tunes but employed lively interactive theatrics to hold the attention of rowdy audiences. While these adaptive practices did not extend to the consumption of alcohol, they were considered to be biblically defensible. For as Catherine was prone to remind critics of the Army, Salvationists 'had never out-Pauled Paul', who became all things to all people to save some (1 Cor. 9:22).[12] Put simply, cultural adaptation was consistent with the central aim of scripture, the salvation of the lost.

Since accommodation to culture already defined the Salvation Army's ministry in Britain, it was only natural that it would be applied to new fields of opportunity overseas. This was strikingly apparent when a small missionary party, headed by Frederick Tucker, was chosen to establish a presence in India.[13] Even before departing from Britain, the Salvationists had appeared in London and elsewhere in Indian attire, not only to advertise their new venture but to demonstrate their sincere desire to adapt to a new culture. As George Scott Railton, a pioneering leader within the Army, said of the missionaries on the eve of their farewell: 'In the strength of God they are resolved to lay aside their Western dignity, and to show by their dress, and in every possible way, that they feel themselves to be the brothers and servants of those to whom God sends them.'[14] These adaptive measures subsequently proved embarrassing to

---

[10] William Booth, 'The Future of Missions and the Mission of the Future [Part 2]', *The War Cry* 25 May 1889, 9

[11] 'Mission Work in East London', *The Nonconformist* 4 November 1868, 1077

[12] Catherine Booth cited in 'An Evening with Mrs. Booth and the Salvation Army', *The Methodist Recorder* 23 December 1881, 922

[13] Tucker, a middle-class gentleman, had been a member of the Indian Civil Service before joining the Salvation Army in 1881. For an informative account of his life see Harry Williams, *Booth-Tucker: William Booth's First Gentleman* (London: Hodder and Stoughton, 1980).

[14] George Scott Railton, 'The Army Going Down!' *The War Cry* 10 August 1882, 1

the British Raj, which likely feared that the religion of the ruling race would be reduced to ridicule, but a number of Indians clearly appreciated them. Especially effusive in its praise was *The New Dispensation*, a Hindu reform paper, which made the following observation shortly after the arrival of Salvationists in Bombay in September 1882: 'You so love us and honor your Master that you are not ashamed for his sake to adopt our dress. . . . You have come to present Christ to us in an oriental garb and devotional enthusiasm, humility, meekness and poverty which are truly oriental.'[15] In the years ahead, as Army missionaries moved into various rural and urban regions, they would embrace additional aspects of the local cultures, from the begging bowl of the religious mendicant to the dietary and social practices of high caste Brahmins. While representing a radical departure from conventional missionary work in South Asia, such actions were a natural extension of the Salvation Army's Pauline approach to evangelism.[16]

The same kind of strategy guided the officers sent to evangelize the Zulus of South Africa in the late 1880s. Headed by Jim Osborne, a former printer's apprentice from the south coast of England, the members of the missionary party simply were instructed by London 'to become as a native to the natives.'[17] Among other things, this entailed residing in beehive-shaped dwellings made of mud, grass and sticks and consuming a traditional African diet of curdled milk and boiled ground corn. Osborne also abandoned his boots and socks in favour of bare feet, although it is unlikely that adaptation in dress was ever complete. Victorian propriety and evangelical morality would have militated against such a practice, because Zulus wore considerably less clothing than the average white person. Even so, Salvationists displayed little interest in changing the attire or social customs of their potential converts, who resided in the Greytown district of northern Natal. As Osborne explained to supporters back in Britain: '[O]ur chief object is to lead [the Zulus] into the light of the Gospel, and we do not interfere with any established law or custom. . . so long as it does not conflict with the spirit of the Scriptures.'[18] By pursuing this culturally sensitive policy, and by appropriating certain features of Zulu life, the Army's missionaries demonstrated that Christianity was not captive to western culture.[19]

---

[15] 'Greetings to the Salvation Army', *The New Dispensation* 24 September 1882, 2

[16] For more on these developments see Andrew Mark Eason, 'Christianity in a Colonial Age: Salvation Army Foreign Missions from Britain to India and South Africa, 1882-1929' (PhD thesis, University of Calgary, Alberta, Canada, 2005), 131-61

[17] 'Zulu Jim. Major Osborne', *All the World* 18, 3 (March 1897), 104-105

[18] Jim Osborne cited in 'Life in Zululand: Being an Account of Staff-Capt. Jim Osborne's Work and Travels [Part 2]', *The War Cry* 17 August 1889, 4 Notwithstanding the title of this article, the subject under discussion was the Salvation Army's missionary work in Natal.

[19] For more on this fascinating chapter in Salvationist missionary history see Andrew M. Eason, '"All Things to All People to Save Some": Salvation Army Missionary Work among the Zulus of Victorian Natal', *Journal of Southern African Studies* 35.1 (March 2009), 7-27

Adaptation to indigenous cultures went hand in hand with a third principle of early Salvationist missiology, an avowed commitment to self-support. For William Booth this meant that 'a large proportion of the money required to maintain and carry on [the Army's work must be] supplied by its own members.'[20] Possessing no guaranteed salaries, officers were expected to trust God for their support.[21] Appeals for divine assistance in Britain typically were answered in two ways, through the collection plates in local corps (mission stations) and from the sale of Army literature to the general public. Circumstances proved more challenging on distant mission fields, but the same standard was supposed to apply. Consequently, even before the first Salvationists set foot in Bombay in 1882, Booth was informing the Indian people that his missionaries would 'depend for their daily bread upon the God who sends them.'[22] Highly critical of the older missionary societies, which paid their western personnel fairly generous stipends, he instructed officers to live humbly in the field, relying upon the local populace for most of their daily needs. The same requirement also distinguished the later mission to the Zulus. Writing to London shortly after he and his colleagues arrived in Natal, Jim Osborne remarked: 'We have told them that we have come to live and work amongst them, and [that] they must keep us, and they are very willing, to all appearances.'[23] While demanding considerable personal sacrifice on the part of missionaries, self-support was viewed as critical to the success of the Salvation Army at home and abroad.

Financial concerns, however, made it extremely difficult to approach the kind of self-support envisioned by William Booth. Speaking of conditions in Britain alone, one informative early pamphlet had to confess that while the 'great majority of [corps] meet their local claims—many do not, and these have to be assisted'.[24] Growing an army of salvation was an expensive undertaking, requiring money for renting and purchasing buildings, training officers, and periodic travel from one location to another. These costs, of course, only multiplied when missionaries were sent to foreign lands. Given that the vast majority of the Army's converts were poor, it was never easy to fund the expanding horizons of the organization in the northern and southern hemispheres. The fiscal burden had become quite heavy by the middle of 1885, necessitating William Booth to place a bold-typed letter of appeal on the front page of *The War Cry*. Addressed to the members and supporters of the organization, it wasted little time in getting to the point: 'We want money. . . . Our present income is below our expenditure.'[25] In addition to meeting the

---

[20] William Booth cited in 'The General at Woolwich', *The War Cry* 14 March 1885, 1
[21] *All about The Salvation Army* (London: S.W. Partridge and Co., 1882), 7
[22] Letter from William Booth, dated 8 August 1882, cited in 'The Salvation Army', *The Times of India* 20 September 1882, 3
[23] 'The Salvation Army among the Zulus', *The War Cry* 8 September 1888, 5
[24] *All about The Salvation Army*, 8
[25] William Booth, 'To the Soldiers and Friends of Salvation', *The War Cry* 8 July 1885, 1. This letter was reproduced several more times in the weeks ahead.

expenses associated with acquiring new properties on the home front, the Army was desperately trying to sponsor a number of new ventures overseas, including a proposed invasion of China by Chinese Salvationists residing in California and Australia.

While entry into China was delayed until the early twentieth century, the Salvation Army's financial health improved somewhat during the second half of the 1880s. To begin with, the organization benefitted from the generosity of Frank Crossley, a wealthy Manchester industrialist, who donated a considerable amount of money to the cause of Salvationist missions. According to Bramwell Booth, Crossley parted with more than £100,000, enabling the Army to rapidly extend its work to various parts of the globe.[26] A second development that proved to be more significant over time was the introduction of a Self-Denial campaign. As William Booth alerted readers of *The War Cry* during the summer of 1886: 'We propose that a week be set apart in which every soldier and friend should deny himself of some article of food or clothing, or some indulgence which can be done without, and that the price gained by this self-denial shall be sent to help us in this emergency.'[27] Even though the scheme raised less than £5,000 in 1886, and did not become a yearly event until 1888, it would gradually become the major source of funding behind the Army's missionary work, bringing in over £170,000 annually by the second decade of the twentieth century.[28] Revenue of this magnitude may have been sorely needed, and therefore greatly appreciated, but the continued existence of Self-Denial testified to the enormous challenges of cultivating any meaningful notion of self-support on the mission field, because the bulk of the money repeatedly came from wealthy western lands.

It was hoped, nonetheless, that a measure of financial independence on the mission field could be attained eventually by the realization of a fourth principle, self-propagation. Such a notion, incidentally, had already met with success on the British home front. From the beginning, members of the Booths' East London mission had been expected to win at least one person to Christ each year, thereby contributing to 'the world's speedy conversion.'[29] According to one religious newspaper, it was the 'employment of the poor as missionaries amongst the poor' that helped to explain the growth of the organization.[30] Local agency held equal promise as the Salvation Army established new bases in

---

[26] E. K. Crossley, *He Heard from God: The Story of Frank Crossley* (London: Salvationist Publishing and Supplies, 1959), 43-44

[27] William Booth cited in 'Self-Denial League', *The War Cry* 21 August 1886, 9. See also Sidney Williams, *Puddings and Policies* (London: Salvationist Publishing and Supplies, 1946), 11-12

[28] 'Origin of Self-Denial Week', *The War Cry* 20 February 1909, 3; 'Self-Denial Blesses All the World', *The War Cry* 26 February 1916, 1

[29] 'The Conversion of the World', *The East London Evangelist* 1 (October 1869), 200. A similar expectation was conveyed years later in William Booth, 'Go!', *All the World* 1, 1 (November 1884), 3-4; and Catherine Booth, 'Our Flag', *The War Cry* 17 December 1884, 1

[30] 'East London People's Mission Hall', *The Christian World* 30 October 1868, 697

foreign lands. There was, for instance, the obvious fact that indigenous personnel were less expensive than foreigners, who incurred the cost of travelling from their home countries to a distant mission field. And, as William Booth readily understood, native-born evangelists possessed a superior knowledge of local languages and cultures. Thus, when given the opportunity to reflect on the ideal missionary society of the future, he believed that it would 'most certainly seek to raise up in every country, from the people among whom she labours, the supplies of men necessary for its conquest.'[31]

Self-propagation on the mission field was obviously not a goal that could be reached overnight, given the time and resources necessary to disciple and train converts. Yet, significant strides in this direction could be detected even during the 1880s. In India, for example, almost fifty per cent of the Salvation Army's officers hailed from South Asia by the end of the decade.[32] Moreover, Arnolis Weerasooriya, a well-educated Christian from Ceylon, rose to second-in-command of the Army's forces on the subcontinent in 1887 before succumbing to cholera a year later.[33] A commitment to local agency also came to characterize the much smaller mission to the Zulus of Natal, which commenced in the summer of 1888. The conversion of an African chief by the name of Ntshibong was especially noteworthy, as he played a leading role in spreading the gospel message among his own people. Henry Thurman, the Army's commander in South Africa, was clearly impressed with the man's evangelistic zeal, reporting in the spring of 1889 that Ntshibong had become 'a real hallelujah preacher'.[34] Remarkable or not, the chief was merely a living embodiment of the Salvationist policy highlighted by George Scott Railton in the movement's annual report: 'We do continually teach our people by example and arrangement, even more than in word, that they are to devote themselves not only to the advancement of their own spiritual interests, but to the salvation of the world.'[35] Here, in particular, was one of the major reasons why the organization could boast of 8,700 officers in thirty-two countries and colonies at the close of this initial chapter in Salvationist missionary history.[36] Making these statistics all the more impressive was the fact that, with the obvious

---

[31] William Booth, 'The Future of Missions and the Mission of the Future [Part 4]', *The War Cry* 8 June 1889, 10

[32] *The Present Position of The Salvation Army* (London: International Headquarters, 1888), 5

[33] For more on the life of this remarkable Salvationist see Frederick Booth-Tucker, *Colonel Weerasooriya* (London: The Salvation Army Book Department, 1905); and Victor Thompson, *Son of Sri Lanka* (London: Salvationist Publishing and Supplies, 1953).

[34] Henry Thurman, '3,000 Miles around the African Battlefield', *The War Cry* 8 June 1889, 4

[35] [George Scott Railton], *Apostolic Warfare: Being the Annual Report for 1889 of The Salvation Army* (London: International Headquarters, 1889), 18. Although this report provided no details about authorship, a review of the book acknowledged that Railton had written it. See 'Apostolic Warfare', *The War Cry* 4 January 1890, 5

[36] Railton, *Apostolic Warfare*, 19

exception of the United Kingdom, these places had been added to the Army fold over the course of the 1880s.

Salvationist Missions between 1890 and 1945

Growth continued to mark the second stage of Salvationist missionary history, despite the challenges brought on by warfare and economic depression. In fact, by the end of this fifty-five year period the Salvation Army had established ministries in sixty-five new lands.[37] Furthermore, approximately two thirds of this expansion took place in the global south and east: Latin America, Africa and Asia. While the pace of extension remained relatively constant between the 1890s and 1930s, it admittedly ground to a halt on the eve of the Second World War (1939-1945). The trauma of this violent conflict, which affected so much of the inhabited world, served, at least momentarily, to place a damper on the organization's evangelistic activities. Conceding as much was the Army's Chief of the Staff, Charles Baugh, who acknowledged in 1944 that the 'missionary urge [was] waning' in Salvationist circles.[38] This development may have been disturbing to Baugh, a former missionary to India, but there still was a great deal to celebrate. Much had been accomplished during this period as a whole, arguably making it the most productive chapter in Salvationist missionary history. Having planted its flag in a total of ninety-seven countries and colonies, the movement was hardly in retreat.

From the perspective of the Salvation Army, such extraordinary enlargement was thanks in large part to its longstanding missionary principles—adaptation, self-support and self-propagation.[39] Evangelism, of course, also remained at the heart of the organization's ministry, finding ample expression in the third tenet, which encouraged all Salvationists to share the Good News with others immediately upon conversion. Increasingly, however, the proclamation of the gospel on the mission field encompassed bodily as well as spiritual needs. The profound poverty of the Army's converts may have warranted this development, but ultimately it reflected the maturing of William Booth's own theology on the British home front. While never without sympathy for the material plight of the masses, Booth adopted a more holistic doctrine of redemption in the late 1880s. In a leading article on the subject, published in January 1889, he stressed that salvation 'meant not only [being] saved from the miseries of the future world, but from the miseries of this [world] also.'[40] This particular conviction culminated, twenty-two months later,

---

[37] The statistical analysis that follows is based upon data found in *The Salvation Army Year Book: 1945* (London: Salvationist Publishing and Supplies, 1945), 17-65

[38] Charles Baugh, 'Go Ye into All the World!', *The Officers' Review* 13, 2 (April-June 1944), 65-68

[39] See 'Principles of Army Missionary Work' in *The Salvation Army Year Book for 1917* (London: The Salvation Army Book Department, 1917), 20, 24; and 'The Evolution of the Army's Missionary Work', *The War Cry* 14 June 1919, 4

[40] William Booth, 'Salvation for Both Worlds', *All the World* 5, 1 (January 1889), 6

in the publication of *In Darkest England and the Way Out*, the Army leader's grand strategy for combatting human misery and vice. Social concerns would now find a place alongside direct evangelism. With the introduction of this bold scheme General Booth made it clear that he had 'no intention to depart in the smallest degree from the main principles on which [he had] acted in the past,'[41] but it is fair to say that the mission field would be impacted, to varying extents, by the proposals emanating from *In Darkest England and the Way Out*.

Precisely how far the Darkest England scheme influenced the Salvation Army's accommodation to local cultures is difficult to assess, but it likely contributed to the dramatic changes witnessed on the African mission field in the early 1890s. Booth himself alluded to what was coming during his first trip to the Cape Colony in August 1891. Speaking to Cape Town's leading citizens, in the hope of securing moral and monetary support for his social scheme, the General announced that the Army was presently devising plans for 'raising [the native population] intellectually, morally, religiously, and materially.'[42] Just what was meant by this was apparent soon after Booth's departure from the continent. As the South African *War Cry* reported in October 1891, a team led by James Allister Smith, an officer from Scotland, was heading to Zululand to establish a missionary settlement on several acres provided by the colonial government. Instead of pursuing a policy of adaptation, the Salvationists would construct 'European-styled houses. . . [and] supplement the Christianising effects of the Gospel with the uses of civilization in the way of trades and agriculture.'[43] Even though this announcement gave no reasons for the sudden reversal in missionary methods, or offered any criticism of the earlier Osborne mission, it generally signalled the demise of accommodation to African culture in Army circles. Apart from language, future adaptation would come from the Zulu side, especially as missionaries encouraged their converts to adopt western forms of life, labour and dress.[44]

Nothing so drastic took place in Asia, although the Salvation Army's principle of cultural adaptation met with only limited success. In India, for example, the extreme asceticism practiced by the earliest officers was modified over time; famine and economic hardship during the 1890s effectively put an end to this kind of lifestyle, especially as sickness and dissatisfaction grew in the missionary ranks.[45] Western officers were still required to wear Indian uniforms—comprised of dhotis and turbans for men and saris for women—but

---

[41] William Booth, *In Darkest England and the Way Out* (New York: Funk and Wagnalls, 1890), iii-iv

[42] William Booth cited in 'General Booth's Visit', *The Cape Times* 28 August 1891, 3

[43] 'The Commissioner in the Editorium', *The [South African] War Cry* 24 October 1891, 5

[44] See, for example, J. Allister Smith, *Zulu Crusade* (London: Salvationist Publishing and Supplies, 1945).

[45] 'Editorial Notes. The Salvation Army', *The Harvest Field* (November 1892), 198-99; Alex M. Nicol, *General Booth and the Salvation Army* (London: Herbert and Daniel, 1911), 164-66

their material conditions improved significantly in the early twentieth century. By the 1920s, such a development was generating considerable resentment among indigenous Salvationists, who juxtaposed the 'miserable lot of the Indian Salvation Army officer' with 'the comforts' of the average missionary officer.[46] Tensions related to adaptation also surfaced in Korea, which joined the family of Salvationist nations in 1908. Successive missionary leaders, chiefly from Britain, were criticized for failing to understand the local language and culture. Demands for greater sensitivity to Korean life eventually led to vocal protests and physical confrontations during Bramwell Booth's visit to the country in 1926.[47] Far better was the experience of the Salvation Army in Japan. The chief difference here was Gunpei Yamamuro, an ambitious and gifted Christian young man, who had joined the organization shortly after its arrival in Tokyo in 1895. Almost singlehandedly, he sought to find various points of contact—literary, social and religious—between the Army's evangelical brand of Christianity and Japanese popular culture. In the process, Gunpei helped missionary officers to overcome their ignorance of the people and their customs.[48]

One challenge that proved harder to surmount was how to achieve a measure of financial independence in missionary lands. As an article in *The War Cry* frankly acknowledged in 1921:

> This has never been completely achieved. In some instances the degree of self-support attained is even yet hardly perceptible; in others it has, practically speaking, covered the cost of general maintenance, without, however, providing anything towards the expenses of oversight and development. [49]

Self-support was difficult enough to reach in the 1880s, when officers lived ascetically and merely preached the gospel, but it had become next to impossible by the early twentieth century.[50] Beyond the rising costs associated with missionary extension and salaries, new expenses were incurred with the introduction of social programs in various parts of the non-western world.[51] Rescue homes for women, industrial homes for the unemployed, shelters for the

---

[46] 'Correspondence. An Open Letter to General Bramwell Booth', *The Christian Patriot* 27 January 1923, 7

[47] Peter H. Chang, *The Salvation Army in Korea* (Seoul: The Salvation Army, 2007), 46-55

[48] R. David Rightmire, *Salvationist Samurai: Gunpei Yamamuro and the Rise of the Salvation Army in Japan* (Lanham, MD: The Scarecrow Press, 1997), 15-18, 45-67, 135-59

[49] 'Why Missionary Work Succeeds', *The War Cry* 26 February 1921, 1. See also Arthur E. Copping, 'The Heathen's Awful Handicap', *The War Cry* 10 March 1923,16.

[50] One notable exception was Japan, which enjoyed periods of intermittent self-support from the late 1920s. See Rightmire, *Salvationist Samurai*, 153

[51] Non-western in this chapter refers to places beyond Europe, the United States, Canada, Australia and New Zealand.

homeless, schools for children, and hospitals for the sick were just a few of the institutions to emerge on the Army mission field, reflecting both the pressing needs of the local people and the evolution in William Booth's understanding of salvation.[52] As important as these developments may have been, they demanded escalating amounts of funding from the Salvation Army's industrialized nations throughout the period under review.[53]

Nevertheless, concerns about money were not meant to distract the Salvation Army from its most important calling, the broadcast of the gospel. All Salvationists—soldiers as well as officers—were expected 'to openly proclaim the great deliverance which has been wrought for them.'[54] In a very real sense, each member of the organization, at home and abroad, was commissioned as a missionary to his or her own people, mirroring the work of the early apostles, who were 'bent upon raising a force from among the sons and daughters of each country'.[55] Among those incarnating this principle of self-propagation were a number of capable African Salvationists. Tom Maqili, who hailed from Portuguese East Africa (Mozambique), was a case in point. While employed on the South African Rand during the 1910s, he evangelized many of his own countrymen, who came in large numbers to work in the local gold mines. Such evangelistic zeal ultimately led the Army to establish a base of operations in Portuguese East Africa in the early 1920s, with Maqili himself being appointed there in 1926.[56] Another fine example of self-propagation came in the person of Maheya Sitoli, who eventually became an officer. Converted through the witness of Salvationists at a South African mine, he returned to his native Rhodesia (Zimbabwe), 'where he won many of his own people for God and opened the Salvation Army work in [his] district.'[57] A similar story saw the extension of the organization into present day Zambia.[58] In all these instances, not to mention countless others around the globe, local agency was responsible for much of the Army's growth.

Even though the militancy and autocracy of the Salvation Army did not allow for self-governing churches, self-propagation was ideally supposed to translate into indigenous leadership in foreign lands. As much was confirmed in the organization's own yearbook in 1928, which noted that it is a 'fundamental principle that, other things being equal, positions of influence, trust, and

---

[52] Henry D. Gore, 'Before—and After', in *The Salvation Army Year Book: 1935* (London: Salvationist Publishing and Supplies, 1935), 7-10

[53] See Edward J. Higgins, 'Responsibility for the Mission Fields of The Army', *The Staff Review* 1, 1 (January 1922), 29-39; and 'Some Financial Needs for the Current Year', in *The Salvation Army Year Book: 1945*, 20

[54] George A. Pollard, 'The Lesson of The Salvation Army', *All the World* 24, 5 (May 1903), 228

[55] Francis Pearce, 'Responsibility for the Maintenance of Missionary Enterprises', *The Officer* 23, 2 (February 1915), 75

[56] 'Many Years of Faithful Service', *The [South African] War Cry* 27 March 1926, 8; Arthur E. Copping, *Banners in Africa* (London: Hodder and Stoughton, 1933), 71-82

[57] 'Who's Who', *The Officer* 38, 8 (August 1930), 121

[58] 'Spreading Salvation in South Africa', *The War Cry* 8 June 1918, 3

authority shall be open alike to all races'.[59] Here, especially, the Army could take some pride, since it had a commendable record of training national officers in a number of missionary lands. Evidence to this effect was particularly striking in Asia. When the Salvation Army celebrated its twenty-fifth anniversary in China in 1941, over three quarters of its officers were Chinese.[60] Japan also claimed an impressive record, eventually possessing more native clergy than any other Christian church in the land.[61] Much the same held true for India, leading one historian to observe that the Army was 'more anti-racist in practice than other missionary societies.'[62] Yet, at the highest levels of governance, the organization fell short of the mark. A careful analysis of its yearbooks from the early to mid-twentieth century reveals that only five to thirteen per cent of senior leadership in missionary countries was indigenous. Dominating the upper echelons were Caucasian officers, the overwhelming majority of whom came from Britain. Thus, at any given time, only a handful of the highest posts (e.g., territorial commander, chief secretary) were filled by national officers in Asia (India, Ceylon, Japan, Korea and China) and Latin America (South America East). Interestingly enough, no black African officer was ever entrusted with a high ranking position during this time period.[63] Self-propagation might have been an admirable Salvationist trait, but it became less and less noticeable as one climbed through the Army's ranks.

Salvationist Missions from 1946 to the Present

Indigenous representation at the uppermost levels of administration only began to improve significantly during the third chapter of Salvationist missionary history. Hastening this development was the drive towards independence in the global south and east, beginning with India in 1947. As more and more European colonies, chiefly in Asia and Africa, sought control over their own affairs, there were mounting petitions from native-born officers to lead their own countries and commands.[64] While moving rather cautiously in this direction, the Salvation Army was generally prone to accept the legitimacy of the nationalism that lay behind these demands. Herbert Lord, a British officer

---

[59] 'Internationalism and The Salvation Army', in *The Salvation Army Year Book: 1928* (London: Salvationist Publishing and Supplies, 1928), 11

[60] Check Hung Yee, *Good Morning China: The Chronicle of The Salvation Army in China, 1916-2000* (Alexandria, VA: Crest Books, 2005), 11

[61] Rightmire, *Salvationist Samurai*, 146-47

[62] Jeffrey Cox, *The British Missionary Enterprise since 1700* (London: Routledge, 2008), 207

[63] This statistical analysis is based upon data found in the command and biographical sections of *The Salvation Army Year Book* for the following dates: 1907, 1913, 1920, 1925, 1930, 1935, 1940, and 1945.

[64] See, for example, Ernest I. Pugmire, 'Home Base and Overseas Needs', *The Officers' Review* 17, 4 (July-August 1948), 197; and Herbert A. Lord, 'A New Look on the Mission Field', *All the World* 13, 2 (April-June 1960), 60

who had spent close to forty years on the mission field, expressed this position well when he said:

> There is no sin in nationality! Such aspirations do not contravene any Christian ethic. There is nothing in Christianity to condemn a claim for recognition to a share of human rights equal to those enjoyed by any other race. . . . A man is no less a good Christian because he claims his civic rights as an individual, or his national rights as a member of a nation.[65]

Lord may have been both sympathetic and correct in his assessment, but, as one Indian officer warned, vigilance would be needed to ensure that nationalism did not swallow up the Army's internationalism.[66]

Regardless of the dangers, nationalism came to have a direct bearing on the governance of the Salvation Army in non-western lands. Postcolonial governments helped to accelerate this process, either by restricting the number of western missionaries in their countries or by expelling them altogether.[67] White Salvationists clearly recognized the urgency of the situation, although some expressed the fear that indigenous personnel lacked the training to rapidly assume positions of authority on the mission field.[68] Perhaps this was a legitimate concern, but it is equally true that missionaries from the west often found it difficult to relinquish the power and privileges they had enjoyed over their converts during the colonial period. Yet, whatever the reluctance, there was no stopping the process of decolonization. Wilfred Kitching, the Army's seventh General, reflected this changing environment when he said: 'I have little sympathy with the critics who suggest that indigenous leadership is a risky thing. . . . It is not the colour of a man's skin that counts, but whether he is of the right calibre for leadership.'[69] By the middle of the 1970s, this particular conviction was finally leaving its mark on the actual numbers—over forty-five per cent of the highest administrative posts in Asia, Africa and Latin America were now being filled by non-western officers.[70] Representing a threefold increase from 1950 and more than a twofold increase from 1965, this statistic

---

[65] Herbert A. Lord, 'At Work in a Changing World [Part 1]', *The Officers' Review* 16, 3 (May-June 1947), 147

[66] Narayana Muthiah, 'The Army's Internationalism', *The Officers' Review* 18, 4 (July-August 1949), 220

[67] Henry Gariepy, *The History of The Salvation Army*, Vol. 8 (Atlanta: The Salvation Army, 2000), 329

[68] See, for example, 'There is Still a Missionary Need', *All the World* 13, 4 (October-December 1960), 141; Caughey Gauntlett, 'The Changing Scene on the Mission Field', *All the World* 16, 3 (July-September 1964), 75-78

[69] Wilfred Kitching, 'The Missionary Outlook', *The Officer* 12, 3 (May-June 1961), 147

[70] *The Salvation Army Year Book: 1975* (London: Salvationist Publishing and Supplies, 1975), 71-194. Only those in command or second-in-command of a non-western territory, command or region are included in this statistic.

ebbed and flowed slightly for the remainder of the twentieth century before rising to over seventy per cent in the 2010s.[71] Given the internationalism of the organization, which fosters the movement of officers, especially from Europe and North America to the global south, it is unlikely that this figure will ever approach one hundred per cent in every place. Nonetheless, the trend towards local or regional control signifies, within a Salvationist context, a greater realization of self-propagation.

Has a similar measure of success been apparent in the area of self-support, another historic aspect of Salvationist missiology? This is a fair question to ask, since the principle is still espoused in the most recent edition of *Orders and Regulations for Officers*: 'Self-support, in terms of human and material resources, is a basic principle of the Army and should be the goal of every territory, corps and centre.'[72] While definitely a laudable ideal, it has remained difficult to achieve in many non-western lands due to extreme levels of poverty, very high rates of inflation, and the enormous costs of funding numerous schools and hospitals.[73] By the early 1970s, self-sufficient territories were sending more than a million pounds sterling each year to the dependent parts of the Salvation Army world, and this influx of money from wealthy regions continues into the present.[74] Some commendable strides, however, have been made to address this matter over the last few decades, as evidenced by the growing number of Army-sponsored development projects in the two-thirds world. Often reaching beyond Salvationists themselves, these partnerships are seeking to promote self-reliance as well as social justice.[75]

Partnership is an important word here, highlighting the need to foster respectful and equitable relationships. A similar desire helped to mould the Salvation Army's third missiological principle, cultural adaptation, which was

---

[71] This statistical analysis is based upon data found in the command and biographical sections of *The Salvation Army Year Book* for the following dates: 1950, 1965, 1975, 1980, 1985, 1990, 1995, 2000, 2005, and 2013.

[72] *Orders and Regulations for Officers of The Salvation Army* (London: International Headquarters, 1997), 85. The same principle was evident at the beginning of this period. See *Orders and Regulations for Officers of The Salvation Army* (London: International Headquarters, 1946), 408

[73] Ernest Bigwood, 'New Emphases in Missionary Affairs', *All the World* 10, 6 (April-June 1957), 200; Herbert Mitchell, 'Financial Implications of Missionary Work', *All the World* 12, 7 (September 1959), 241; Devavaram, 'India: A New Maturity', *The Officer* (December 1999), 7

[74] Arnold Brown, 'One Salvation Army', in *The Salvation Army Year Book: 1973* (London: Salvationist Publishing and Supplies, 1972), 8; Henry Gariepy, *Christianity in Action: The International History of The Salvation Army* (Grand Rapids, MI: Eerdmans, 2009), 113, 136; *The Salvation Army Year Book: 2013* (London: The Salvation Army International Headquarters, 2012), 38-40

[75] Harry Williams, 'We're All for Development', in *The Salvation Army Year Book: 1981* (London: Salvationist Publishing and Supplies, 1981), 21-25; Leigh O'Donoghue, 'Training for Life', *All the World* 40, 4 (October-December 2002), 4-5; 'A Tale of Three Women', *All the World* 51, 1 (January-March 2013), 10-15

meant to foster oneness between missionaries and their converts. Salvationist adaptability, however imperfect in practice, proved particularly useful on the eve of Indian independence, eliciting praise and goodwill from the nationalist politicians about to assume power.[76] In Africa, however, officer missionaries pursuing a more westernized agenda were likely to find their motives 'very much under suspicion.'[77] Perhaps it was this failure to adapt in some decolonizing regions of the globe that explained the 'fairly widespread [opinion] in certain hostile quarters that the Salvation Army is not international at all but British.'[78] In any event, circumstances increasingly dictated a more sensitive and welcoming approach to indigenous cultures. As Herbert Lord conceded in 1968: 'The gospel today should be proclaimed as a positive and creative force, not [as] a weapon for the destruction of a great deal that is precious and indeed constructive in the life and history of a people.'[79] Echoing this sentiment six years later was another officer, Ernest Yendell, who forcefully argued that 'it is no part of our Christian mission to attempt a cultural change in the areas in which we serve.'[80] Such a position, of course, had been held by Jim Osborne in Natal almost a century earlier. Those at work on the mission field today may not be required to adopt indigenous forms of dress and habitation—due in large part to the forces of globalization—but they do need to follow in the footsteps of Army pioneers by contextualizing the gospel.

The third chapter of Salvationist missionary history amply demonstrates the enduring relevancy of the gospel—its message is eminently translatable, capable of being communicated through any culture on the face of the earth.[81] Africa, Asia and Latin America have become especially fertile ground for the Good News, as most of the Salvation Army's growth since 1946 has been found in these regions of the world, continuing a trend set in motion during the organization's second chapter of missionary history.[82] This development, of course, is not unique to the Army. It mirrors the larger patterns of world Christianity described so well in recent years by religious historians such as Philip Jenkins and Dana Robert.[83] Put simply, the Christian heartland

---

[76] 'S.A. Wanted in India', *The War Cry* 15 March 1947, 3.
[77] Kathleen Kendrick, 'Missionary Education', *All the World* 13, 3 (July-September 1960), 80
[78] Gilbert Abadie, 'Internationalism—True and False', *The Officer* 1, 1 (January-February 1950), 31
[79] Herbert A. Lord, 'Missionary Purposes and Claims Today', *The Officer* 19, 2 (March-April 1968), 123
[80] Ernest Yendell, 'The Missionary Message Today', *The Officer* 24, 1 (January 1974), 33
[81] For more on this process see Lamin Sanneh, *Translating the Message: The Missionary Impact on Culture*, 2nd ed. (Maryknoll, NY: Orbis Books, 2009).
[82] 'Countries Where The Salvation Army is at Work', in *The Salvation Army Year Book: 2013*, 18-19; Gariepy, *The History of The Salvation Army*, Vol. 8, 308, 330-32
[83] See Philip Jenkins, *The Next Christendom: The Coming of Global Christianity*, 3rd ed. (New York: Oxford University Press, 2011); and Dana L. Robert, 'Shifting Southward: Global Christianity since 1945', in Robert L. Gallagher and Paul Hertig (eds.),

has shifted to the global south and east during the last century, away from Europe and European-derived societies. Even allowing for the growth that has taken place in eastern and central Europe since the fall of Communism, the most impressive gains for the church, the Salvation Army included, have come from the non-western world, particularly Africa. If predictions for the future hold true, then Africa, Asia and Latin America will be the most Christianized parts of the world by 2050, outpacing not only Europe but North America.[84]

Conclusion

Are western countries therefore destined to become increasingly secularized? While some scholars continue to answer in the affirmative, others are beginning to paint a less dire picture. One of the chief reasons for hope lies with immigration, given that Christians represent a significant proportion of those moving from the global south and east to the more affluent west. Immigrants are making their presence felt in western churches, including the Salvation Army, but much more needs to be done to harness the potential of this growing segment of the population. As one officer serving in the American state of New York noted recently: 'With the exception of the USA Eastern Territory. . . Western territories in Europe, Canada and the USA remain predominantly white, representing an insignificant number of non-white officers and members due to the lack of a strategic plan for reaching immigrants.'[85] Even though ethnic Salvationist ministries have existed in some large urban centres for decades, the long-term survival of the Salvation Army in western lands will undoubtedly require more intentional, inclusive and integrative efforts, not only in corporate worship and fellowship but in mission and leadership.

Present-day Salvationists looking for resources to assist them in this crucial endeavour would be wise to draw upon the principles first employed by the Salvation Army's founders and missionary pioneers. There are, for instance, ongoing calls to adapt to ever-changing cultures, both at home and abroad. How these demands will shape or transform the culture of the Army remains to be seen, but one hopes that spiritual discernment will guide the process. What must never change, however, is the Salvationist emphasis upon the propagation of the gospel. Winning the world for God, through a myriad of ministries to the disadvantaged, will surely require much more in the way of self-support, for as one early report plainly and unapologetically put it, '[t]o save men and women means—money!'[86] But rising to this biblical and financial challenge is imperative for each new generation. There can be no other alternative

---

Landmark Essays in Mission and World Christianity (Maryknoll, NY: Orbis Books, 2009), 46-60
[84] Jenkins, *The Next Christendom*, 3
[85] Daniel Diakanwa, 'Cultural Mosaics', *The Officer* (January-February 2013), 17
[86] 'The Finances of The Army', in *On Salvation Battlefields: Being a Brief Account of Some Salvation Army Activities* (London: The Salvation Army International Headquarters, 1928), 88

according to the great twentieth-century missiologist David Bosch, who reminds us that 'Christianity is missionary by its very nature, or it denies its very *raison d'être*.'[87] If the church fails to heed the Great Commission, then it will gradually wither away and eventually perish. Yet, as the Army's own imperfect experiences testify over the last century and a half, astonishing results are possible when men and women of different races are mobilized by Jesus Christ to make disciples of all nations.

Successes of this magnitude have already left their mark on the missionary enterprise, which is now more global, inclusive and complex than ever before. As Stanley Skreslet, a Presbyterian missiologist, has pointed out recently:

> The flow of mission no longer moves exclusively or even predominantly from North to South or from West to East, which means that it cannot be conceptualized as a North Atlantic project... Mission now is truly "from everywhere to everywhere." It involves many laypersons and a relatively few full-time professionals, who share faith and give witness in their own neighborhoods and around the world.[88]

It will be interesting to see how these seismic shifts impact the work of the Salvation Army in the decades ahead. One suspects that when the fourth chapter of Salvationist missionary history is finally written, the narrative will differ in conceptual, thematic and geographical ways

---

[87] David J. Bosch, *Transforming Mission: Paradigm Shifts in Theology of Mission* (1991; reprint, Maryknoll, NY: Orbis Books, 2011), 9
[88] Skreslet, *Comprehending Mission*, 15

13. 'Heart to God, Hand to Man'[1]

What is The Salvation Army's theology as we serve suffering humanity?

Campbell Roberts[2] *& Denis Metrustery*

General Arnold Brown summarised the Army's global mission, declaring that 'the front lines of the Salvation Army run through the tragedies of our world'.[3] This is no more apt than when applied to the vital work the movement carries out in the realms of social services and humanitarian aid. We are also reminded of the importance of an integrated, holistic approach, for 'we need to affirm the importance of serving suffering humanity, not as an end in itself, but because that is what Christians do as a response from the local worshipping community... too many of our Army social centres have been set apart from the worshipping community. This is not healthy for corps or centre'.[4] This sets apart the Army's social and humanitarian involvement from that of NGOs and other agencies; the Army's approach is not simply altruistic, but driven by a deep compassion for fellow humanity, inspired by an appreciation of God's love and commitment to his creation, and the hope of redemption through Christ 'from the uttermost to the uttermost'. No-one is beyond hope in the scope of God's cosmic salvation. Ray Harris suggests that the Army should 'embrace the whole [breadth] of salvation, and we will embrace the whole of our mission'.[5]

William Booth typified a postmillennial eschatology, where the evangelical revivals and social reforms of mid-nineteenth century England engendered a sense of optimism that the world could be conquered in Christ's name. Positively, such a perspective seeks the engagement of men and women in the realisation of God's kingdom spiritually and socially, while its negative connotations can stress human agency too heavily – only God can ultimately

---

[1] One of the Army's slogans which reinforces the integration of spirituality and practical service

[2] Campbell Roberts' contribution to this chapter is based largely on a paper he presented at the USA Salvation Army Conference for Social Work and Emergency Disaster Services 25-28 March 2014, Orlando, Florida; he focuses particularly on the experience of The Salvation Army in New Zealand where, although 'retired' he continues to serve in the Social Policy and Parliamentary Unit

[3] Henry Gariepy, *Mobilized for God: The History of the Salvation Army*, Volume Eight 1977-1994, (Grand Rapids MI: Eerdmans/Salvation Army Southern Territory, 2000), 7

[4] Dean Pallant, 'A church or a corporation?', *The Officer*, September/October 2002, 15

[5] Ray Harris, 'The Salvation Army: Its Name and Mission', *The Officer*, May/June 2003, 11

bring about the fullness of his kingdom. Booth wanted his Army to work for the establishment of God's kingdom on earth, and insisted that 'Salvationism means simply the overcoming and banishing from the earth of wickedness, inward and outward, from the heart and life of man, and the establishment of the principles of purity and goodness instead'.[6]

Millennial themes can be found in the writings of Wesley and Fletcher, with the anticipation that Methodism was a precursor to a new Pentecost and the millennial reign of Christ.[7] Such anticipation, however, is a common element in most revival movements. Influenced by the American holiness revivalists, Booth's own postmillennial theology evidences a strong pneumatological emphasis, with the Spirit's indwelling received for sanctification, and his presence empowering believers to establish the kingdom. He suggests that

> The unutterable longings, and hopes and beliefs of many of God's most faithful people seem to signify the near approach of His universal kingdom. Some say that the general triumph of godliness will be ushered in by the reign of Christ. We Salvationists, however, expect it to be preceded by further and mightier outpourings of the Holy Ghost than any yet known... [8]

In Booth's mind, it was his Salvation Army that would usher in the Millennium, and he understood its mission as nothing less than global redemption, for God's grace – through Christ's sacrifice – was available to all.

While postmillennialism attempted to pull the kingdom into the present, the concept of inaugurated eschatology noted the 'already-but-not-yet' quality of the kingdom. Through Christ's death and resurrection, and the continuation of his mission through his Spirit-empowered church, God's kingdom was breaking into our world; this was proleptic as the ultimate realisation of the kingdom and its messianic blessings remains part of a yet future consummation.

The 'not yet' element of the kingdom gives us consolation when we fail in our efforts to bring healing, restoration and justice, for these will only be realised in full in the eschaton. In the interim, we rightly continue to pray that God's 'kingdom [will] come on earth as in heaven'.[9]

---

[6] William Booth, '"Fight!" *All The World I* (May 1885), 111
[7] See Laurence W. Wood, *The Meaning of Pentecost in Early Methodism: Rediscovering John Fletcher as John Wesley's Vindicator and Designated Successor* (Lanham: The Scarecrow Press, 2002), 145-162
[8] William Booth, 'The Millennium; or, The Ultimate Triumph of Salvation Army Principles', *All The World 6* (August 1890), 338
[9] Matt. 6:10; it is interesting that 'our daily bread' (6:11) can also be rendered 'the bread of tomorrow' thus praying for the future blessings of the kingdom to be made present in our day, where we can 'taste the powers of the coming age' (Heb. 6:5)

The history of Israel, as recorded in the Old Testament, is replete with divine instruction that God's people are to model his mercy, compassion, and justice, giving refuge to the foreigner and the excluded, safety to the oppressed, grace and assistance to the poor and exploited, and succour to the destitute, the widows and orphans. The prophets frequently rebuked the people for their failure to exemplify the high standards of justice and righteousness to which they were called.

Christ's kingdom manifesto[10] offers not only the possibility of ethical living, but a blueprint for the transformation of society; it addresses both the spiritually poor and the socially poor. This transformation is, however, only truly possible in the context of the arrival and expansion of the kingdom of God.

Karen Shakespeare proposes that

> The outworking of the response to this command reaches beyond the confines of church disciple-making, vital though this may be, to prophetic word and action, particularly with, and on behalf of, the poor and oppressed, so that justice can be restored. Put simply, the disciples of a just and righteous God have no choice but to pursue justice and righteousness in their personal, social and political lives.[11]

As part of its remit, the International Spiritual Life Commission included a call to 'Our Life in the World' in its report:

> "The 'healing of a hurting world' and the need for prophetic witness in the face of social injustice'... must be seen as more than wishful thinking... We who have received complete love from Christ are called to give transparent witness to justice, peace, equality and holiness through actions which redeem and re-order the world.[12]

Geanette Seymour, a former Director of the International Social Justice Commission, comments that

> To William Booth, advocacy for change in social systems was an imperative to his vision. [He] initiated the mandate for system change, explaining in principle that responding to initial need only begins the recovery. Altered conditions are required to sustain it. Still today The Salvation Army understands that charity and goodwill are simply not

---

[10] Lk. 4:16-21, Matt. 5:1-20
[11] Karen Shakespeare, 'Fulfilling the Great Commission in the 21st Century: Outworking of the response – The Salvation Army and Social Justice', (February 2009), a paper presented to the International Doctrine Council, http://www1.salvationarmy.org/IHQ/www_ihq_isjc.nsf/vw-sublinks/B3DB4808441E738E802575EE0009F92F?openDocument (accessed 18 June 2012)
[12] Street, *Called to be God's People*, pp. 69-70

enough. Effectiveness for the Army requires that conscience and conviction spur us to social action, where mercy meets the cause of justice in the world.[13]

We will now explore how The Salvation Army in New Zealand has responded to its holistic mission.

The Army's response to human need – the New Zealand experience

For most of us the everyday reality of our ministry is serving a never-ending queue of suffering humanity. People impacted by the scourges of poverty, loneliness, addiction, criminal offending, homelessness, human trafficking, illness, illiteracy, social isolation, unemployment, abuse, and other human suffering.

Internationally, this torrent of human need is responded to by a Salvation Army ready with immediate care, crisis management, practical love, and professional skills and training. Motivating Salvationists to make such a response is the impact and reality of God's love and salvation operating in their individual lives. Salvationists are pragmatic people, and The Salvation Army a pragmatic organisation keen to respond immediately to need rather than spend time reflecting on the theology that might lead to this serving of suffering humanity.

From the post-war period to the 1990s, the approach of The Salvation Army in New Zealand in meeting need was similarly pragmatic, albeit using where possible the best of healing therapies and professionally competent staff. Although leadership would have denied it, the link between serving humanity and biblical theology had become organisationally isolated and theologically tentative.

Over the past ten years in New Zealand a change has occurred that has seen a stronger link between the Army's theology and the services meeting need. A closer alignment between evangelistic and social theology, corps and social services, theology and practice, social service and social reform has occurred to the point that it could be said the link between the theology of the Army and suffering humanity is strong.

This change had mixed drivers, including: a more aggressive and comprehensive territorial mission setting process that has unified theology and practice; an organisational change that has seen most corps embracing Community Ministries (the name of our frontline welfare centres), Just Action social justice conferences, the birth of Recovery Churches in addiction services, a deliberate Christian mission focus on social services, and the establishment of The Salvation Army Social Policy and Parliamentary Unit (SPPU).

---

[13] Geanette Seymour, 'How can we make our voice heard and speak prophetically from our experience?' - a paper presented at the USA Salvation Army Conference for Social Work and Emergency Disaster Service, March 2014

Theologically-based approaches to serving suffering have developed as Salvationists have more deeply understood and appreciated The Salvation Army's historical mandate and theology.

At this stage it is too early in the change process to know whether what we are observing is a permanent change in how The Salvation Army in New Zealand undertakes its ministry, or whether other environmental or international factors may arrest this approach.

Offered, therefore, in this chapter is a description of the New Zealand journey in this change as an example of what Salvation Army theology can look like when serving suffering humanity.

Integration of spiritual and social

From an early period, The Salvation Army in New Zealand—in line with international trends—separated its evangelistic and social wings administratively, financially and missionally. This separation became entrenched, to the point where the social and evangelical work of the Army happened in two entities with Salvation Army officers divided into either 'field officers' or 'social officers'.

This divide increased in the 1950s to 1970s as social and health services in New Zealand moved to more strongly specialise and professionalise. The result was an external environment demanding more professional practice, staff better educated in social sciences and the requirement of more accountability in government funding contracts.

The Salvation Army's theological imprimatur on its social service operation at this time could best be described as a loose belief that loving God meant loving others—hence, 'social services' were justified as Christian acts of love. While this practical model of Christian love was appropriate overall, the theological understanding and rationale for service was not well articulated or understood. Christian pragmatism rather than Christian theology influenced how The Salvation Army undertook its social and public ministry.

In the 1980s a rethinking of the integration between service and theology commenced in The Salvation Army. Contributing to this change were external environmental factors and greater concentration on biblical truth.

Strangely, an economic philosophy contributed to The Salvation Army reconnecting in greater depth to its theological foundations The dominance of economic liberalism as the major public policy doctrine in New Zealand came with a Labour Government in 1984 and changed how New Zealand acted as a society and how individual 'Kiwis' treated each other. Self-interest, individualisation, dominance of the market, secularism, competitiveness rather than cooperation, and an increasing gap between rich and the poor became increasingly the markers of New Zealand life.

These economically liberal policies resulted in a new poor. People found themselves in poverty, disenfranchised from the norms of New Zealand society, in low-quality housing, with limited employment opportunities, often victims of crime, and susceptible to social hazards.

One impact on Army corps of this altered New Zealand, was a reinterpretation of corps mission, worship and service. This following what had been a loss of certainty in corps ministry created by the church growth movement and theological uncertainty. There were obvious links in this new economic liberalism to the situation for the poor in Booth's London. Salvationists became more interested in embracing the historical mandate of the Army and the theological roots of Wesley and Booth. Similarly, in social services, a new emphasis on creating Christian community was added to professional practice and therapies.[14]

The result of weaving people into a patchwork of Christian community means the marginalised have become known, named and included within Salvation Army communities in corps and social centres. Our congregations in New Zealand have become less middle class, with many congregations increasingly comprising people (clients) from Salvation Army social services work. The embracing of economic liberalism in public policy was a wakeup call that helped the Army in New Zealand rediscover its theological roots.

Cultural contextualisation

Another external factor influential in the reconnection of Salvationists with their faith taproots has been increased awareness in New Zealand public life of bi-culturalism and the honouring of the Treaty of Waitangi. The Treaty of Waitangi is the founding document of New Zealand and was between indigenous New Zealanders, Māori, and the British Crown. In recent years, New Zealand has been challenged to better recognise the bi-cultural partnership created by the Treaty in public policy and in its social and economic life.

Although New Zealand is traditionally a very secular state, to more fully recognise Māori people, there has needed to be greater regard for faith and the spiritual dimension of life. These are two essentials elements of *Māoritanga*.

One public aspect of this is in the Māori religious ceremony and prayer (*karakia*) associated with *pōwhiri* (welcomes) at government occasions. This recognition also provides new opportunities for faith communities to receive public acknowledgement of their own faith heritage. An example of this is found in a Memorandum of Understanding between The Salvation Army and the Ministry of Social Development. The document reads:

> The Ministry of Social Development acknowledges that The Salvation Army is an evangelical church and human resources provider, with its message based on the Bible, its ministry motivated by the love of God

---

[14] 'Shaping the Future of the Army, Territorial Strategic Mission Plan' (Wellington, 2006)

and its mission to preach the gospel of Jesus Christ and meet human need without discrimination. This involves The Salvation Army in caring for people, transforming lives through God in Christ in the power of the Holy Spirit and working for the reform of society by alleviating poverty, deprivation and disadvantage and by challenging evil, injustice and oppression. [15]

This statement is a significant acknowledgement of the faith tradition and motivation of The Salvation Army in its contracts with Government. By incorporating The Salvation Army mission in its partnership agreement, Government not only recognises the right to encompass spiritual processes in the transformation and care of people, but also recognises that on occasions the Army will change and oppose government policy and practice in seeking the reform of society. I suspect this opportunity to have Government sanction and encouragement of our spiritual as well as humanitarian purposes is reasonably unique internationally in The Salvation Army.

The Treaty of Waitangi, then, is another example of an external influence that has served to nurture a rediscovery and reemphasis of The Salvation Army's theological story and journey.

Theological roots

Internally, the rediscovery of theological roots includes: a greater understanding of the biblical theme of justice, a deeper faith-to-life connection, increased biblical literacy, and a desire to be missional in a way that makes a real difference in people's everyday lives. As a result, social service work is now largely integrated into Salvation Army corps. Ten years ago, few Salvation Army corps included social service expressions as part of their congregational life. Where social assistance was given, it would have been undertaken by a corps officer. Now, nearly all New Zealand corps have a community of social expression, with appropriate training and engagement of soldiers and adherents. Increasingly, the community is seen as the centre of corps mission.

Salvationists seem willing to actively embrace that part of our theological DNA which understands that no-one is beyond redemption or separated from the grace and love of God. Five years ago, the territory commenced addiction rehabilitation work alongside the Mongrel Mob, one of New Zealand's largest and most troublesome criminal gangs.

This work was difficult for Salvation Army Addiction Services to undertake because of the almost universal community rejection of these gang members by New Zealanders and the gang's insistence on contributing and commenting on all treatment methodologies. Without a strong connection to our theological and biblical mandate, this work would have failed. Professional treatment methodologies alone could not have been effective or sustained what

---

[15] 'Memorandum of Understanding between the Ministry of Social Development and The Salvation Army' (2006)

turned out to be a very challenging journey. The faith component and theological touchstone enabled officers and staff to remain 'with' the Mob despite immense hurdles. Through this programme, numbers of the Mob have turned their lives around and beaten their drug and alcohol habits.

As The Salvation Army in New Zealand has rediscovered its Wesleyan and Booth roots, the territory has focused its ministry on the causes, and not just the effects, of poverty and need. Nine years ago, the territory was led to question the effectiveness of its social services operation in achieving real change for those it served. In a 2003 survey it found that despite significant efforts in social provision, the Salvation Army had failed to arrest a decline in the social circumstances of New Zealand's most vulnerable groups in all the areas in which it was working.[16] Although some people came to faith and thousands were cared for, with regard to the gospel imperative to create a more just society, we were achieving little.

Engaging with causes of injustice

To change this situation, Salvation Army leadership established a specialist unit focused on engaging with social policy and the causes of injustice. This new entity, 'the Social Policy and Parliamentary Unit' was deliberately housed in a Salvation Army social service centre in South Auckland where some of New Zealand's most deprived neighbourhoods were located. The Unit's purpose was defined as 'working towards the eradication of poverty in New Zealand'. It undertook this mandate by working with New Zealand's social and economic policy-makers. These individuals were generally leaders in the community, government, politics, business and commerce.

The methodologies used in the engagement with these leaders included:

- an annual programme of social policy research
- regular publications to provoke and stimulate debate from our theological and biblical understandings around issues of social policy and social justice
- deliberate engagement with four hundred or so individuals seen to be the most influential in creating public policy
- organisation of an annual national (Just Action) conference focused on issues of biblical justice, social policy and social justice
- judicious use of the media to raise public awareness on key social policy issues
- the establishment of relationships with individual politicians and political parties represented in the New Zealand Parliament.

---

[16] Work undertaken by Bonnie Robinson in 2001 looking at the effectiveness of Salvation Army Social Services in South Auckland

One of the most influential pieces of work undertaken by the Unit is the publication of its annual State of the Nation report. Six of these reports have now been published. At the beginning of each year the Army brings its theological and biblical framework alongside public policy, examining: the state of New Zealand's children, the adequacy of work and incomes policies, adequacy of housing provision, progress in eliminating crime and moving towards a more rehabilitative punishment regime, and progress on a range of social hazards. Evidence is that Government is increasingly introducing policies to address these areas.

Increasing awareness

Apart from its external influence, the work of the Social Policy and Parliamentary Unit has been influential in supporting a renewed understanding and outworking of the foundational beliefs of biblical justice in the life of Salvationists. Deepening awareness of injustice has caused an increasing group of Salvationists to be attracted to the area of social justice. Social justice has become part of the territorial mission agenda, with one of four mission goals being to fight injustice. Ten years ago such a social reform mission goal would never have been accepted as a strategic goal of The Salvation Army in New Zealand.

Without at all diminishing its place as an evangelical church and social service provider, the Salvation Army in New Zealand has become increasingly known as a movement for social justice and institutional change. Recently, the head of a leading government ministry said, 'The Salvation Army is the strongest church body in New Zealand in terms of advocating for socio-economic change. MPs get jittery when they know a SPPU report is imminent'.

There is no doubt that The Salvation Army in New Zealand is more intentionally integrating its theology with its mission to serve suffering humanity. It better articulates the truths of the gospel in collective situations and environments. In doing so, it has found it is possible to be a provider of social services receiving government funding and still provide robust evaluation and critique from our theological and biblical understandings of that government's social policy. We are making a pastoral response by linking people to communities of hope, and to social and spiritual holiness in new and exciting ways. This linking of theology and service has produced an Army willing to fight for what it believes and prepared to challenge the leadership of the nation. For many, this has been a welcome development in our public ministry that they feel is worthy of their support.

Additionally, as Salvationists have reflected more deeply on the genesis of their faith they have been drawn to a more integrated community approach that sees holiness not only in individual but also in collective terms. As there has been an increasingly outward focus, with faith re-energised in the lives of Salvation Army worshipping communities.

In New Zealand the better integration of Salvation Army theology in our mission of serving suffering humanity is contributing to a unification and renewal of the missional purpose of The Salvation Army in New Zealand. It is helping us bridge the great divide between church congregations and social expression by returning us to the intention of God for the Church: that we would be integrated in our mission expression, and that we would proclaim the actuality of God's integration with the social and public spheres of his world. God is present and invites us to be present also.

Conclusion

Frederick Coutts reminds us of the integrative imperative for the two major elements of the Army's mission:

> If we, ourselves, for want of a better way of speaking, refer to our evangelical work and to our social work, it is not that these are two distinct entities which could operate one without the other. They are but two activities of the one and same salvation which his concerned with the total redemption of man. Both rely on the same divine grace. Both are inspired with the same motive. Both have the same end in mind. And, as the gospel has joined them together, we do not propose to put them asunder.[17]

Perhaps some of the final words attributed to William Booth[18] serve to best sum up the Army's commitment to social justice:

> While women weep, as they do now, I'll fight; while children go hungry, as they do now I'll fight; while men go to prison, in and out, in and out, as they do now, I'll fight; while there is a poor lost girl upon the streets, while there remains one dark soul without the light of God, I'll fight, I'll fight to the very end!

---

[17] Cited in Philip D. Needham 'Toward a Reintegration of the Salvationist Mission' in John D. Waldron, (Ed)   *Creed and Deed: Toward a Christian Theology of Social Services in The Salvation Army,*(Ontario, Canada: The Salvation Army Canada and Bermuda Territory, 1986), 145; see also *Jesus and Justice*, (New York, NY: The Salvation Army International Social Justice Commission, 2010)

[18] Although this stirring challenge is usually attributed to Booth's final speech to his followers, it perhaps derives from earlier sources. See Sven Ljungholm,'He said what', http://fsaof.blogspot.co.uk/2012/05/he-said-what.html (accessed 25 March 2015). In any case, the words provoke a call to action to which Booth himself would not object!

14. Warriors in the Salvation War

Who are these Primitive Salvationists?

Aaron White

Primitive Salvationism (noun): Charismatic-flavoured, mission-focused heroism. A term describing a strain of Salvation Army philosophy based on the 19th century fundamentals of Booth, Railton, Booth-Tucker, and others, and re-emerging in the late 20th century throughout the western Salvation Army world.[1]

There was a popular idea in the time of Jeremiah (roughly 600 BCE), called "Zion Theology." This theology affirmed that Yahweh would always fight for Zion. Those in Jerusalem believed they could act in whatever manner they saw fit - including idolatry, oppressing the fatherless and the sojourner, abusing the poor, stealing, murdering, adultery, and swearing falsely - and still trust that God would not let Zion fall.[2]

Jeremiah 7 reveals that this way of thinking and acting was far more dangerous than any invading army. Yahweh warns the people that their history, geography, and reputation were not enough to save them; only obedience to their covenant relationship with Yahweh held any hope for salvation. Yahweh had raised them up to be his obedient children who would faithfully fulfill his mission on the earth, but they had rebelled against their very identity. When Babylon came to conquer Jerusalem, God did not fight for them. He allowed the city to fall, the Temple to be destroyed, and the people to be slaughtered or carried off into exile.

A variation on Zion Theology was reproduced in the early Church. John's letter to the Church in Ephesus (Rev 2:1-7) has Jesus rebuking them for abandoning their first love, and telling them to repent and do the works they had done at first or he would remove their lampstand. They had forgotten their purpose, their identity. The same applied to the Church in Sardis (Rev 3:1-6) which had the reputation of being alive, but was dead. Again, if they did not wake up and repent, Jesus would come against them like a thief. These churches seemed busy, dutiful, and pious; but they had lost something vital, and were not living up to the identity they had been given in Christ. Zion Theology did not save ancient Jerusalem from falling, nor would an updated

---

[1] http://primitivesalvationism.wordpress.com/?s=holiness&submit=Search Quote is originally attributed to Major Stephen Court
[2] W.J. Wessels, "Zion, Beautiful City of God: Zion Theology in the Book of Jeremiah", *Verbum et Ecclessia*, Volume 27, Issue 2, 2006.

Zion Theology save the first century churches if they failed to faithfully persevere.

What if The Salvation Army in the Western world were facing its own Zion Theology, its own crisis of identity and purpose? This is the concern of Primitive Salvationism, and this is why the emphasis of Primitive Salvationists is on the renewal of The Army's first love. Lilian Taiz notes that

> During the 20th century the Army ceased to be a working-class dominated religious organization. Its social institutions offered temporal salvation to the poor while its spiritual work ministered to the upwardly mobile. In contrast to the blood-washed warriors of the 19th cent, the SA of the 20th gradually regarded themselves as a church that sponsored professionalized Christian social services to the downtrodden.[3]

As The Salvation Army in the global West faces internal struggles, plummeting attendance, and declining soldier's rolls and officer candidates, it is very common to hear the confident assertion that 'God raised up The Salvation Army'.[4] Most, if not all, Salvationists would agree. But does this mean God will continue to bless and uplift The Salvation Army if it fails to faithfully persevere in the mission and identity it has been given? The idea that The Salvation Army's future is divinely secure no matter how far it strays from what God raised it up to be is just a version of Zion Theology with epaulets on. General William Booth, foreseeing this possibility, proclaimed: 'When The Salvation Army ceases to be a militant body of red hot men and women whose supreme business is the saving of souls, I hope it will vanish utterly'. If The Salvation Army has indeed strayed from its roots, and if Booth's words are to be taken seriously, should Salvationists now look to find or create another movement? Or is the reclamation of our birthright a possibility? The hope for the latter is what gave birth to Primitive Salvationism.

To call something primitive is usually an insult. It refers to something basic, simple, old, antiquated. If something is primitive it means that the times have passed it by, that there are new realities, new iterations and adaptations which have made the primitive obsolete. When the term 'primitive' is self-applied, however, the meaning shifts from one that is pejorative to one that takes delight in associations with what has gone before. Primitive Salvationists are hardly the first to take on this designation. The Franciscan Order were considered dangerously primitive as they spread out all over Europe with their message of simple love, devotion, compassion, and the denial of wealth, scholarship, power and prestige for the love of Christ. The early Methodists,

---

[3] Lillian Taiz, *Hallelujah Lads and Lasses: Remaking The Salvation Army in America, 1880-1930*, (UNC Press, 2001)

[4] Stephen Court,
http://armybarmyblog.blogspot.ca/2014_03_01_archive.html#6316040615466983131.
Court notes that worldwide, The Salvation Army has 356 fewer Corps in 2014 Yearbook than it did in 2013 Salvation Army Yearbook. Much of that loss (along with declining Senior Soldier, Junior Soldier, and Cadet numbers) has taken place in the Global West.

committed as they were to reforming the nations and the Church through Scriptural holiness, were viewed as primitive by the Church hierarchy. There were even Primitive Franciscans (*Fratecelli*) and Primitive Methodists who sprang up when they felt their respective movements had lost the original mission and vision, and who focused on less formal and more democratic organisation, greater simplicity, and more involvement with the destitute and the working poor.[5]

Primitive Salvationists look to the early Salvation Army and find there a very primitive movement. Catherine Booth, speaking of recruitment, said: 'He may not be able to put together two sentences of the Queen's English, but if he can say that he has been born again, if he can say "once I was blind but now I see", he will do for The Salvation Army'.[6] Samuel Logan Brengle reminds us that

> The Salvation Army was born, not in a cloister, nor in a drawing-room, but on a spiritual battlefield – at a penitent-form. It has been nourished for spiritual conquests, not upon speculative doctrines and fine-spun verbal distinctions, but upon these great doctrines which can be wrought into and worked out in soul-satisfying experience. Hence, The Army compels the attention of all men everywhere and appeals to the universal heart of humanity.[7]

At its heart The Salvation Army was a prophetic movement – calling sinners to salvation but also calling the Church back to the essentials, to its first love. It was not trying to be a new Church denomination, but understood itself instead as an actual army, challenging the Church and the world with its words and actions: 'We are an army of soldiers of Christ, organised as perfectly as we have been able to accomplish, seeking no church status, avoiding as we would the plague of every denominational rut, in order perpetually to reach more and more of those who live outside every church boundary'.[8] It was a clarion call to entire sanctification, to aggressive evangelism, and to radical acts of mercy and justice. Their innovation was not theological subtlety so much as the marriage of belief and action, the holistic union of spiritual and social concern incarnated in the slums, the pubs, the mines, the street corners and under the bridges. Here were a people who embodied, to the best of their abilities, what they believed.

---

[5] Frank Whaling, *John and Charles Wesley: Selected Writings and Hymns,* (New York, NY: Paulist Press, 1981), p. 61. It should be noted that neither the *Fratecelli* nor the Primitive Methodists were ultimately successful in their attempts to bring their respective movements back to their understanding of the original vision. It may be, however, that their influence within the movements preserved more of the original purposes than would otherwise have been possible.
[6] Catherine Booth, http://primitivesalvationism.wordpress.com/page/6/, April 4, 2013
[7] Samuel Logan Brengle, *Love-Slaves*, (London: Salvationist Publ. and Supplies Ltd., 1923), Chap. IX, 68
[8] George Scott Railton, *Heathen England*, (London: The Salvation Army, 1887), 145

And they believed that in so doing they were taking shape as the Army of the Lord that would bring revival to the ends of the earth.

Primitive Salvationists look to emulate the prophetic primitivism of the early Army. In so doing, they try to position themselves as prophets to the prophetic movement, calling the Army back to its first love: back to blood and fire; back to covenant; back to holiness; and back to holistic love in action. Their call is not new by any means, as many Salvationists have been living out this first love across the world since the Army's founding. Primitive Salvationists are simply looking and working and praying for the renewal of that which is already deep within the DNA of The Salvation Army. In a digital age where ideas are transmitted much more quickly and widely than previously, it could be that this message is getting some traction, particularly amongst the younger generation. The call has manifested itself in a renewed emphasis on the early Salvation Army's understanding and application of full salvation, spiritual warfare, missional community, justice, prayer and worship.

Full Salvation

'Every Salvationist should be a living, walking, fighting Bible, which can be seen, read and felt by every soul around him'. (General William Booth)

The Salvation Army was never simply a mission of evangelism and social concern. At the very heart of early Salvationism was a commitment to Wesleyan holiness, or entire sanctification. (William Booth is remembered for saying, 'There is one God, and John Wesley is his prophet'.[9]) Made in the image of God, the purpose of humanity is to be freed from the guilt *and* the power of sin, and to be conformed or re-made into to the likeness of Jesus Christ. This "full salvation" means the growth of perfect, holy love for God and for fellow humans as an essential part of Christian life. This is more than a 'fire-insurance' salvation message, this is Doctrine 10: 'We believe that it is the privilege of all believers to be wholly sanctified, and that their whole spirit, soul and body may be preserved blameless unto the coming of our Lord Jesus Christ'. The early Salvationists took their cue from John Wesley, who preached:

> There is scarce any expression in Holy Writ which has given more offence than this. The word perfect is what many cannot bear. The very sound of it is an abomination to them. And whosoever preaches perfection (as the phrase is,) that is, asserts that it is attainable in this life, runs great hazard of being accounted by them worse than a heathen man or a publican.[10]

---

[9] Frederick Booth-Tucker, *The Life of Catherine Booth: The Mother of the Salvation Army*, Volume 1 (New York, NY: Flemming H. Revell Co., 1872), 74

[10] Howard Snyder, 'What is Unique About a Wesleyan Theology of Mission?' accessed 28 July, 2011, available from http://www.wineskins.net/pdf/wesleyan_mission.pdf

Salvationist leaders such as Samuel Logan Brengle clearly *did* believe that sanctification was attainable in this life, and the theology and practice of the early Salvation Army was built upon the idea that holiness – the separation of the soul from sin, and the maturation of perfect love - was possible for all.

This kind of holiness teaching has not been abandoned by The Salvation Army, as evidenced by worldwide Brengle Holiness Institutes for officers. Yet it must be said that Wesleyan holiness is in danger of becoming increasingly marginalised. Salvationist preachers and teachers will confidently exclaim that 'they know they will sin tomorrow', and at conferences and retreats across the Western world this author has heard time and again the despairing resignation that sin is simply a normal part of life, something that will continue to have a fearsome hold over us until glory. This is a far cry from Brengle's assertion: 'We do not say that it is not possible to sin, but we do say that it is possible not to sin'.[11] The message of entire sanctification is as offensive today as it has ever been.

Primitive Salvationists view entire sanctification as a theological necessity. There is no hint in the New Testament that Christians ought to go on sinning, that this is to be accepted as the norm. Christians rather are described as 'dead to sin and alive to Christ' (Romans 6:1-14). Nor is there the kind of theology which has God redeeming the soul but leaving the body and the mind to continue on in depravity. This dualism, often the result of an eschatology that disdains the body and elevates the soul at its expense, does not contain within it the beauty, power and truth of The Salvation Army's holistic mission.[12] As Howard Snyder puts it:

> Salvation-as-healing makes it clear that God is intimately concerned with every aspect of our lives; yet, biblically understood, it also makes clear that the healing we most fundamentally need is spiritual: Our relationship to God. Biblically grounded (and as Wesley understood it), the salvation-as-healing motif is no concession to pop psychology; it is an affirmation of who God is, what it means to be created in God's image, and what it takes for that image to be restored in Jesus Christ by the power of the Holy Spirit.[13]

This commitment to full salvation is at the heart of The Salvation Army's identity and mission, and Primitive Salvationists see it as a key marker for gauging the movement's faithful obedience.

---

[11] http://primitivesalvationism.wordpress.com/page/5/, April 4, 2013
[12] Jonathan Evans, *Training Warriors to Win the World for Jesus:The Salvation Army's 'War College' Wesleyan Missiology*, (Vancouver, 2011), 12
[13] Quoted in Evans, *Training Warriors,* 13

Discipleship and Spiritual Warfare

Alongside the re-emphasis of Wesleyan holiness is a renewed interest in more radical forms of discipleship, at the heart of which is a recommitment to spiritual warfare. Commissioner Booth-Tucker once declared that 'there is a danger of the old clergy and laity idea creeping in amongst us. The common church idea is that of a minister doing all the fighting and feeding, while his congregation does all the looking on and swallowing. We are an Army. Every soldier is expected to fight'.[14] There are simply too many examples to cite of the early Salvationists employing militant language and highlighting the need for true soldiers to join in the fight against sin and the devil. Nor has this belief ever fully fled, as shown by Commissioner Phil Needham's distinguishing between 'soldiers' and 'members':

> [Describing Soldiership as Membership] means that there is no room for passive membership. In this sense, 'soldier' is a better word than 'member'. Members can be passive or active; they may do no more than belong on the rolls. Soldiers cannot only belong; they are either fighting or maintaining readiness for battle – otherwise, they are not really soldiers.[15]

There is some opposition in The Salvation Army now to the so-called 'military metaphor'. In some cases this is related to the form of military structure and bureaucracy within the organisation, in other cases to a deeper disagreement with the language of spiritual warfare and the idea of aggressive evangelism. Primitive Salvationists, however, put great stock in the making, discipling and deploying of soldiers, and in the use of militant language as an expression of spiritual realities. Many Corps around the Western world expect recruits – and transferring soldiers – to demonstrate that they have read the whole Bible, memorised the doctrines, been clean and saved for a year, are willing to wear uniform, and are an active participant in the mission of the Corps before joining the ranks. Soldiers are also taking up ministry positions once reserved for officers. They do not consider themselves 'lay leaders' that are somehow substantially different from 'ordained ministers'. Rather, they identity as covenanted soldiers doing exactly what they should be doing: engaging the enemy on their front, and leading the charge when commissioned to do so. Again, this is neither new nor unique, but it does represent a reaction to the neglect of soldier-making in some locations, and the perceived low bar set for soldiers in others. It also speaks to a belief that officers are soldiers first, and that the concept of 'officers' is not exactly interchangeable with that of

---

[14] http://primitivesalvationism.wordpress.com/page/2/ 4 April, 2013
[15] http://primitivesalvationism.wordpress.com/page/3/ 4 April, 2013

'pastors'. Officers are honoured and recognised for their leadership role, but they are not expected to do all the fighting, leading or ministering.

Accompanying this push for soldiers are the multitude of gap year training programs now available, such as the UK Territory's Timothy Program/Mission Team/Alove team; Revolution Hawaii; Order 614 in Melbourne; Ignite in Toronto; and The War College in Vancouver. All of these discipleship programs have their own unique contexts and methods, but underlying each of them is a desire to take people deeper into the understanding and application of radical holiness, sacrifice and mission. These are just some of the training grounds for new Primitive Salvationists.

Missional Community

'*I say to my officer who is going to Holland: "Can you be a Dutchman?" To the man who is going to Zululand: "Can you be a Zulu?" To the one going to India: "Can you be an Indian?" If you cannot, you must not go at all*' (General William Booth)

One of the more exciting aspects of Primitive Salvationism is that missional communities are forming as a context for this renewed discipleship and understanding of spiritual warfare. A missional community can be described as a 'salvific community which is sent out into the world with a gospel invitation'.[16] It is a renewal, in a sense, of the original idea of a *Corps*. William Booth defined a Corps in this way: 'a band of people united together to attack and Christianise an entire town or village'.[17] Clearly mission was at the very heart of Booth's understanding of Corps, but it was a mission that steered a course between the extremes of a soulless social gospel on one side and a disembodied spirituality on the other. Booth-Tucker famously inhabited this concept of incarnational mission in India, adopting Indian name, dress and custom in his desire to speak the gospel into a culture not his own.[18]

Commissioner Needham's excellent 1987 work, *Community in Mission: A Salvationist Ecclesiology*, demonstrates that the idea of Corps as communal centres of mission is one that has held on through the years, though it has been gradually replaced by the language of 'Church'.[19] The newest *Handbook of Doctrine* accepts the identification of The Salvation Army as a mission, but also argues for a more ecclesiastical understanding of the movement in the modern era.[20] Primitive Salvationists highlight the vital

---

[16] Evans, *Training Warriors*, 12
[17] http://armybarmyblog.blogspot.ca/2013_12_01_archive.html#5850414686906632858
[18] Harry Williams, *Booth-Tucker: William Booth's First Gentleman*, (London: Hodder and Stoughton, 1980); F.A. Mackenzie, *Booth-Tucker: Sadhu and Saint,* (London: Hodder and Stoughton, 1930).
[19] Phil Needham, *Community in Mission: A Salvationist Ecclesiology,* (London: The Salvation Army International Headquarters, 1987)
[20] *The Salvation Army Handbook of Doctrine,* Salvation Books, (London: The Salvation Army International Headquarters, 2010), 265-267. The 2006 Theology and Ethics

importance of Corps, not simply as places of worship and preaching, and not as 'churches' *per se,* but as strategic centres of discipleship and mission that are part of a wider Army movement.

The '614' model is one modern example of Corps as missional communities. The first 614 began in Toronto in 2000 when officers and soldiers intentionally moved into Regent Park, an inner city area of Toronto well-known for generational poverty, gang violence, and remarkable ethnic diversity. Their purpose was to live out their founding verse: 'They will rebuild the ancient ruins and restore the places long devastated; they will renew the ruined cities that have been devastated for generations' (Isaiah 61:4). This required incarnation - taking on the neighbourhood's 'flesh' by living there and encountering the same concerns their neighbours encountered; a deep connection between 'social' work and 'spiritual' work that ran counter to separation of the social units and Corps that had been more the norm in the West; and a commitment to sacrificial evangelism. It also required a new understanding of and dedication to community, one based around the nature of God. This harkens back to The Salvation Army's Wesleyan roots: 'John Wesley's emphasis was on God's Triune essence as love. The community of three and one permits loving interaction to a fullness that an individual could not express'.[21] According to this theology, salvation, while being at one level an individual event, is also fundamentally a corporate reality:

> God wants to save us from sin so that he can bring creation to a higher purpose. God wants us to participate in an eternal community. 'God's desire is to create a redeemed humankind, dwelling within a redeemed creation, and enjoying the presence of the Triune God'. Such a community rightfully holds an *imago Dei*, a corporate reality rather than a 'human-spirit-after-the Holy-Spirit-in-me theology'.[22]

614 Corps endeavour to incarnate in the footsteps of Jesus, and to be united in community as bearers of the Trinitarian image of God.

The 614 model has extended around the Western world, first to Vancouver, Canada, and then to locales such as Melbourne, Australia; Chattanooga, Tennessee; Charlotte, North Carolina; Chemnitz, Germany;

Symposium in Johannesburg had this to say on the topic: 'Through the years Salvationism has moved on in its emerging self-perception, and in the perception of others, from being a para-church evangelistic revival movement...to being a Christian church with a permanent mission to the unsaved and the marginalised. Salvationists remain comfortable in being known simply as "the Army", or a "mission", or a "movement", or for certain purposes as a "charity". All of these descriptors can be used alongside "church". With this multi-faceted identity the Army is welcomed to, and takes its place at, the ecumenical table at local, national and international levels'.

[21] Evans, *Training Warriors,* 2

[22] Evans, *Training Warriors,* 13, quoting Peter R. Holmes, *Becoming More Human: Exploring the Interface of Spirituality, Discipleship and Therapeutic Faith Community* (Waynesboro, GA: Paternoster Press, 2005), 57

Wellington, New Zealand; and all over the UK. Each 614 Corps, while differing in context, commits to a series of 'essentials':

- Worship with commitment and integrity
- Transformational prayer
- Preaching for all by all
- Radical discipleship
- Redemptive theology of salvation
- Holistic mission of redemption
- Prophetic engagement with culture
- Passionate pursuit of justice
- Commitment to lifestyle simplicity
- Incarnational community life
- Affirmation of all peoples equally
- Rooted in mission not maintenance[23]

The 614 model is, again, far from the only example of missional community in The Salvation Army world. Corps, at their best, have always exemplified The Salvation Army's identity through incarnation, social and spiritual connection, and radical evangelism. Primitive Salvationists acknowledge and encourage these Corps everywhere they are found, be they in urban, suburban or rural settings.

Justice

The Primitive Salvationist renewals in the areas of holiness teaching, discipleship, and missional communities have been accompanied by a renewed emphasis on justice. Justice must be seen as part of the core identity of The Salvation Army, past, present and future. The early Salvationists were risky, entrepreneurial fighters for justice. From establishing safe match factories, to redeeming Devil's Island, to famously fighting against sex slavery in Europe and Japan, The Salvation Army was not just active in mercy, charity and evangelistic work, but took on social and systemic inequalities with a boldness and effectiveness that inspire modern activists to this day. Booth's *In Darkest England and the Way Out*, while never fully realised, presents a vision of a transformed, redeemed, and just society that helped pave the way for modern social safety nets.

The Salvation Army is internationally renowned for its ongoing mercy and charity work, but it has rarely matched its early efforts to combat injustices. Yet in recent years there has been an upswing in Salvationist consciousness around justice issues, something that Primitive Salvationists help initiate, participate in, and applaud. The Salvation Army's International Social Justice Commission, which takes an active role in UN discussions, is 'the Salvation

---

[23] http://www.614network.com/essentials/

Army's strategic voice to advocate for human dignity and social justice for the world's poor and oppressed'.[24] Territorial justice initiatives have also been created, and The Salvation Army worldwide has helped bring awareness to the abomination of Human Trafficking. Many resources, months of prayer, conferences and think-tanks have been produced within Army circles to work for the creation of a more just and sustainable world.[25] Jonathan Evans of The War College, contemplating both The Army's and the Wesleys' approach to justice, argues that 'the universal human endeavour is in reflecting the political image of God by stewarding (ruling and keeping) over all the earth...working within the created order to bring God's loving rule into all aspects of life'.[26] Just as Jeremiah warned Israel:

> If you really change your ways and your actions and deal with each other justly, if you do not oppress the foreigner, the fatherless or the widow and do not shed innocent blood in this place, and if you do not follow other gods to your own harm, then I will let you live in this place, in the land I gave your ancestors for ever and ever. (Jeremiah 7:5-7)

So must The Salvation Army live up to its identity as a movement of justice-fighters, or it may lose its crown.

Prayer and Worship

Finally, out of the overflow of holiness theology, radical discipleship, missional communities and justice has come a renaissance of Primitive Salvationist prayer and worship forms. Many attribute The Salvation Army's early successes to the priority they placed on radical, persevering prayer, or 'Knee Drill' as they called it. Brengle believed that 'all great soul-winners have been men of much and mighty prayer, and all great revivals have been preceded and carried out by persevering, prevailing knee-work in the closet'.[27] Salvationists have never lost the sense of the importance of prayer and worship, but it is easy to relegate these to the sideline when there is so much other work to be done. Thus, in 1999 the *International Spiritual Life Commission* challenged

---

[24] http://www.salvationarmy.org/isjc
[25] The following are some excellent books on Justice and The Salvation Army: Danielle Strickland, Campbell Roberts, *Just Imagine: The world for God,* (Melbourne: SALVO Publishing, 2008); S. Carvosso Gauntlett, Danielle Strickland, *Challenging Evil,* (2010); Danielle Strickland, *The Liberating Truth: How Jesus Empowers Women,* Oxford: (Monarch Books, 2011); Wesley Campbell, Stephen Court, *Be A Hero*, (Shippensburg, PA: Destiny Image Publishers, Inc., 2004).
[26] Evans, *Training Warriors,* p. 17, referencing John Wesley's Sermon 45, 'The New Birth' *Works*, 2: 188
[27] http://associate.com/groups/anzac/0::760read.html

Salvationists everywhere to live up to their spiritual heritage through "a renewal of faithful, disciplined and persistent prayer."[28]

That same year the 24-7 Prayer movement arose out of the south of England, and quickly took root in Salvation Army circles, particularly amongst those longing for a greater emphasis on sacrificial spirituality in the movement. The very first Salvation Army 24-7 Prayer room was run out of a portacabin behind the Salvation Army Mission Team offices in London, after Salvo representatives had been present at the launch of 24-7 Prayer in Southampton. The next was run at the *Roots* conference in Southport, England, an event notable for its exploration of ways to renew the original vision of The Salvation Army. This prayer room was actually a double-decker bus, filled night and day with (primarily) teens and young adults, praying with fervour and experiencing something very old, but brand new to them. After this there was no stopping the prayer movement. The UK territory hosted a full year of non-stop prayer, linking up Corps that prayed 24-7 for one week at a time. This was followed by similar years of prayer in Australia, the US, and Canada, until finally the international Salvation Army committed to a full year of non-stop prayer in 2011 and another full year beginning July 2014.

The 24-7 Prayer movement itself could not quite fathom how or why this form of prayer was so immediately accessible to Salvationists, who had a reputation for good works but not, in modern times, for radical prayer. The key was likely *The Vision*, a poem written by Pete Greig in the first 24-7 Prayer room. *The Vision* seemed to stream directly out of the subconscious of Salvation Army spirituality, with lines such as:

> The vision is JESUS – obsessively, dangerously, undeniably Jesus / The vision is an army of young people. / You see bones? I see an army...This is an army that will lay down its life for the cause. A million times a day its soldiers choose to lose that they might one day win the great 'Well done' of faithful sons and daughters....And the army is discipl(in)ed. / Young people who beat their bodies into submission. / Every soldier would take a bullet for his comrade at arms. The tattoo on their back boasts "for me to live is Christ and to die is gain.[29]

The Vision struck a chord deep inside many Salvationists, and the response of radical committed prayer became the norm. 24-7 Prayer rooms have since become a hallmark of Primitive Salvationist communities, with some even becoming officially recognised 24-7 Prayer 'Boiler Rooms'. This form of prayer has also been easily accepted into mainstream Salvation Army ranks. Many Youth Councils, Young Adult retreats, and Officers' Councils now carry the expectation of 24-7 prayer rooms.

---

[28] Robert Street, *Called to be God's People*, International Headquarters, London, 1999, 39

[29] Pete Greig, "The Vision", Read the full poem here: http://www.24-7prayer.com/about/thevision-en.

Renewed worship has also emerged in Primitive Salvationist circles. New musical forms are being embraced by Salvation Army bands and songsters, while contemporary Army worship groups such as *The Singing Company* and *Transmission* have written music that re-digs old wells of songbook hymns and Wesleyan theology. These songs teach a new generation of Salvationists to sing their doctrine, but also attempt to capture the passionate heart of Army pioneers. Early Salvation Army worship was, by all accounts, a lively affair, filled with manifestations of the Holy Spirit, loud singing, tears, wails, and a cacophony of various instruments.[30] Catherine Booth noted how many 'unkind things have been said of The Salvation Army, because people have fallen on their faces under the convicting power of the Spirit at our meetings'.[31] The Salvation Army has not ceased to give joyful expression in worship through the years; even C.S. Lewis commented (somewhat) favourably on the 'rowdiness' or 'gusto' present in Salvation Army worship in the mid-20th century.[32] The 1960's witnessed the cultural phenomenon that was the *Joystrings*, a Salvationist musical group that managed to break into the pop mainstream and show the world the kind of innovation and joy The Salvation Army at its best really does possess.

Of course, the importance of worship is not in its popular appeal, and the 1960's (and 1860's) are a long time ago. The Salvation Army cannot rest on old glories and stories if it wishes to see true spiritual renewal. This is why Primitive Salvationism must never take a solely doctrinal or missional approach. If it cannot connect with the spiritual life of The Salvation Army, if its passion is never embodied in the prayers and worship of the rank and file, then it will not, and should not, survive. Below is an example of a contemporary worship song - also a prayer - that encapsulates the dream of Primitive Salvationism as well as any can:

Soldiers Hymn (by t*ransMission*)

Father of this Army, Captain of our soldiers
May Your glory fill the earth
As this world grows colder, may Your troops be bolder
May we fight with only love
May the crosses we bear be the weapons of our warfare
May we even more dare for You
May we even more dare for You

---

[30] See an excellent overview of early, charismatic worship in The Salvation Army by Lt-Col Max Ryan: http://salvationist.ca/2011/03/signs-and-wonders/

[31] Catherine Booth, *Papers on Aggressive Christianity*, 1880, accessed at http://www.gospeltruth.net/booth/cath_booth/agressive_christianity/cbooth_3_adaptation.htm

[32] C.S. Lewis, "'The Fair Beauty of the Lord,'" Reflections on the Psalms (1958) as republished within C.S. Lewis: Selected Books (London: HarperCollins, 2002) 336-337.

Let our uniform be holiness and mercy
Justice clothed with grace and truth
Those who speak be fearless, those who serve be blameless
Dreamers old and visioned youth
Save us when we look past Jesus as an outcast
Shining, let us hold fast to You
Shining, let us hold fast to You

Breathe onto these dry bones, search the Spirit's deep groans
Speak into these calloused minds
Faith to make our dreams new, hope as we await You
Love to serve with joy and might
Onward to the conquest, north to south and east to west
Forward to the glorious fight of love
Forward to the glorious fight of love [33]

Onward

A chapter of this size and nature only allows for the broadest of brush strokes to paint a picture. There is of course a danger in this, as there is in any discussion of Primitive Salvationism. Some will be inspired, others repulsed, but still others will wonder if they are being rejected, excluded, or ignored. From what this author has seen, Primitive Salvationists celebrate *all* advances in the Salvation War, and recognise that there are many different fronts on which the battle is being fought, each front requiring different tactics. Primitive Salvationists are looking to influence The Salvation Army towards a faithful pursuit of the Army's original call and mission, and against any hint of the dangerous 'Zion Theology' mindset. They know that in this work they stand on the epaulet-engraved shoulders of giants. They have no interest in constructing a new denomination, nor in denigrating or neglecting the work of those thousands of officers and soldiers in the field who are quietly giving of themselves and living the mission every day, and have for years, decades, and generations. To these faithful warriors all Primitive Salvationists would say: 'We are one Army, with one mission, and one hope. No task is too small. No prayer is unheard. No advance in holiness is unimportant. Carry on! Fight the fight of faith, and do not stop until the hour of death! We are in this Salvation War together, and we are bound together by the holy bonds of Christ's love and sacrifice for us. All to the glory of God! Hallelujah! Amen!'

---

[33] Phil Laeger and Marty Mikles, *Soldier's Hymn,* 2009,
http://transmission.virb.com/charts

Epilogue

This book has been structured around General John Gowans' statement of The Salvation Army's purpose. We will conclude with a reflection on this statement and encouragement for the renewal of the Army's mission, by Gowans' colleague John Larsson, who succeeded him in the role of General.

> To save souls — The Army is called to proactive evangelism that adapts to changing times and circumstances. It is essential that we remain focussed on both the goal and the need for continual adaptation of our means in order to attain that goal.
>
> To grow saints — The Army is called to proclaim the doctrine **that believers can be Christlike... As a movement we must never forget the 'fire' in our motto ['Blood & Fire']** — the fire of the Holy Spirit that not only empowers but also sanctifies and purifies.
>
> To serve suffering humanity — The Army is called to be at the forefront of meeting the human needs of today — not those of yesterday. If we are to remain at the cutting edge of meeting human need we have to continually review for relevance the areas of our social service and action.

We need to encourage the renewal of vision of what the Army is meant to be. I believe that in this process of renewal we are rediscovering the genius of the original **vision... It is important that we all encourage the renewal of confi**dence in the unique contribution that the Army was raised up to make.

We are part of a dynamic process. And if in this process of renewal, we as an Army, succeed in recapturing our passion for mission and develop a new self-understanding of the unique contribution we are meant to make, even greater things await the Army in the future.[1]

> *So we'll lift up the banner on high,*
> *The salvation banner of love;*
> *We'll fight beneath its colours till we die,*
> *Then go to our home above.*[2]
>
> *The World for God! The world for God!*
> *I give my heart! I will do my part!*[3]

---

[1] John Larsson, 'Renewal!', The Officer (November/December 2002), 4.
[2] The Song Book of The Salvation Army, 782 (chorus) — William Thomas Giffe.
[3] The Song Book of The Salvation Army, 830 (chorus) — General Evangeline Booth (1895-1950).

Appendix A
The international mission statement of The Salvation Army

The Salvation Army, an international movement, is an evangelical part
of the universal Christian Church. Its message is based on the Bible.
Its ministry is motivated by love for God.
Its mission is to preach the gospel of Jesus Christ and meet human needs
in His name without discrimination.

Appendix B
The Doctrines of The Salvation Army

We believe that the Scriptures of the Old and New Testaments were given by inspiration of God, and that they only constitute the Divine rule of Christian faith and practice.

We believe that there is only one God, who is infinitely perfect, the Creator, Preserver, and Governor of all things, and who is the only proper object of religious worship.

We believe that there are three persons in the Godhead - the Father, the Son, and the Holy Ghost, undivided in essence and co-equal in power and glory.

We believe that in the person of Jesus Christ the Divine and human natures are united, so that He is truly and properly God and truly and properly man.

We believe that our first parents were created in a state of innocency, but by their disobedience, they lost their purity and happiness, and that in consequence of their fall, all men have become sinners, totally depraved, and as such are justly exposed to the wrath of God.

We believe that the Lord Jesus Christ has by His suffering and death made an atonement for the whole world so that whosoever will may be saved.

We believe that repentance toward God, faith in our Lord Jesus Christ and regeneration by the Holy Spirit are necessary to salvation.

We believe that we are justified by grace through faith in our Lord Jesus Christ and that he that believeth hath the witness in himself.

We believe that continuance in a state of salvation depends upon continued obedient faith in Christ.

213

We believe that it is the privilege of all believers to be wholly sanctified, and that their whole spirit and soul and body may be preserved blameless unto the coming of our Lord Jesus Christ.

We believe in the immortality of the soul, the resurrection of the body, in the general judgement at the end of the world, in the eternal happiness of the righteous, and in the endless punishment of the wicked.

Appendix C
Soldier's Covenant

HAVING accepted Jesus Christ as my Saviour and Lord, and desiring to fulfil my membership of His Church on earth as a soldier of The Salvation Army, I now by God's grace enter into a sacred covenant.

I believe and will live by the truths of the word of God expressed in The Salvation Army's eleven articles of faith:

We believe that the Scriptures of the Old and New Testaments were given by inspiration of God: and that they only constitute the Divine rule of Christian faith and practice.

We believe that there is only one God, who is infinitely perfect, the Creator. Preserver, and Governor of all things, and who is the only proper object of religious worship.

We believe that there are three persons in the Godhead—the Father, the Son and the Holy Ghost—undivided in essence and coequal in power and glory.

We believe that in the person of Jesus Christ the Divine and human natures are united, so that He is truly and properly God and truly and properly man.

We believe that our first parents were created in a state of innocency. but by their disobedience they lost their purity and happiness; and that in consequence of their fall all men have become sinners, totally depraved. and as such are justly exposed to the wrath of God.

We believe that the Lord Jesus Christ has, by His suffering and death, made an atonement for the whole world so that whosoever will may be saved.

We believe that repentance towards God, faith in our Lord Jesus Christ and regeneration by the Holy Spirit are necessary to salvation.

We believe that we are justified by grace, through faith in our Lord Jesus Christ; and that he that believeth hath the witness in himself.

We believe that continuance in a state of salvation depends upon continued obedient faith in Christ.

We believe that it is the privilege of all believers to be wholly sanctified, and that their whole spirit and soul and body may be preserved blameless unto the coming of our Lord Jesus Christ.

We believe in the immortality of the soul; in the resurrection of the body; in the general judgment at the end of the world; in the eternal happiness of the righteous; and in the endless punishment of the wicked.

THEREFORE

I will be responsive to the Holy Spirit's work and obedient to His leading in my life, growing in grace through worship, prayer, service and the reading of the Bible.

I will make the values of the Kingdom of God and not the values of the world the standard for my life.

I will uphold Christian integrity in every area of my life, allowing nothing in thought, word or deed that is unworthy, unclean, untrue, profane, dishonest or immoral.

I will maintain Christian ideals in all my relationships with others: my family and neighbours, my colleagues and fellow Salvationists, those to whom and for whom I am responsible, and the wider community.

I will uphold the sanctity of marriage and of family life.

I will be a faithful steward of my time and gifts, my money and possessions, my body, my mind and my spirit, knowing that I am accountable to God.

I will abstain from alcoholic drink, tobacco, the non-medical use of addictive drugs, gambling, pornography, the occult, and all else that could enslave the body or spirit.

I will be faithful to the purposes for which God raised up The Salvation Army, sharing the good news of Jesus Christ, endeavouring to win others to Him, and in His name caring for the needy and the disadvantaged.

I will be actively involved, as I am able, in the life, work, worship and witness of the corps, giving as large a proportion of my income as possible to support its ministries and the worldwide work of the Army.

I will be true to the principles and practices of The Salvation Army, loyal to its leaders, and I will show the spirit of Salvationism whether in times of popularity or persecution.

I now call upon all present to witness that I enter into this covenant and sign these articles of war of my own free will, convinced that the love of Christ, who died and now lives to save me, requires from me this devotion of my life to His service for the salvation of the whole world, and therefore do here declare my full determination, by God's help, to be a true soldier of The Salvation Army.

Junior Soldier's Promise

Having asked God for forgiveness, I will be his loving and obedient child. Because Jesus is my Saviour from sin, I will trust him to keep me good, and will try to help others to follow him. I promise to pray, to read my Bible and, by his help, to lead a life that is clean in thought, word and deed. I will not smoke, take harmful drugs or drink alcoholic drinks.

Appendix D

Officer's Covenant

My Covenant

Called by God to proclaim the gospel of our Lord and Saviour Jesus Christ as an officer of The Salvation Army, I bind myself to him in this solemn covenant: to love and serve him supremely all my days, to live to win souls and make their salvation the first purpose of my life, to care for the poor, feed the hungry, clothe the naked, love the unlovable, and befriend those who have no friends, to maintain the doctrines and principles of The Salvation Army, and, by God's grace, to prove myself a worthy officer.

Appendix E

A Call to Salvationists

As part of the report of the International Commission on Spiritual Life (1996-97)

WORSHIP

1. We call Salvationists worldwide to worship and proclaim the living God, and to seek in every meeting a vital encounter with the Lord of life, using relevant cultural forms and languages.

2. We call Salvationists worldwide to a renewed and relevant proclamation of and close attention to the word of God, and to a quick and steady obedience to the radical demands of the word upon Salvationists personally, and upon our movement corporately.

3. We call Salvationists worldwide to recognise the wide understanding of the mercy seat that God has given to the Army; to rejoice that Christ uses this means of grace to confirm his presence; and to ensure that its spiritual benefits are fully explored in every corps and Army centre.

4. We call Salvationists worldwide to rejoice in our freedom to celebrate **Christ's real presence** at all our meals and in all our meetings, and to seize the opportunity to explore in our life together the significance of the simple meals shared by Jesus and his friends and by the first Christians.

5. We call Salvationists worldwide to recognise that the swearing in of soldiers **is a public witness to Christ's command to make disciples and that** soldiership demands ongoing radical obedience.

THE DISCIPLINES OF LIFE IN THE SPIRIT

6. We call Salvationists worldwide to enter the new millennium with a renewal of faithful, disciplined and persistent prayer; **to study God's word consistently and to seek God's will earnestly; to deny self** and to live a lifestyle of simplicity in a spirit of trust and thankfulness.

7. We call Salvationists worldwide to rejoice in their unique fellowship; to be open to support, guidance, nurture, affirmation and challenge from each other as members together of the body of Christ; and to participate actively and regularly in the life, membership and mission of a particular corps.

8. We call Salvationists worldwide to commit themselves and their gifts to the salvation of the world, and to embrace servanthood, expressing it through the joy of self-giving and the discipline of Christ-like living.

TRAINING IN GOD'S WORD

9. We call Salvationists worldwide to explore new ways to recruit and train people who are both spiritually mature and educationally competent; to develop learning programmes and events that are biblically informed, culturally relevant, and educationally sound; and to create learning environments which encourage exploration, creativity, and diversity.

10. We call Salvationists worldwide to restate and live out the doctrine of holiness in all its dimensions — personal, relational, social and political — in the context of our cultures and in the idioms of our day while allowing for and indeed prizing such diversity of experience and expression as is in accord with the Scriptures.

11. We call Salvationists worldwide to join in the spiritual battle on the grounds of a sober reading of Scripture, a conviction of the triumph of Christ, the inviolable freedom and dignity of persons, and a commitment to the re-demption of the world in all its dimensions — physical, spiritual, social, eco-nomic and political.

12. We call Salvationists worldwide to restore the family to its central position in passing on the faith, to generate resources to help parents grow together in faithful love and to lead their children into wholeness, with hearts on fire for God and his mission.

[Editor's emphases]

The following officers and soldiers were appointed to serve as members of the International Spiritual Life Commission. Ranks given are as they applied at the time:

Lieut-Colonel Robert Street (Chairman), Lieut-Colonel Earl Robinson (Secre-tary), Lieut-Colonel Linda Bond, Captain Teofilo Chagas, Commissioner Doreen Edwards, Dr Roger Green, Lieut-Colonel Margaret Hay, Sister Susan Harris, CSM Warren Johnson, Lieut-Colonel David Lofgren, Colonel Emman-uel Miaglia, Lieut-Colonel Stuart Mungate, Colonel Phil Needham, Major Ly-ell Rader, Captain John Read, Captain Oscar Sanchez and Major N.M. Vijaya-lakshmi.

Corresponding members who also **attended some of the Commission's delib**-*erations were:*

Commissioner Ian Cutmore (former Chairman), Colonel Shaw Clifton, Major Ian Barr and Envoy William van Graan.

Other corresponding members who assisted:

Lieut-Colonel David Kim, Chong-won, Colonel Douglas Davis, Commissioner Peter Chang and Recruiting Sergeant John Bayliss.

The Commission met on five occasions; each meeting lasted for five days and there were five of them. They took place during July and November 1996, and in March, July and September/October 1997. Each meeting was held in London and hosted at either the International College for Officers, the William Booth Memorial Training College or Sunbury Court.

Appendices

Appendix F
Ecclesiological Statement

The Salvation Army in the Body of Christ

An Ecclesiological Statement
A statement issued by the International Headquarters of The Salvation Army in 2008 by authority of the General, in consultation with the International Doctrine Council and the International Management Council

Summary Statement
1. The Body of Christ on earth (also referred to in this paper as the Church Universal) comprises all believers in Jesus Christ as Saviour and Lord.

2. Believers stand in a spiritual relationship to one another, which is not dependent upon any particular church structure.

3. The Salvation Army, under the one Triune God, belongs to and is an expression of the Body of Christ on earth, the Church Universal, and is a Christian denomination in permanent

mission to the unconverted, called into and sustained in being by God.

4. Denominational diversity is not self-evidently contrary to God's will for his people.

5. Inter-denominational harmony and co-operation are to be actively pursued for they are valuable for the enriching of the life and witness of the Body of Christ in the world and therefore of each denomination.

6. The Salvation Army welcomes involvement with other Christians in the many lands where the Army is privileged to witness and serve.

This Statement, accompanied by an Amplified Statement, are contained in *The Salvation Army Handbook to Doctrine* (2010)

Appendix G
International Statistics

International statistics (as at 1 January 2014)

Number of corps: 15,636
Number of officers: 26,497
Number of employees: 107,918

Soldiers: 1,174,913
Adherent members: 169,491
Junior soldiers: 385,994
Senior band musicians: 30,151
Songsters: 114,402
Sunday school members: 630,060

Community development programmes: 11,570 (number of beneficiaries: 1,891,877)
Homeless hostels: 446 (capacity: 24,148)
Residential addiction dependency programmes: 234 (capacity: 14,108)
Children's homes: 222 (capacity: 9,913)
Homes for elderly persons: 158 (capacity: 11,309)
Mother and baby homes: 41 (capacity: 1,163)
Refuges: 65 (capacity: 2,140)

Community day care centres: 603
Non-residential addiction rehabilitation programmes: 74

Services to the armed forces: 31 clubs, canteens, mobile units; 31 Chaplains
Disaster rehabilitation schemes: 100
Prisoners visited: 272,593

General hospitals: 19
Maternity hospitals: 26
Specialist hospitals: 12

Source: *Salvation Army Year Book 2015*

Appendix H
The International Social Justice Commission

The International Social Justice Commission is the Salvation Army's strategic voice to advocate for human dignity and social justice with the world's poor and oppressed.

Purpose

Believing that everyone is created in the image of God but that global economic and political inequity perpetuates human injustice, the ISJC exercises leadership in determining the Army's policies and practices in the international social arena. Lamenting the abusive and unethical behaviour imposed on vulnerable people in today's world, the Commission assists the Territories and engages with like-minded organizations and other world forums to advance the cause of global justice.

In pursuit of its stated purpose, the International Social Justice Commission has established five measurable goals:

1. Raise strategic voices to advocate with the world's poor and oppressed.
2. Be a recognized center of research and critical thinking on issues of global social justice.
3. Collaborate with like-minded organizations to advance the global cause of social justice.
4. Exercise leadership in determining social justice policies and practices of The Salvation Army
5. Live the principles of justice and compassion and inspire others to do likewise.

Initiatives and Responsibilities

Mandated by the General as a permanent body under the leadership of the Director, the ISJC's initiatives and responsibilities will include the following:

- Advise the General of global matters of social justice and poverty;
- Consult with territories on present social justice practices and programmes;
- Develop expertise on selected global issues and key concerns;
- Represent the Army at the United Nations (New York, Vienna, Geneva);
- Maintain a commitment to current priorities e.g., human trafficking;
- Coordinate the development of ethical and moral positional statements;
- Produce justice related biblical and theological resources;
- Propose policy and positioning strategy to address critical concerns.

http://www1.salvationarmy.org/IHQ/www_ihq_isjc.nsf/vw-dynamic-index/24062DEBBB9B2F138025755800580A76?openDocument

Appendix I
International Vision Statement: One Army, One Mission, One Message

The Vision Statement and underlying Mission Priorities were launched by General Linda Bond in October 2011

ONE ARMY: We see a God-raised, Spirit-filled Army for the 21st century – convinced of our calling, moving forward together

We will...

- deepen our spiritual life
- unite in prayer
- identify and develop leaders
- increase self-support and self-denial

ONE MISSION: Into the world of the hurting, broken, lonely, dispossessed and lost, reaching them in love by all means

We will...

- emphasise our integrated ministry
- reach and involve youth and children
- stand for and serve the marginalised
- encourage innovation in mission

ONE MESSAGE: With the transforming message of Jesus, bringing freedom, hope and life

We will...

- communicate Christ unashamedly
- reaffirm our belief in transformation
- evangelise and disciple effectively
- provide quality teaching resources

http://www.salvationarmy.org/ihq/vision

Bibliography

Note - *where 'SA' is shown as Author, this indicates a Salvation Army volume published under the Copyright of the 'General of the Salvation Army' at the time of publication*

PRIMARY SOURCES

Salvation Army History

Coutts, F., *No Discharge in this War* (London: Hodder & Stoughton, 1974).

—. *The Better Fight – The History of The Salvation Army*, Volume Six: 1914-46 (London: Hodder & Stoughton, 1973).

—. *The Weapons of Goodwill – The History of The Salvation Army*, Volume Seven: 1946-77 (London: Hodder & Stoughton, 1986).

Gariepy, H., *Christianity in Action: An International History of The Salvation Army* (Grand Rapids, MI: Eerdmans, 2009).

—. *Mobilized for God: The History of the Salvation Army*, Volume Eight 1977-1994 (Grand Rapids MI: Eerdmans/Salvation Army Southern Territory, 2000).

Green, R.J., *Catherine Booth: A Biography of the Co-founder of The Salvation Army* (Grand Rapids MI: Baker Books, 1996).

—. *The Life and Ministry of William Booth: Founder of the Salvation Army* (Nashville, TN: Abingdon Press, 2006).

Larsson, J., *1929: A Crisis that shaped The Salvation Army's Future* (London: Salvation Books, 2009).

—. *Inside a High Council: How Salvation Army Generals are Elected* (London: Salvation Books, 2013).

McKinley, E.H., *Marching to Glory: The History of the Salvation Army in the United States 1880-1992* (Grand Rapids, MI: Eerdmans, 1995, 2nd ed.).

Merritt, J.G. (ed)., *Historical Dictionary of The Salvation Army* (Lanham, MD: Scarecrow Press, 2006).

Railton, G.S., *The Authoritative Life of General William Booth* (New York, NY: Hodder & Stoughton, 1912).

SA, *The Salvation Army Yearbook 2015* (London: Salvation Books, 2014).

—. *The Salvation Army Yearbook 2014* (London: Salvation Books, 2013).

Sandall, R., *The History of The Salvation Army*, Volume One: 1865-1878 (London: Thomas Nelson, 1947).

—. *The History of The Salvation Army*, Volume Two: 1878-1886 (London: Thomas Nelson, 1950).

—. *The History of The Salvation Army*, Volume Three: Social Reform and Welfare Work (London: Thomas Nelson, 1955).

Watson B., *Soldier Saint* (London: Hodder & Stoughton, 1970).

Wiggins, A.R., *The History of The Salvation Army*, Volume Four: 1886-1904 (London: Thomas Nelson, 1964).

—. *The History of The Salvation Army*, Volume Five: 1904-1914 (London: Thomas Nelson, 1968).

Salvation Army Leaders – Autobiography/Biography

Barnes, C. (ed.), *The Founder Speaks* (London: Salvationist Publishing and Supplies, Ltd., 1960).

Bate , J.M., *Destination Unknown: Memoirs of a private secretary to the General of The Salvation Army* (Long Beach, CA: Frontier Press [Salvation Army USA Western]), 2012 (Kindle edition).

Begbie, H., *Life of William Booth, Founder of the Salvation Army* (London: MacMillan, 1920).

Booth, C.B., *Bramwell Booth* (London: Rich and Cowan, 1932).

Brown, A., *The Gate and the Light* (Toronto, Canada: BookWright, 1984).

Clifton, S., **Something Better...** *Autobiographical Essays* (London: Salvation Books, 2014).

—. *Selected Writings* Volume I (1974-1999) (London: Salvation Books, 2010).

—. *Selected Writings* Volume II (2000-2010) (London: Salvation Books, 2010).

Eason, A M & R Green (eds), *Boundless Salvation: The Shorter Writings of William Booth* (New York, NY: Peter Lang, 2012).

Ervine, St. John, **God's Soldier, General William Booth** (London: Heinemann, 1934).

Gariepy, H., *General of* **God's Army: The Authorized Biography of General** *Eva Burrows* (Wheaton, IL: Victor Books/SP Publishers, 1993).

Gowans, J., **There's a boy here... The Autobiography of John Gowans** (Amersham, Bucks: Halstan, 2002).

Howes, T. & P. Mortlock (eds), *From Her Heart - Selections from the Preaching and Teaching of Helen Clifton* (London: Salvation Books, 2012) (Kindle Edition)

Hunt, C.F., *If Two Shall Agree: The Story of Paul A. Rader and Kay F. Rader of the Salvation Army* (Kansas City, MO: Beacon Hill Press, 2001).

Larsson, J. *Saying YES to LIFE: An Autobiography* (London: Salvation Books, 2007).

—. *Those Incredible Booths* (London: Salvation Books, 2015).

le Feuvre, C., *William and Catherine: The Love Story of the Founders of the Salvation Army Told Through Their Letters* (Oxford: Monarch Books, 2013).

—. *A girl with a mind of her own: The story of Gisèle Gowans* (London: Shield Books, 2015).

Strachan, J., *The Marechale* (Minneapolis, MN: Bethany Fellowship, 1966).

Watson, B., *The 9th General: A profile of Erik Wickberg* (London: Oliphants, 1970).

Doctrine/Salvation Army Distinctives

Barr, I., **'Is The Salvation Army still a Holiness movement?'** http://therubicon.org/2007/04/supper-club-series-3-barr/ (accessed June 15, 2012).

Booth, C., *Papers on Aggressive Christianity* (London: International Headquarters, 1891). London: S.A. Books — http://www.sabooks.org.uk (accessed January 28, 2013)

Bovey, N., *The Mercy Seat Revisited* (London: The Salvation Army United Kingdom Territory, 2010).

Brengle, S.L., *The Way of Holiness* (London: Salvationist Publishing & Supplies Ltd., 1966).

—. *Heart Talks on Holiness* (London: Salvationist Publishing & Supplies Ltd., 1897).

—. *Helps to Holiness* (London: Salvationist Publishing and Supplies Ltd., 1955 [first publ. 1896])

—. *When the Holy Ghost is Come* (New York, NY: Salvation Army Printing and Publishing House, 1909, Seventh ed.).

—. *The Soul-Winner's Secret* (New York, NY: Salvation Army Printing and Publishing House, 1900).

—. *Love-Slaves* (London: Salvationist Publishing & Supplies Ltd., 1929 – Third ed.).

—. 'The Holiness Standard of The Salvation Army in Teaching and Practice' in John D. Waldron (ed.), *The Privilege of All Believers* (Atlanta, GA: The Salvation Army Supplies and Purchasing Department, 1987).

Calvert, G. (ed.), *Health, Healing & Wholeness: Salvationist Perspectives* (London: The Salvation Army, 1997).

Carpenter, M.L., *Salvationists and the Sacraments* (London: Salvationist Publishing and Supplies Ltd., 1945).

Clifton, S. (ed.), *Who are these Salvationists? An Analysis for the 21st Century* (Alexandria, VA: Crest Books, 1999).

—. *New Love: Thinking Aloud About Practical Holiness* (Wellington, New Zealand: Flag Publications (SA), 2004).

—. 'Who do we think we were, and who do we think we are?' (International Heritage Centre, Cyril Barnes Memorial Lecture, April 2013) https://s3-eu-west-1.amazonaws.com/uki-cache.salvationarmy.org/ddbeb87d-5067-4291-83e3-bf32a63533e9_International+Heritage+Centre+-+Barnes+Memorial+Lecture+-+%E2%80%A6.pdf (accessed, November 17 2013).

Court, S. (ed.), *Boston Common: Salvationist Perspectives on Holiness* (Melbourne, Australia: Salvo Publishing, 2010).

Coutts, F., *The Splendour of Holiness* (St Alban's: Campfield Press, 1983).

—. *The Doctrine of Holiness* (London: SP&S, 1955; web edition 2003) http://archive.salvationarmy.org.uk/uki/www_uki.nsf/vw-dynamic-index/6C83335AB22267AD80256F960053213A?Opendocument (accessed January 2, 2012)

Coutts, J., *This We Believe* (London: Challenge Books/The Salvation Army, 1976, reprinted 2001).

—. *The Salvationists* (London: Mowbrays, 1977).

Davies-Kildea, J., 'What is the meaning of salvation in The Salvation Army today? Exploring a theology of Social **Service and Holistic Mission**' (MTh

thesis, Melbourne College of Divinity)
http://www.salvationarmy.org.au/salvwr/_assets/main/lib60633/salvationthe
sis_jdk.pdf (accessed June 18, 2012)

Dean, H., *The Faith We Declare: Brief Studies in Salvation Army Doctrine*
(London: Salvationist Publishing and Supplies Ltd., 1955 [Third Impression
1962]).

Gariepy, H. & S Court (eds), *Hallmarks of The Salvation Army* (Blackburn,
Victoria, Australia: Salvo Publishing, 2009).

Hedgren, S. & R. Lyle., *Mapping the Salvationist DNA: beliefs, values,
behaviours* (West Nyack, NY: The Salvation Army USA Eastern Territory,
2012 [Kindle Edition]).

Howard, T.H., *Standards of Life and Service* (London: The Salvation Army
Book Dept., 1909 [Kindle edition]).

Kew, C., *Closer Communion* (London: Salvationist Publishing and Supplies
Ltd., 1980, reprinted 1986).

Krommenhoek, V., J. Kleman & A. Puotiniemi, *A Sacramental Army: A
Salvationist View of Sacramental Living in a Nordic Context* (Helsinki,
Finland: Suomen Pelastusarmeijan Säätiö, 2011).

Lawson, K., **'Sacraments and Symbols in The Salvation Army'** (MA Thesis,
Durham: University of Durham, 1996)
http://etheses.dur.ac.uk/5017/1/5017_2469.PDF (accessed January 30,
2013)

Layton, P., *The Sacraments and the Bible* (London: Shield Books, The
Salvation Army UK, 2007).

Metcalf, W., *The Salvationist and The Sacraments* (London: Challenge Books,
1965).

Needham, P., *Community in Mission: A Salvationist Ecclesiology* (**St Alban's:**
Campfield Press, 1987).

Rader, P.A. & K.F. Rader, *To Seize this Day of Salvation* (London: Salvation
Books, 2015).

—. **'Reaching for Metaphors of Grace'** (Sydney, Australia: Booth College,
Coutts Memorial Lecture August 2010)
http://salvos.org.au/boothcollege/events/archives-coutts-memorial-lecture/
(accessed January 27, 2012)

Read, J., *Catherine Booth: Laying the Theological Foundations of a Radical
Movement* (Eugene, OR: Wipf & Stock Publishers, 2013).

Rhemick, J.R., *A New People of God: A Study in Salvationism* (Des Plaines, IL:
The Salvation Army, 1984).

SA, *Conversations with The Catholic Church* (A record of the papers presented
and recommendations made during the informal conversations between The
Catholic Church and The Salvation Army 2007-2012: London: Salvation
Books, 2014).

—. *Handbook of Doctrine* (**St Alban's: Campfield Press, 1969**).

—. *Handbook of Doctrine* (London: Salvation Books, 2010).

—. *One Faith, One Church: The Salvation Army's Response to 'Baptism,
Eucharist and Ministry'* (St Alban's: Campfield Press, 1990).

—. *Salvation Story: Salvationist Handbook of Doctrine* (London: UK Territory Print & Design Unit, 1998).

—. *The Salvation Army in the Body of Christ: An Ecclesiological Statement* (London: Salvation Books, 2008).

—. *The Songbook of The Salvation Army* (London: International Headquarters of The Salvation Army, 1986, reprinted 1987 **(a revised edition of the Song Book was launched at the Boundless! Congress in London, July 2015)**

Sandercock-Brown, G., *21 Questions for a 21st Century Army: Being the Salvos Now* (Freemantle, Western Australia: Vivid Publishing, 2013 [Kindle edition]).

Satterlee, A., *Turning Points* (Alexandria, VA: Crest Books, 2004).

Street, R., *Love Right at the Heart* (London: Salvation Books, 2011).

Swan, W.F., **'Grace**-based Practices of an Emergent Community – An Army is **Born'** (Wesleyan Studies Symposium, Toronto, Canada) http://www.tyndale.ca/sites/default/SwanW%20-%20Symposium%20Paper.pdf (accessed February 22, 2013)

Taylor, D., *Like A Mighty Army? The Salvation Army, the Church, and the Churches* (Eugene, OR: Pickwick, 2014) (Kindle edition)

—. **'Marching Orders'** A Theological reflection upon the origin and development of Salvation Army ecclesiology in an ecumenical context, and the implications for its future in the 21st century (MTh dissertation, Oxford: University of Oxford, 2005) (accessed July 7, 2012).

—. **'Autocratic Personal Holiness: A recipe for decline in postmodernity?'** http://therubicon.org/2007/03/supper-club-series/ (accessed January 30, 2013).

Wall, P., *"I'll Fight..." – Holiness at War* (Tonbridge, Kent: Sovereign World, 1998).

Webb, G. (ed), *Mission Mandates: McPherson Lectures 2008-2011* (Melbourne, Australia: Salvo Publishing/The Salvation Army Australia Southern Territory, 2011).

Yuill, C., *We Need Saints: A Fresh Look at Christian Holiness* (London: Salvation Army International Headquarters, 1988).

Ministry/Leadership

Burrows, E. & S. Court (eds), *A Field for Exploits: Training Leaders for The Salvation Army* (London: Salvation Books, 2012).

Clarke, D., **'Female Ministry in The Salvation Army'** *The Expository Times* 95 (May 1984): 232-35.

Eason, A.M., *Women in God's Army: Gender and Equality in the Early Salvation Army* (Canadian Corporation for Studies in Religion / Studies in Women and Religion 7 Ontario, Canada: Wilfrid Laurier University Press, 2003)

Green, R.J., 'Settled Views: Catherine Booth and Female Ministry' *Methodist History*, 31:3 (April 1993): 131-47.

Hill, H.I.W., *Leadership in the Salvation Army: A Case Study in Clericalisation* (Milton Keynes: Paternoster, 2006).

Mitchinson, N.J., 'A Study of the Influential Levers used by The Salvation Army in the United Kingdom to Secure Local Centre Outcomes in Conurbations Consistent with its Mission and Objectives' (PhD Thesis, Edinburgh Business School, Heriot-Watt University, 2012) http://www.ros.hw.ac.uk/handle/10399/2536 (accessed, January 20, 2014)

Munn, J Theory and Practice of Gender Equality in The Salvation Army, (Ashland, OH: Gracednotes Ministries, 2015)

Murdoch, N.H., 'Female Ministry in the Thought and Work of Catherine Booth' *Church History* 53 (September 1984): 348-62.

SA, *Servants Together: Salvationist Perspectives on Ministry* (London: Salvation Books, 2002 – Rev. Ed. 2008).

——. *Orders & Regulations for Officers of The Salvation Army* (London, SA International Headquarters, 1974, 2nd ed 1987).

——. 'International Commission on Officership: Final Report and The General's Consultation with Officers' (London: The Salvation Army International Headquarters, 2000).

Shakespeare, K., 'Knowing, Being, and Doing: The Spiritual Life Development of Salvation Army Officers' (Doctorate in Practical Theology Thesis, Anglia Ruskin University, 2011). http://angliaruskin.openrepository.com/arro/bitstream/10540/211700/1/ShakespeareK_Thesis_2011.pdf (accessed May 9, 2012)

Sious, J.A., *Preaching a Disturbing Gospel* (Toronto, ON: The Salvation Army Canada & Bermuda, 2012).

Strickland, D., *The Liberating Truth: How Jesus Empowers Women* (Oxford: Monarch Books, 2011).

Yuill, C., *Leadership on the Axis of Change* (Alexandria, VA: Crest Books, 2003).

Missiology

Burns, A., *Founding Vision for a Future Army: Spiritual Renewal and Mission in The Salvation Army* (London: Shield Books, 2013).

Cleary, J., 'Boundless Salvation: An Historical Perspective on the Theology of Salvationist Mission' – 6th draft, June 2012 http://www.google.co.uk/url?sa=t&rct=j&q=john%20cleary%20boundless%20salvation%20sixth%20draft&source=web&cd=2&ved=0CFIQFjAB&url=http%3A%2F%2Fwww.salvationarmy.org.au%2Fsalvwr%2F_assets%2Fmain%2Flib60633%2Fboundlesssalvationdraftv6.doc&ei=myfnT53MLMGw0AXO9KH2CA&usg=AFQjCNEgv4QielTTY1ouv4LmiJirtrICcA (accessed June 18, 2012)

de Sousa, M.M., *Parceiros na Missão* (São Paulo, Brazil: The Salvation Army, 2003) *Partners in Mission: An Introduction to Salvationist Missiology* (Eng Trs M. McLaughlin & H.A. Ward; Atlanta, GA: The Salvation Army, 2011).

Larsson, J., *How Your Corps Can Grow: The Salvation Army and Church Growth* (London: The Salvation Army, 1998).

Mitchinson, J. (ed.), *Call to Mission: Your Will Be Done* (The Salvation **Army's Mission Symposium 2013**; London: Shield Books, 2013) (Kindle edition).

Yuill, C., *Others: The Insistent Challenge to a Reluctant Church* (Milton Keynes: Authentic Media, 2007).

Spirituality/Discipleship

Booth, W., *Salvationist Soldiery* (London: John Snow, 1889).

Gowans, J., *O Lord!* **(St Alban's: Campfield Press, 1982)**.

Larsson, J., *Spiritual Breakthough* **(St Alban's: Campfield Press, 1983)**.

—. *The Man perfectly filled with the Spirit* (1986; electronic ed 2011) http://www2.salvationarmy.org.uk/uki/www_uki.nsf/vw-sublinks/1B0EAB4295B0F9A1802578640059D089?openDocument (accessed October 3, 2011)

Munn J. & S. Court, *Army on its Knees* (London: Salvation Books, 2012).

SA, *Chosen to be a Soldier: Orders and Regulations for Soldiers of the Salvation Army* **(St Alban's: Campfield Press, 1977)**.

Street, R., **Called to be God's Pe**ople: *The International Spiritual Life Commission: Its report, implications and challenges* (London: Salvation Books, 1999).

Tillsley, B.H., *Life in the Spirit* (Atlanta, GA: The Salvation Army Supplies, 1986).

Social Justice/Humanitarian Advocacy

Booth, William, *In Darkest England and the Way Out* (London: The Salvation Army, First Ed 1890) (Kindle edition).

Bonner, A. & C. Luscombe, *The Seeds of Exclusion* (London: The Salvation Army United Kingdom with the Republic of Ireland Territory, 2008).

Clifton, S., *Crown of Glory, Crown of Thorns* (London: Salvation Books, 2015).

Fairbank, J., **Booth's Boots: Social Service Beginnings in The** *Salvation Army* (London: International Headquarters of The Salvation Army, 1983).

Needham, P.D., **'Redemption and Social R**eformation: A Theological Study of William Booth and his **Movement'** (Princeton Theological Seminary, Th.M Thesis, 1967).

Pallant, D., *Keeping Faith in Faith-Based Organizations: A Practical Theology of Salvation Army Health Ministry* (Eugene, OR: Wipf & Stock Publishers, 2012).

Waldron, J.D. (ed.), *Creed and Deed: Toward a Christian Theology of Social Services in The Salvation Army* (Ontario, Canada: The Salvation Army Canada and Bermuda Territory, 1986).

Woodall, A. M., *What Price the Poor? William Booth, Karl Marx and the London Residuum* (Aldershot, Hampshire: Ashgate, 2005)

Music/Worship

Boon, B., *The Best of Both Worlds* (Wellingborough: World of Brass, 2009).
—. *Sing the Happy Song* (London: SP&S, 1978).
—. *Play the Music, Play* (London: Salvation Army, 1966).
Cox, G., *The Musical Salvationist: The World of Richard Slater (1854-1939)* (Woodbridge: Boydell Press, 2011).
Holz, R.W., *Brass Bands of The Salvation Army: Their Mission and Music, Volumes 1 and 2* (Streets Publishers, 2006, 2007).
Steadman-Allen, R., *History, Harmony and Humanity* (London: Salvation Army, 2012).
Taylor, G., *Companion to The Song Book of The Salvation Army* (London: SP&S, 1989).

Salvation Army Periodicals/Journals/Online

Journal of Aggressive Christianity http://www.armybarmy.com/jac.html Published online from #1 June/July 1999.
Court, S., Blog at http://www.armybarmy.com/blog.html '...dedicated to the Glory of God and the Salvation of the world'.
Word & Deed: A Journal of Salvation Army Theology and Ministry http://www.salvationarmyusa.org/usn/www_usn_np.nsf/vw-sublinks/B398C75F2EB4AE048525770600679216?openDocument
The Officer Private circulation bi-monthly communication forum magazine (Salvation Army International Headquarters, London). International Headquarters – website: http://www.salvationarmy.org/
Salvationist (Published separately by Territory; accessible via main Territorial websites).

SECONDARY SOURCES

Salvation Army History

Hattersley, R., *Blood & Fire: William and Catherine Booth and Their Salvation Army* (London: Little, Brown, 1999).
Horridge, G.K., *The Salvation Army, Origins and Early Days: 1865-1900* (Godalming: Ammonite Books, 1993).
Ocheltree, C., **'Wesleyan Methodist Perceptions of William Booth'** *Methodist History* 28:4 (July 1990): 262-76.
Winston, D.H., *Red-hot and Righteous: The Urban Religion of the Salvation Army* (Cambridge, MA: Harvard University Press, 1999).
Walker, P.J., ***Pulling the Devil's Kingdom Down: The Salvation Army in Victorian Britain*** (Berkeley, CA: University of California Press, 2001).

Bibliography

Doctrine

Bloesch, D., *The Essentials of Evangelical Theology* (San Francisco, CA: Harper Collins, 2006).

Hart, L.D., *Truth Aflame: A Balanced Theology for Evangelicals and Charismatics* (Nashville TN: Thomas Nelson, 1999).

Kärkkäinen, V-M., *Pneumatology: The Holy Spirit in Ecumenical, International, and Contextual Perspective* (Grand Rapids, MI: Baker Academic, 2002).

Larsen, T. & D.J. Treier (eds), *The Cambridge Companion to Evangelical Theology* (Cambridge: Cambridge University Press, 2007).

McGrath, A.E. (ed.), *The Blackwell Encyclopedia of Modern Christian Thought* (Oxford: Blackwell, 1993).

Ecclesiology

Dulles, A., *Models of Church* (New York, NY: Image Books/Doubleday, 1978).

Stevenson, G.J., *Methodist Worthies* (London: Thomas Jack, 1884).

Ministry/Leadership

Anderson, R.S. (ed.), *Theological Foundations for Ministry* (Edinburgh: T&T Clark, 1979).

Missiology

Bosch, D.J., *Transforming Mission: Paradigm shifts in Theology of Mission* American Society of Missiology Series, No 16 (Maryknoll, NY: Orbis Books, 1991).

Gibbs, E., *I Believe in Church Growth* (London: Hodder & Stoughton, 1981).

Kirk, J.A., *What is Mission?* (London: Darton, Longman and Todd, 1999).

McKnight, S., *The King Jesus Gospel: The Original Good News Revisited* (Grand Rapids, MI: Zondervan, 2011).

Moreau, A.S. (ed.), *Evangelical Dictionary of World Missions* (Grand Rapids, MI: Baker Books, 2000).

Peskett H. & V. Ramachandra, *The Message of Mission* (Nottingham: IVP, 2003).

Wright, C., *The Mission of God: Unlocking the Bible's Grand Narrative* (Nottingham: IVP, 2006).

Wright, N.T., *Surprised by Hope: Rethinking Heaven, the Resurrection, and the Mission of the Church* (New York: HarperOne, 2008).

Spirituality/Discipleship

Bonhoeffer, D., *The Call to Discipleship* (New York, NT: Macmillan, 1965).

Bruce, A.B., *The Training of the Twelve* (Edinburgh: T&T Clark, 1911).

Clark, R. (ed.), *Power, Holiness and Evangelism* (Shippensburg, PA: Destiny Image, 1999).

Fee, G.D., ***God's Empowering Presence: The Holy Spirit in the*** *Letters of Paul* (Peabody, MA: Hendrickson, 1994).

Foster, R., *Celebration of Discipline* (London: Hodder & Stoughton, 1978, 1980).

Gillett, D., *Trust and Obey: Explorations in Evangelical Spirituality* (London: Darton, Longman & Todd, 1993).

Gundry, S.N. & B. Demarest (eds), *Four Views on Christian Spirituality* (Grand Rapids, MI: Zondervan, 2012).

Mannoia, K.W. & D. Thorsen (eds), *The Holiness Manifesto* (Grand Rapids, MI: Eerdmans, 2008).

McGrath, A.E., *Christian Spirituality* (Oxford, Blackwell, 1999).

Smith, R., *Christ and the Modern Mind* (Downers Grove, IL: IVP, 1973)

Holt, B. P., A Brief History of Christian Spirituality (Oxford: Lion, 1993, 1997)

Social Justice/Humanitarian Advocacy

Watson, R.A. & B. Brown, *The Most Effective Organization in the U.S. – Leadership Secrets of The Salvation Army* (New York, NY: Crown Business, 2001)

ND - #0085 - 090625 - C0 - 229/152/14 - PB - 9781842278451 - Gloss Lamination